GUIDE TO THE ARCHIVES AND

MANUSCRIPT COLLECTIONS

MEMOIRS OF THE

AMERICAN PHILOSOPHICAL SOCIETY

Held at Philadelphia

For Promoting Useful Knowledge

VOLUME 66

Guide to the

ARCHIVES

and

MANUSCRIPT COLLECTIONS

of the

AMERICAN PHILOSOPHICAL SOCIETY

Compiled by

WHITFIELD J. BELL, JR.
Librarian

and

MURPHY D. SMITH
Assistant Librarian

THE AMERICAN PHILOSOPHICAL SOCIETY
INDEPENDENCE SQUARE · PHILADELPHIA
1966

FOREWORD

The manuscript holdings of the American Philosophical Society have accumulated over a period of nearly two centuries. The Society, formed largely on the model of the Royal Society of London, was the first scientific academy in this country; and its archives and other early documents illuminate the beginnings of organized science and scholarship in America.

As Dr. Bell and Mr. Smith point out in the Introduction which follows, the Society's interest in acquiring manuscripts reached its first high point between 1800 and 1830, when Jefferson was for a time President of the Society as well as of the United States, and when the Historical and Literary Committee served as an embryonic historical institute. A second period of enthusiasm for a manuscripts program followed after 1940, when Dr. William E. Lingelbach was appointed Librarian and more adequate funds for purchases became available. Since that time, the acquisition of materials relating to the history of science has been emphasized; but such other fields as early American history and American Indian studies—of great interest to the Society's early collectors—have by no means been abandoned. This is evident in the acquisition since 1940 of two of the Library's chief collections, the films of the Stephen Girard Papers (ca. 1790-1830), and the original papers of the anthropologist Franz Boas.

As in other libraries, the need for making guides or indexes to manuscript holdings became more obvious in the present century. Certain published guides of this nature must have long been known to the Society's Committee on Library, though most such publications related to larger and more general collections than those possessed by the Society. As the latter's holdings became more extensive, however, so likewise did concern about aiding scholars in using them. About 1950, for example, Dr. St. George L. Sioussat—who had served as chief of the Manuscripts Division of the Library of Congress and was an active member of the Society's Committee—proposed that a guide to "our historical manuscript material" be prepared and published.

A decade later, the Library's collections were growing more rapidly, were housed in a new fireproof, air-conditioned vault, and literally called for an adequate introduction to scholars at large. This was all the more true because many persons still seemed uncertain whether the Library was open to all readers. No doubt the misunderstanding arose, at first, from the fact that the Library is part of a private Society and not an autonomous institution. Hence, to this day, it is not a circulating library except for members—though it does provide interlibrary loan services for books. Moreover, the Library always has welcomed serious readers, and it is in order to assist them that the present Guide has been prepared.

We were fortunate in securing the services of Dr. Bell as Associate Librarian in 1961. His experience as Associate Editor of the Franklin Papers provided an excellent background for editing the present Guide—in collaboration with Mr.

v

Smith, who had long served as Manuscripts Librarian. Dr. Bell and Mr. Smith modestly omit, in their Introduction, any reference to the thorough and imaginative work which they have devoted to this arduous task. But they do make clear just what the Guide is, what it is not, and how it can be used to best advantage. They assume—even in this day of elaborate bibliographies and extraordinary "communication" techniques—that scholars, given good "leads" and copying facilities, will do much of the final, detailed searching for themselves.

The editors note that the Society has also published guides to two special collections of manuscripts during 1966. One, edited by Dr. John F. Freeman, relates to our American Indian holdings, and the other, prepared by Dr. Thomas S. Kuhn, to the Archive for the History of Quantum Physics. It may be added that other special guides will be made available in the near future, though not necessarily in letterpress form. In preparation, for example, is a topical guide to our large collection of eighteenth- and early nineteenth-century pamphlets—a type of literature which has been relatively neglected by bibliographers. But the "Bell and Smith" here presented will serve as the most complete introduction to the Library's resources in unpublished materials.

RICHARD HARRISON SHRYOCK

CONTENTS

	PAGE
Introduction	1
Archives of the American Philosophical Society	4
Manuscript Collections	21
Index	150

GUIDE TO THE ARCHIVES AND

MANUSCRIPT COLLECTIONS

INTRODUCTION

Official records and papers of the American Philosophical Society—what we now call "archives"—began to accumulate with the first establishment of the institution. So did the manuscript collections. Year after year for two centuries the regular round of Society business, a flow of communications from members and would-be members, many gifts and occasional bequests have brought a steady increase to the papers which secretaries and librarians had to preserve. Sometimes, as in the early nineteenth century when the Historical and Literary Committee flourished, there was a period of vigorous collection, and then manuscripts seemed to pour in. Since 1940 acquisitions of manuscripts have been more numerous, more constant, more intelligently planned. As it approaches the end of its second century, the Library of the Society has developed into a center for research in the history of science, especially science in America.[1]

This is the first general guide to the archives and manuscript collections in the Library that has been prepared.[2] Despite the many lists of names and topics in its descriptive notes, this is not an index or a catalogue or even a shelf list of the collection, but an introduction which should give scholars, for whom it is intended, a good idea of what the Library has that may interest them or their students. In many instances the scholar will find in the *Guide* exactly everything he wants; in most cases, however, he will need to consult the Library's card catalogue of manuscripts for more complete and detailed information about particular persons and topics. (Not every collection has been catalogued item by item, of course; but many collections long in the Library's possession have been so analyzed.)

Readers of the *Guide* will notice that some entries describe collections of thousands of pieces, while others are for only a handful of documents or even a single one. This inequality of treatment is owing to some extent to cataloguing idiosyncrasies in times long past. In some cases the compilers of the *Guide* have ignored or overcome the unsystematic classifications of their predecessors by bringing together items logically or historically related. In other cases, however, it seemed there would be no gain, except to logic, by submerging individual pieces or small lots of manuscripts into the anonymity of the Archives (No. 9) or Miscellaneous Manuscripts (No. 462); while scholars would lose the benefit of having such items presented to their attention. Should there be a second edition of the

---

[1] For a short history of the Society's manuscript holdings, see Whitfield J. Bell, Jr., "Archives and Autographs in the American Philosophical Society Library," APS *Proc.* **103** (1959): pp. 761-767.

[2] For accounts of problems and procedures in making this guide, see Murphy D. Smith, "Preparing a Manuscript Guide for a Learned Society," *American Archivist* **25** (1962): pp. 323-330; and John F. Freeman, "The American Indian in Manuscript: Preparing a Guide to Holdings in the American Philosophical Society," *Ethnohistory* **8** (1961): pp. 156-178.

Guide, some of the inequalities remaining will be corrected, especially by describing the larger collections at greater length.

The Library's Manuscript Collection contains some items which are manuscripts only technically, because they were written by hand; they are in fact copies of printed works (e.g., No. 696) and therefore not likely to interest anyone but students of penmanship. Most such "manuscripts" have been ignored here, but a few have been mentioned.

Only the longer and more significant films in the Library's collection are listed. Those omitted are mostly short strips, selections of documents made by scholars for their particular researches; and the individual items on each film are accessible through the card catalogue. A few collections, especially in anthropology and American Indian linguistics, include recordings of songs and speech, but tapes and records have not been specifically described in this *Guide.*

A few things should be said about the form and content of the entries:

Author. Authors of manuscript collections have been briefly identified wherever possible. Dates of election to American Philosophical Society are given. Sketches in readily accessible biographical encyclopedias are cited; the principal dictionaries mentioned are:

Appleton.	*Appleton's Cyclopaedia of American Biography,* 6 vols., 1888-89.
DAB.	*Dictionary of American Biography.*
DNB	*Dictionary of National Biography.*
Hoefer.	*Nouvelle Biographie Universelle depuis les temps les plus reculés jusqu'à nos jours,* 46 vols., 1852-66.
Larousse.	*Grand Dictionnaire Universel du XIXe Siècle,* 15 vols. and supplements, 1866-76.
Year Book.	*American Philosophical Society: Year Book,* 1937- .

Tables of contents. Some manuscript collections are provided with tables of contents. (Others will be so provided as time and staff allow.) The fact is noted under each entry, with the length of the table given, so that readers may estimate its fullness. Photoprints and Xerox copies may be obtained at the usual per page charges.

Restrictions. Microfilm, photostat and other copies of manuscripts not belonging to the Society, and manuscripts of persons still living or but recently dead are usually under restrictions concerning use and reproduction. In general, such materials may be consulted in the Library; for extensive use, reproduction, or publication, however, prior permission of the owner or donor is usually required. The terms controlling any collection may be learned from the Manuscripts Librarian.

Other Guides. All the Society's manuscript collections are at least briefly described in the present *Guide.* The American Indian manuscript materials, however, are fully described and indexed in John F. Freeman, *A Guide to Manuscripts Relating to the American Indian in the Library of the American Philosophical Society,* APS *Memoirs* **65** (Philadelphia, 1966). The large collection on the history of quantum physics (No. 104) is described and analyzed in Thomas S. Kuhn and others, *Sources for the History of Quantum Physics: an Inventory and Report,* APS *Memoirs* (in press). Both these guides are published by the Society.

As is usually the case with such works as this, the *Guide* incorporates the work and interest of many persons whom we here gratefully recall: Dr. Richard H. Shryock, who, as Librarian of the Society, appreciated the usefulness of a printed guide and encouraged its preparation at every step; Mrs. Gertrude D. Hess, Associate Librarian, who prepared the original descriptions and tables of contents of some of the collections; and Miss Marion Fawcett, who gave the manuscript many useful editorial attentions.

ARCHIVES

The archives of the Society are extraordinarily complete. They appear to contain almost every written record of the members' labors from scientific communications and minutes of meetings (including the secretary's rough drafts) to a run of receipted bills for the semi-annual cleaning of the privy. The reasons for this unusually full documentation are not hard to find: since 1789 the Society has occupied the same building; it has never had a fire; and its secretaries routinely saved check stubs, dinner invitations, and mailing lists as well as important things. Even when, as sometimes happened, a secretary or committee chairman kept official papers in his private office, such is the continuity of old Philadelphia law firms, they have ultimately been returned to the Society.

In bulk the Society's archives are the largest collection in the Library, and they offer perhaps the richest and most varied materials for relating and illustrating the development of science in the United States. Except for studies of the Society and its members in the eighteenth century and of a few special topics, such as the Lewis and Clark expedition, the archives have been little used. At present, however, a history of the Society and a biographical dictionary of the members are in preparation; both will make full use of the records and papers described below.

The archives are arranged in this guide in the following order:

     I. Minutes and By-Laws
    II. "Archives"
   III. Communications
    IV. Members
     V. Officers
    VI. Curators
   VII. Library
  VIII. Committees
    IX. Financial Records
     X. Miscellaneous
    XI. Wistar Association
   XII. History

Readers of the guide will notice that some records of currently functioning committees have not been deposited in the Library. The minutes of the Research Committee and the several prize committees are examples. In addition, some other records, usually less than twenty years old, which may be described properly as "archives," are in current use, and also have not yet been deposited in the Library. Inquiries about these kinds of records and requests for permission to consult them should be addressed to the Executive Officer of the Society.

I. MINUTES AND BY-LAWS

The Archives contain minutes of both the American Society and the American Philosophical Society, which united in 1769 to form the American Philosophical Society, held at Philadelphia, for Promoting Useful Knowledge. The records of the first-named give its title variously as American Society for Promoting and Propagating Useful Knowledge, held at Philadelphia; and American Society held at Philadelphia for Promoting Useful Knowledge. For convenience, it is referred to here simply as the American Society. In addition, the Archives have minutes of a predecessor of the American Society, which was sometimes called the "Young Junto," but is here identified by the binder's title as the "Junto."

1. JUNTO

Minutes, 1758-62

2. AMERICAN SOCIETY

Minutes, 1766-68.

The above two sets of minutes were bound together in one volume in 1838.

3. ————

Rules and statutes, 1766-68. 1 vol.

Contains also the Society's Obligation, with the signatures of the members subscribing it.

4. AMERICAN PHILOSOPHICAL SOCIETY

Minutes, 1768. 1 vol.

Contains also the signatures of members under each of the six standing committees.

5. AMERICAN PHILOSOPHICAL SOCIETY, HELD AT PHILADELPHIA, FOR PROMOTING USEFUL KNOWLEDGE

Minutes, 1769– . 18 vols. (to 1915) are in the Library.

The minutes of 1768-1837 have been extracted and abstracted by Henry Phillips, Jr., in "Early proceedings of the American Philosophical Society . . . 1744 to 1838," APS *Proc.* **20**, 3 (1885). Beginning in 1838 abstracts were printed in the current APS *Proc.* until 1937, since which date they have appeared in the *Year Book.*

6. ————

Rough minutes, 1771-1804, 1819-1927. 1 box, 38 vols.

In particular instances the rough minutes are fuller than the minutes as finally transcribed. After about 1900 the principal articles in the minutes were prepared in advance of meetings.

7. ————

Laws and regulations, 1804. 1 vol.

A formal record, required by the by-laws of 1804, of the Fundamental Laws of 1769; the Act of Incorporation of 1780; the Act of Assembly of 1785 granting the Society a piece of State-House Square, with its supplements; the conditions of the award of the Magellanic Premium; and the by-laws adopted May 4, 1804.

8. ————

Standing orders, 1885-1925. 1 vol.

A compilation from the minutes.

II. "ARCHIVES"

9. AMERICAN PHILOSOPHICAL SOCIETY

"Archives," 1768-1965. 112 boxes.

This group of miscellaneous materials, called "Archives," consists of some 12,000 pieces; each is separately filed and catalogued. A few large, well-defined groups of papers, such as those of the printer and binder Jane Aitken, have been removed from the "Archives" and constituted as independent collections under their own name; while some single pieces, such as John Vaughan's history of the Society, which are properly part of the "Archives," were removed years ago, separately bound and catalogued, and do not call for return. From time to time small lots of manuscripts are absorbed into the "Archives."

The collection contains every sort of material relating to the business of the Society, such as drafts of minutes, committee reports, letters to officers and others, memoranda, scientific papers and proposals, orders, receipts, etc. A sample from a six-months period in 1820 shows letters to John Vaughan from J. B. Sevry, the Sociedad de la Havana, George Ord, Jonathan Russell, John Quincy Adams, and Lambert Cadwalader; letters to Robert Patterson from Nicholas Fuss, J. B. T. Harmand de Montgarny, William Vaughan, the Royal Horticultural Society of London, the Imperial Academy of Sciences of St. Petersburg, and Nicholas Collin; letters to Peter S. DuPonceau from J. A. Albers; notes by Frederick Adelung on books sent to the Society; memorandum of purchases by the Society through Ferdinand R. Hassler; reports of committees on the following papers: Robert McWilliams' on dry rot, C. A. Busby's on telescopes, Nicholas M. Hentz' on alligators, on resin made from the Lombardy poplar, John B. Gibson's on geology, T. G. Mower's on meteorological observations in Missouri, on varnish from poplar buds; and a report of the Library Committee on classification and location of books.

III. COMMUNICATIONS

10. AMERICAN PHILOSOPHICAL SOCIETY

Manuscript communications, 1748-1837. 11 vols.

Upwards of 560 scientific communications and letters to the Society, its officers, or members, removed from the "Archives" and arranged chronologically under one of seven series:

1. Mechanics, Machinery, and Engineering
2. Trade, Navigation, Manufactures, Agriculture, Economics
3. Medicine, Anatomy, Physiology
4. Natural History, 2 vols.
5. Philology, Literature, Antiquities, Geography, Education, 2 vols.
6. Natural Philosophy, 2 vols.
7. Mathematics and Astronomy, 2 vols.

Many of the papers are mentioned in the Minutes (see "Early Proceedings"), and some were printed in the *Transactions*. Several papers are those submitted in the Society's contest for the best essay on education in a republic, 1795-97. Authors of communications include:

Benjamin S. Barton	Oliver Evans
Moses Bartram	Richard Harlan
Samuel Brown	Ferdinand R. Hassler
John Churchman	Benjamin Latrobe
William Dunbar	Peter Legaux
Pierre S. du Pont	George Logan
Andrew Ellicott	Stephen H. Long

Timothy Matlack
Lewis Nicola
John Page
Robert M. Patterson
Joel R. Poinsett
Joseph Priestley
David Rittenhouse
James Rumsey

Benjamin Rush
Thomas Say
Benjamin Silliman
William Thornton
J. Rudolph Valltravers
Charles Varlé
David Bailie Warden
Hugh Williamson

11. ―――

Verbal communications, 1801-07. 1 vol.

Notes of observations, discoveries, publications, and other facts communicated to the Society by members. Among these are reports by Robert Patterson, Benjamin H. Latrobe (on bilious and noxious gas in wells), Caspar Wistar, John Wister (on tree growth), Thomas Gilpin (on placing rafters), Jonathan Williams, and Benjamin S. Barton; also extracts from letters to Barton from Sir Joseph Banks, Peter Curtis, and Richard P. Barton; also extracts from letters from James Winthrop to Francis Nichols, from Thomas Cooper to John Vaughan, and from John Clifford to Caspar Wistar; and also James Wright's (not James Logan's) description of the mastodon, copied from *Philadelphia Medical and Physical Journal* 1, 1 (1804): p. 154.

IV. MEMBERS

12. AMERICAN PHILOSOPHICAL SOCIETY

Membership and attendance lists, 1792-1942.

Several kinds of membership lists have been prepared from time to time; all have been superseded in completeness or accuracy of detail by the lists of living and deceased members printed annually in the *Year Book* and by the card files kept by the Executive Officer and in the Library. The following lists are in the archives: Lists of members, 1792, 1846, 1874, and undated, 4 vols; List of surviving members, 1885, 1 vol.; List of resident members, 1842-86, with record of attendance and payment of dues, 4 vols.; Roll of members present at meetings, 1845-50, 1929-42, 7 notebooks, 1 ledger.

13. ―――

Nominations for membership, 1773– . 3 boxes, 6 vols. (to 1931) in the Library.

Principally of the period after 1815, the papers are arranged chronologically, but they are accompanied by alphabetical indexes. The papers for 1891-98 are missing. Nominations of persons not subsequently elected are, by Society rule, destroyed. (An exception is listed below.) By the middle of the nineteenth century, nominations were usually conventionally phrased; after 1888 printed forms were often used. Among those nominated before 1837 are:

John Quincy Adams
John J. Audubon
Alexander Dallas Bache
Jean-Pierre Blanchard (not elected)
Daniel Drake
Princess Dashkova
Edward Everett
Richard Harlan
Abiel Holmes
Louis Philippe

Charles-Alexandre LeSueur
John Marshall
M. S. Navarette
Joel R. Poinsett
William Roxburgh
Henry R. Schoolcraft
Jared Sparks
Henry Vethake
Daniel Webster
Noah Webster

14. ——

Letters acknowledging election, 1840– . 6 vols. (to 1930) in the Library.

Letters of acceptance, mostly formal, addressed to the secretary; chronologically arranged. Letters in the first volume (to 1874) are from, among others, the following:

Cleveland Abbe	Arnold Guyot
Elizabeth C. Agassiz	Edward Everett Hale
George Bancroft	Hermann von Helmholtz
Benjamin S. Butler	Edward Hitchcock
James Dwight Dana	John Lawrence Le Conte
Charles Darwin	Joseph Le Conte
Charles W. Eliot	Joseph Leidy
Michael Faraday	Sir Charles Lyell
Wolcott Gibbs	Othniel C. Marsh
James M. Gilliss	Samuel F. B. Morse
Ulysses S. Grant	Alexis de Tocqueville
Asa Gray	Coleman Sellers
F. P. G. Guizot	John Greenleaf Whittier

15. ——

Rolls of members, 1743– . 2 vols. (to 1898) in the Library.

One volume, containing the Act of Incorporation and obligation of 1780 on extra pages bound into a copy of APS *Transactions*, o.s., **1** (1771), has signatures of hundreds of members from Thomas Bond to Emlen Hutchinson in 1898; these pages were reprinted in facsimile in a volume without title, 1896. The second volume, entitled "Laws and Rules of Order of the American Philosophical Society . . . followed by a Complete List of the Members," prepared by William Fite, an expert calligrapher, 1837, contains similar material and also the name and style of every elected member. After 1837 members (including some elected before that date) signed this roll upon being admitted into the Society. This volume was closed in 1889, when it was superseded by a similar volume, which is still in use. Some members signed both books.

16. ——

Membership certificates, 1786– . *ca.* 60 pieces.

In 1786 the Society for the first time provided members with a formal, engraved certificate of election. This is a collection of such certificates, issued to about 60 different members, signed by Benjamin Franklin and other presidents and officers from 1786 to the present time.

17. ——

Record of the decease of members, 1837. 1 vol.

An alphabetical list of members whose dates of death had been ascertained. See the printed list in *Laws and Regulations* (1860), p. 25. The record is in John Vaughan's hand.

18. ——

Memoirs of deceased members, 1783-1855. 1 vol.

The volume contains the following memoirs:
Frederick Beasley, by George Bacon Wood
Clement C. Biddle, by George Ord
Mathew Carey, by Isaac Lea
Redmond Conyngham, by Alonzo Potter

William H. Dillingham, by Charles B. Trego
Louis Stephen Duhail, by M. Davezac
William Gaston, by William H. Dillingham
John Gummere, by Robert M. Patterson
Justus Heinrich Christian Helmuth, by his son
Joseph Hopkinson, by John Kintzing Kane
Isaac Rand Jackson, by John Kintzing Kane
William Stephen Jacobs, by William E. Horner
Severin Lorich, by F. S. Lorich, with a note by Condy Raguet
William McIlvaine, by George Ord
Christian Mayer, by J. M. Buthe
Joseph Nicholas Nicollet, by John J. Abert
William Peter, by Job R. Tyson
Philip Syng Physick, by William E. Horner
Joseph Priestley, by Joseph Priestley, Jr.
Christian Rask by George B. Depping
Henry Reed, by John F. Frazer
Benjamin Wood Richards, by John Kintzing Kane
John Sanderson, by John Seely Hart
Francisco Borja Garçao Stockler, by José Maria Dantas Pereira
William Strickland, by John Kintzing Kane
Lardner Vanuxem, by Isaac Lea
Daniel Webster, by Henry A. Boardman
John Price Wetherill, by John Kintzing Kane
William White, by William Heathcote DeLancey
Caspar Wistar, by José Francesco Corrêa da Serra

19. ——

Autographs of members, *ca.* 1876-90. 1 vol.

Scrapbook of signatures of members, alphabetically arranged, clipped from return postal cards and acknowledgments of receipt of the Society's publications.

20. ——

Photograph albums, 5 vols.

Photographs of members, collected *ca.* 1880-1900, including some photographs of paintings. A few are autographed. The photographs are in no order, but each volume is indexed.

V. OFFICERS

President

21. BACHE, FRANKLIN. President, 1853-55. *DAB;* APS *Proc.* **10** (1865)

Presidential addresses, 1853 and 1854. 1 vol.

The address of 1853 is principally on scientific associations; that of 1854 is on APS business. Brief résumés are printed in APS *Proc.* **5** (1848-53): p. 360, and **6** (1854-58): p. 67.

22. CONKLIN, EDWIN GRANT. President, 1942-45, 1948-52. *Year Book* 1952

Miscellaneous papers, 1913-21. 9 folders.

Principally routine correspondence, including notices of committee appointments and meetings, concerning Society business.

23. DERCUM, FRANCIS X. President, 1927-31. *DAB;* APS *Proc.* 71 (1932)

Correspondence, 1921-31. 7 boxes, 2 folders.

Letters and copies of letters, programs, news releases, addresses, etc., principally as president of APS. One folder contains correspondence with Richard A. F. Penrose, Jr., including notes on it by Edwin G. Conklin; the other folder contains correspondence with the Penn Club about a reception for Denis Cardinal Dougherty, 1921.

24. KEEN, WILLIAM WILLIAMS. President, 1908-18. *DAB;* APS *Proc.* 72 (1933)

Presidential reports, 1908-09, 1911-16. 1 package.

Manuscripts of reports read at the annual meetings of APS. These do not appear in the printed minutes in APS *Proc.* of the period.

25. WOOD, GEORGE BACON. President, 1859-79. *DAB;* APS *Proc.* 19 (1880)

Presidential address, 1860. 1 vol.

Discusses hasty generalizations in science, and also Society business. Printed in APS *Proc.* 7 (1859-61): p. 331.

Secretary

26. CORRESPONDING SECRETARY

Journal of the proceedings, 1789-1823, 1827-52. 3 vols.

Drafts and copies of outgoing letters, principally to newly elected members and to booksellers and agents; mostly in the hand of John Vaughan (to 1841) and Charles B. Trego. Table of contents, 1789-1823.

27. SECRETARY

Correspondence, 1897– . 9 vols., 14 boxes (to 1921) in the Library.

Press and carbon copies of outgoing letters, mostly of a routine character.

28. ―――

Letters, 1900-21. 39 boxes.

Variously labeled "Secretaries' Correspondence" (1900-07), "Secretaries' Letters" (1908-21), and "Daily Correspondence" (1921), this is miscellaneous incoming correspondence, mostly on routine Society business. One box for 1904 contains letters from, among others:

Charles C. Abbott	William W. Keen
Alexander Agassiz	S. Weir Mitchell
Franz Boas	Simon Newcomb
Edwin G. Conklin	Sir Ronald Ross
Horace H. Furness	Josiah Royce
Daniel C. Gilman	Woodrow Wilson
John Hay	

Treasurer

The Treasurer's records constitute a vast mass of material, most of it routine and of little value, since it can be assumed that the Society was charged for, and in turn paid for, everything it required, and that some record of these transactions was made at the time and has probably survived. They can be grouped as follows:

29. Treasurer's accounts, 1782-1920. 11 vols.

Later called Cash Books. In the first volume are memoranda on leases of space to the College of Physicians, the Philadelphia Society for promoting Agriculture, the Pennsylvania Horticultural Society, Athenaeum of Philadelphia, Historical Society of Pennsylvania, Kappa Lambda fraternity, Charles Willson Peale, and Thomas Sully; accounts with Robert Aitken and George Turner; subscriptions for the portrait of Joseph Priestley; accounts of the Observatory Fund and the Magellanic Fund.

30. Ledgers, 1844-1919. 5 vols.

31. Miscellaneous financial records, 1798-1937. 3 boxes.

Bank books (1798-1863), check books (1836-1920), canceled checks (1837-1920), bills and receipts (1834-1937).

32. Subscription books, 1817-26, 1838. 6 vols.

Three volumes, 1817-26, kept by John Vaughan, contain records of subscriptions for (1) the purchase of Gotthilf H. E. Muhlenberg's herbarium, 1817, and for the works of Buffon in 127 vols., 1817-18; (2) for the second volume of the *Transactions* of the Historical and Literary Committee and for the Philadelphia Chamber of Commerce, 1825; and (3) for the Chamber of Commerce (the latter apparently one of Vaughan's other interests). Two volumes containing subscriptions for the publication of *Transactions*, n.s., 3 (1826); and one for the publication of Du Ponceau's treatise on the Chinese language, 1838.

In addition, there are invoices (2 vols.), receipts (2 boxes), records of members' annual contributions, lists of securities, and "Contingent Expenses and Post Office" (1 vol.) which records expenditures for printing and postal expenses, and minutes of the auditing committee, 1922-37 (1 vol.).

Officers and Council

33. OFFICERS AND COUNCIL

Minutes, 1804– . 2 vols. (to 1926) in the Library.

The officers and council acted as a kind of executive committee of the Society, under the by-laws of 1804.

VI. CURATORS

34. CURATORS

Curators' material, 1793-1953. 4 boxes.

Correspondence on gifts, loans, deposits, etc.; lists of specimens of natural history, coins, portraits; receipts; annual reports of curators, etc.

35. ——

Donation book, 1818-31. 1 vol.

Rough notes by John Vaughan, with miscellaneous letters, of gifts to the cabinet of APS.

36. ——

Donations to the cabinet, 1834-99. 1 vol.

A continuation of the Donation book; a record of gifts of fossils, minerals, coins, medals, etc., by Thomas Jefferson, Joseph Sansom, William Short, Joel R. Poinsett, William H. Keating, and others.

37. ——

Curators' records, 1769-1900. 6 vols.

A record of gifts to the cabinet and of all actions of the Society respecting its collections, abstracted from the minutes; with indexes of donors and of gifts.

38. SACHSE, JULIUS F.

Portraits and busts in the collection of the American Philosophical Society, 1898. 1 vol.

69 prints from negatives made by Sachse, most of them superior to the photographs reproduced in *Catalogue of Portraits . . . in the . . . American Philosophical Society* (APS *Memoirs* 54), which otherwise supersedes it.

39. PETTIT, HENRY

Preliminary notes for Curators' catalogue of portraits, busts, and bas-reliefs in the collection of the American Philosophical Society, 1898-1900. 1 vol.

Biographical sketches and memoranda.

VII. LIBRARY

40. LIBRARIAN

Annual and special reports, 1862-1936. 1 box.

41. ——

Correspondence, 1900– . 44 boxes (to 1921) in the Library.

Routine correspondence, principally about purchases and gifts to the Library.

42. LIBRARY

Bills of parcels of books, 1815-32. 1 vol., with loose papers.

Records and receipts of books from booksellers and at auction, including purchases from the libraries of Benjamin Smith Barton, Nicholas Collin, Alexander J. Dallas, and Joseph Priestley.

43. ——

Donation books, 1809-1954. 10 vols. and an index vol.

Record of gifts to Library and Cabinet, including books, portraits, busts, medals, artifacts, specimens of natural history, mechanical models, etc.

44. ——

Loan books, 1803-1941. 3 vols.

Record of borrowings from the Library by members and others. The first and third volumes, 1803-35 and 1889-1941, are in the form of printed promissory notes to return the volume or forfeit a sum of money (the financial forfeiture was disregarded after about 1900). The first volume is indexed by borrower: the heaviest users included:

Alexander Dallas Bache	Thomas T. Hewson
Benjamin Smith Barton	Thomas C. James
Charles Caldwell	Robert Patterson
Zaccheus Collins	Jonathan Williams
Peter S. Du Ponceau	Caspar Wistar
Anthony Fothergill	John Vaughan
Richard Harlan	

This volume also contains a copy of the library regulations drawn from the minutes and by-laws, 1802-16, and several pages headed "Account of Importation of Journals by the Treasurer," 1803-31.

45. ——

Catalogues.

The following manuscript catalogues of the Library are preserved:

1. Catalogue of the Library, 1798. 2 vols. Apparently prepared with a view to publication.

2. Nicholas Collin, Catalogue of the Library, 1799. 2 vols.

3. Catalogue of the Library, 1814. 1 vol. The titles are arranged alphabetically by author, with case and shelf number of the volume, and the name of the donor. A notation explains: "This Book was delivered by the Stationer on Tuesday 18th of January 1814—the Catalogue was finished on Friday the 25th of February 1814, i.e., a Space of 33 days (Sundays excepted.)"

4. Numerical catalogue of the Library, 1836. 2 vols., one rough, the other fair. Begun by John Vaughan.

5. Catalogue of manuscripts register, [ca. 1840]. 1 vol. An alphabetical list of authors, translators, editors, etc.

6. Index to catalogue of Library, Vol. 2. List of authors, translators, &c., [ca. 1840]. 1 vol.

7. Author index to Catalogue of the American Philosophical Society Library, 1863-64. 1 vol.

8. Index to catalogue of Library, list of authors, translators, &c., n.d. 1 vol.

46. ——

Library withdrawals, 1915-49. 1 vol.

Record of books, mostly periodicals, withdrawn from the catalogue, principally for sale or gift to other institutions. The most unusual item is the Tribute Roll of Montezuma, presented to the National Museum of Mexico, 1942.

47. ——

Library book, 1873-83, 1885-88. 1 vol.

Record of letters, accessions, borrowings, and other library business.

48. ——

Correspondence on the Library building, 1954-60. 4 boxes, 1 bundle.

On specifications, equipment, and servicing the new library building, opened 1959.

49. ——

Miscellaneous records.

Many records and series of records have to do with the routine work of the Library in past years and at the present time. Among these may be cited the Binding Records, 1803-22, 1842-46, in 2 vols., and 1909-41 in 15 vols.; also Accession Books, 10 vols.;

also List of Purchases, 1922-38; also Monthly Statistics on Library use, 1941-61; also 15 vols. of miscellaneous notes and records. Most of these records have as much value for the historian as the Register of Attendance in the Library, 1935-66, 4 vols., which each of the many casual visitors to the building was asked to sign: among these, on January 14, 1960, according to the manuscript record, were Thomas Jefferson and two Franklins, each of whom gave his address as Elfreth's Alley.

VIII. COMMITTEES

50. COMMITTEE RECORD, 1793-1869, 1908-15. 4 vols.

A record of committees, their members, duties, dates of report, and disposition. The second volume contains a record of members' attendance, 1804-33; and one volume—"Committees special"—lists three committees on "the State of the manuscripts," "the Franklin Mss.," and the revision of the Society's laws and regulations, 1840-42.

50a. ADVISORY COMMITTEE

Minutes, 1933-36. 1 vol.

The committee was appointed to consider nomination of members.

50b. COMMITTEE ON REVISION OF LAWS

Minutes, 1933. 1 vol.

With letters and papers on the question whether residents of the District of Columbia were qualified, under the terms of the Society's charter, to vote and hold office in the Society.

51. HISTORICAL AND LITERARY COMMITTEE

Minutes, 1815-41. 2 vols.

The record of a committee which, under the leadership of Peter S. Du Ponceau, collected a large quantity of historical documents and letters of the colonial and Revolutionary periods of American history, and of materials on Indian languages. An index of names and principal topics has been prepared.

52. ———

Letter books, 1816-26. 3 vols.

Copies of letters sent by the committee to owners of historical manuscripts and to scholars and others interested in the early history of America, soliciting their cooperation, asking for the gift of documents, thanking them, and the like. Among those to whom the committee wrote are:

John Quincy Adams	Alexander von Humboldt
Frederick Adelung	Thomas Jefferson
Elias Boudinot	George Logan
Redmond Conyngham	Rejoice Newton
Mahlon Dickerson	Joseph P. Norris
Albert Gallatin	Caesar A. Rodney
Alexander Graydon	John Sibley
John Heckewelder	Horatio Gates Spofford
David Hosack	Isaiah Thomas
Abiel Holmes	John Vaughan

53. FINANCE COMMITTEE

Minutes, 1826- . 5 vols. (to 1941) are in the Library.

Established January 20, 1826, the committee was directed "to take charge, in conjunction with the Treasurer, of the investment of the Society's monies; and to have the general superintendence and management of the funds."

54. ——

List of securities, 1898-1902.

54a. COMMITTEE ON GRANTS

Minutes, 1933-35. 1 vol.

Originally the Committee on the Use of Funds for the Advancement of Knowledge through Investigation; now the Committee on Research.

54b. COMMITTEE ON HALL

Minutes, 1907-15, 1922– . 2 vols. (to 1939) in the Library.

The committee was responsible for the physical structure.

55. COMMITTEE ON PUBLICATIONS

Minutes, 1826– . 3 vols. (to 1939) in the Library.

The committee was established by resolution of April 21, 1826.

56. ——

Papers and records, 1899– . 7 boxes (to 1921) in the Library.

Principally correspondence about publications, printing, and related topics.

57. ——

Charles B. Trego's account, 1852-73. 1 vol.

Financial record of the APS *Transactions*.

58. ——

Papers for publication, 1897-1927. 1 vol.

An office record of papers submitted to the Society, with dates of reading, approval for printing, return of galleys, etc.

59. ——

Requests for Society publications, 1866-77. 1 box.

60. ——

Acknowledgments of publications, 1922-25. 1 box.

61. ——

Exchanges, 1871-79, 1884, 1898. 2 boxes.

Lists of institutions and journals with which the Society exchanged publications.

62. ——

Mailing lists, 1817-74, 1885-1912. 2 boxes, 4 vols.

Record of members, institutions, and others receiving the APS *Proceedings* and *Transactions*.

63. ——

Hays Calendar material, 1946. 1 box.

Correspondence with the office of the Executive Officer about gifts to institutional libraries of copies of I. Minis Hays' *Calendar of the Papers of Benjamin Franklin.*

63*a*. COMMITTEE ON EDUCATION AND PARTICIPATION IN SCIENCE
Papers, 1941-43. *ca.* 1,500 pieces.
For the committee's study of amateur scientists and their organizations, see W. Stephen Thomas, ed., *The Layman Scientist in Philadelphia* (Philadelphia, 1940).

64. COMMITTEE ON MECHANICAL AND PHYSICAL SCIENCE
Minutes, 1834. 2 leaves.

65. LIBRARY COMMITTEE
Minutes, 1897– . 6 boxes, 2 vols.
Original manuscript and typed copies.

66. COMMITTEE ON HISTORICAL MANUSCRIPTS
Minutes, 1897-1904. 1 vol.
Authorized December 17, 1897, "to examine the historical manuscripts and early American imprints in the Library of the Society," the committee was responsible for the following publications by the Society or commercial publishers: George Weedon's *Valley Forge Orderly Book* (Dodd, Mead, 1902); *Calendar of the Correspondence Relating to the American Revolution* . . . (The Society, 1900); "Calendar of the Papers of Richard H. Lee," *APS Proc.* 38 (1899): p. 114; Reuben G. Thwaites, ed., *Journals of Lewis and Clark* (Dodd, Mead, 1904-05); and *Documents Relating to the Purchase & Exploration of Louisiana* (Houghton Mifflin, 1904). The minutes relate principally to these publications.

67. COMMITTEE ON THE FRANKLIN BICENTENARY
Minutes, 1903-07. 1 vol.
Bound with the minutes of the Committee of the Arrangement of the Bicentenary of the Society; the minutes of the Franklin Bicentenary Committee are concerned with the program, proceedings, and expenses of the anniversary meetings, and with the preparation of the *Calendar of the Papers of Benjamin Franklin* (5 vols., Philadelphia, 1905-08). For the record of the anniversary, see *The Record of the Celebration of the Two Hundredth Anniversary of the Birth of Benjamin Franklin* . . . *April the seventeenth to April the twentieth, A.D. Nineteen Hundred and Six* (Philadelphia, 1906), and the profusely illustrated scrapbook on the celebration, compiled by G. Albert Lewis (1829-1915) and presented by him to the Society, 1906.

68. ——
Papers and records. 11 boxes.
Correspondence, invitations and acceptances, bills, menus, plans for receptions, etc.

69. COMMITTEE ON PAPERS
Minutes, 1909-20. 1 vol.
This committee was virtually a program committee; its minutes record its efforts to secure papers and lectures for the regular meetings of the Society.

69*a*. COMMITTEE ON GENERAL MEETING
Minutes, 1901-23. 2 vols.
This was a kind of program committee.

69*b*. Committee on Nominations of Officers
   Minutes, 1914-40. 1 envelope.

70. Committee on South Polar Exploration
   Papers, 1909-10. 1 vol.
   Minutes, correspondence, reports, and newspaper clippings of a committee appointed in response to the Society's resolution of April 22, 1909, that the Society "request the cooperation of the scientific and geographical societies in the Country to urge the Government of the United States that it send a vessel . . . to thoroughly explore and survey the coast of Wilkes Land, and other parts of Antarctica."

71. Committee of the Arrangement of the Bicentenary of the Society
   Minutes, 1923-26. 1 vol.
   Bound with the minutes of the Committee on the Franklin bicentenary. For the program marking the 200th anniversary of APS (then believed to have been founded in the Junto of 1727), see "Record of the Celebration of the Two Hundredth Anniversary . . . of the American Philosophical Society . . . April 27 to April 30, 1927," published as APS *Proc.* **66** (1927).

72. ———
   Engrossed congratulations, 1927. 1 box.
   Formal felicitations from learned societies and their appointed delegates to the APS bicentenary.

73. Magellanic Premium
   Prize questions, *ca.* 1820. 1 vol.
   Questions—35 in all—under consideration for the Magellanic Premium.

74. ———
   Magellanic premium entries, 1884-1913. 3 folders.
   Notes, memoranda, and essays submitted to the committee.

75. Phillips Prize Essay Committee
   Papers, 1888-1921. 8 boxes.
   Minutes, reports of committee, and copies of essays submitted for this prize in jurisprudence.

IX. FINANCIAL RECORDS

76. Trustees of the Building Fund
   Minutes and accounts, 1866-1900. 1 vol.
   Authorized by resolution of October 5, 1866, to raise and hold money to construct a fireproof building for the Society, the trustees in 1900 turned over to the Society's general fund the small amount they had collected.

77. Building and Endowment Fund
   Papers, 1911-57. 2 vols., 4 boxes.
   Minutes, correspondence, signed pledges, vouchers for payment of expenses, newspaper clippings relating principally to the Society's plan to erect a hall on the Benjamin Franklin Parkway. The committee was first called Committee on Site for a New Hall.

78. ――――

    Ledgers, 1928-33. 2 vols.

    Principally a record of receipts during a financial campaign. For the inception and plan of this campaign, see the Society's prospectus, *When Aristotle Comes Again* (Philadelphia, 1929). The campaign was abandoned, the Society did not move, and the subscriptions, with the donors' permission, were eventually used to erect the Library, 1959.

79. ――――

    Scrapbooks, 1929-31. 11 vols.

    Newspaper cuttings, supplied by a clipping bureau engaged in connection with the fund-raising campaign of 1929.

X. MISCELLANEOUS

80. Letters and documents relative to a petition to the Legislature for an appropriation for a "Franklin House," 1911-13. 1 package.

    Contains a circular letter to members, 1911; circular letter to the Legislature, 1913; and related correspondence on one of the Society's many efforts to move from Independence Square to a more advantageous address in Philadelphia.

81. Miscellaneous legal papers, 1794-1963. 10 boxes.

    Deeds, title searches, agreements to sell or buy, mortgages concerning the Society's lot on State-House Square and the site of a proposed building on the Benjamin Franklin Parkway; leases of rooms in Philosophical Hall to the Athenaeum of Philadelphia, the Pennsylvania Horticultural Society, the University of Pennsylvania, Charles Willson Peale, Thomas Sully, the United States marshal, and others; papers concerning Dunn's Chinese Museum property, 1839-42; papers on the will of François André Michaux; correspondence and papers on the Magellanic Premium, the purchase of Franklin's books and manuscripts from Franklin Bache, 1936, the restoration of Franklin's house, construction of the library building; also material about bequests and gifts of I. Minis Hays, E. R. Johnson, R. A. F. Penrose, Jr., J. E. Whitfield; insurance policies.

82. Philosophical questions, 1801-05. 1 vol.

    Queries by Robert M. Patterson and James Woodhouse.

82a. Weekly Broadcasts, 1942-43.

    The Society sponsored, in cooperation with the World Wide Broadcasting Foundation, a series of lectures, principally on internationalism in sciences, "to those countries overseas where there is still interest in the progress of science and learning." Speakers include:

Charles G. Abbot	Kirtley F. Mather
Francis Biddle	Elmer D. Merrill
Edwin G. Conklin	Robert A. Millikan
Edward S. Corwin	Harlow Shapley
Karl K. Darrow	Horace W. Stunkard
Sir Angus Fletcher	W. F. G. Swann
Philip C. Jessup	T. Wayland Vaughan
William Draper Lewis	

82b. Reports of General Meetings, 1936-45. 11 fascicules.

    Stenographic reports of informal discussions and addresses at general meetings and executive sessions of the Society. One is the report of a joint meeting with the National

Academy of Sciences on "Atomic Energy and Its Implications," 1945; another contains the texts of after-dinner addresses by James T. Shotwell on world peace, Agnes Repplier on science and research, and Dugald C. Jackson on Elihu Thomson, 1937.

83. Correspondence on the 150th anniversary of the Society, 1893. 1 box.

Contains printed invitations, programs, letters of acceptance and congratulation from other societies and from individuals. For an account of the celebration, see APS *Proc.* **32** (1893): p. 5.

84. Visitors at the centennial celebration, 1843. 1 vol.

85. Register of visitors, 1870-1920. 1 vol.

XI. WISTAR ASSOCIATION

Composed originally of eight Philadelphia members of APS, the Wistar Association was organized in 1818 to continue the agreeable social entertainments which the Society's late president Caspar Wistar had held regularly for many years for members and distinguished strangers in the city. The Association suspended meetings during the Civil War, and did not meet after 1866. In 1884 the Fortnightly Club was formed for purposes similar to those of the old Wistar Association, although not all its members were also members of APS. When the Fortnightly sought to change its name to the Wistar Club, two ancient survivors of the older group revived the Association, elected new members, and absorbed the upstart. In 1898 membership in APS was restored as a prerequisite for election. The Association has met regularly since 1886. Its membership is now 24, and modern transportation has made it feasible to include persons not residents of Philadelphia.

86. WISTAR ASSOCIATION

Manuscript archives, 1818– . 1 vol. (to 1910) in the Library.

Contains a copy of the 1842 constitution; miscellaneous minutes; membership lists; memoranda and receipts; and letters, principally of acceptance and resignation, from such persons as: Franklin Bache, John C. Cresson, Jacob M. Da Costa, Robley Dunglinson, Robert Hare, John Kintzing Kane, William M. Meredith, William Pepper (1843-98), Moncure Robinson, and George Sharswood.
Deposited by the Association, 1911.

87. ———

Annual lists of the Wistar Party, 1824-42. 2 vols.
Deposited by the Association, 1911.

88. FORTNIGHTLY CLUB

Minutes, 1884-87. 1 vol.
Deposited by the Wistar Association, 1911.

XII. HISTORY

89. DU PONCEAU, PETER STEPHEN (1760-1844). *DAB*

An historical account of the origin and formation of the American Philosophical Society, 1840. 1 vol.

On a careful examination of the records, the author concluded that APS was founded in the Junto of 1727. This volume also contains a letter of Du Ponceau to a committee of the Society relative to publication of the paper, 1841; the report of the committee which considered this paper and one by J. Francis Fisher on the founding of the Society; a statement on the attendance of members at meetings, 1758-68; abstracts from the minutes of the Junto; and a chronology of the history of the Society. The author withdrew his essay for the purpose of revising it, 1841.

Du Ponceau's essay, the related documents mentioned above, and additional evidence and arguments were published by the Society in 1914 as part of the report of a committee, appointed 1910, "to investigate and determine the date of the foundation of the Society." Upon their recommendation the Society adopted 1727 as its founding date. In 1948, however, it accepted again the more historically defensible date of 1743.

90. HINDLE, BROOKE (1918-)

The rise of the American Philosophical Society, 1766 to 1787. 1 vol. Typed, carbon.

Doctoral dissertation, University of Pennsylvania, 1949. Some of the material and conclusions of this authoritative study were used in the author's full account of *The Pursuit of Science in Revolutionary America, 1735-89* (Chapel Hill, 1956).

91. VAUGHAN, JOHN (1756-1841)

An account of the American Philosophical Society. 1 vol. Copy.

A brief history and description of the Society sent to Baron Roenne, Prussian minister to the United States, 1841, in response to a query from the Prussian minister of public instruction.

MANUSCRIPT COLLECTIONS

92. ACADEMY OF NATURAL SCIENCES OF PHILADELPHIA
    Minutes, 1812-46. Film. 4 reels.
    From Academy of Natural Sciences of Philadelphia.

93. ——
    Miscellaneous letters. Film. 1 reel.
    From Academy of Natural Sciences of Philadelphia. Selections from the miscellaneous collection of the Academy; correspondents include:

Louis Agassiz	Samuel G. Morton
Zaccheus Collins	George Ord
Peter S. Du Ponceau	Charles Pickering
Elie M. Durand	Constantine S. Rafinesque
Asa Gray	Benjamin Silliman, Sr.
William Hembel	John Torrey
Alexander von Humboldt	Charles Waterton
William H. Keating	Alexander Wilson
James Mease	

94. ACCADEMIA DELLE SCIENZE, TURIN
    Correspondence with Philadelphia institutions, 1824-1912. Film. 1 reel.
    From Accademia delle Scienze. Letters, principally of a formal character, from APS, Academy of Natural Sciences, Wistar Institute, Wagner Free Institute of Science, and other learned societies and institutions; also a letter from John Vaughan to Prospero Balbo, 1832; with drafts of some replies. Table of contents (3 pp.).

95. ADAMS FAMILY
    Adams Papers. Film. 608 reels.
    From Massachusetts Historical Society. Papers of John Adams, John Quincy Adams, Charles Francis Adams, their wives, children, and others. See Wendell D. Garrett, "Opportunities for Study: The Microfilm Edition of the Adams Papers," *Dartmouth College Library Bulletin*, n.s., 5 (1962): pp. 26-33. Table of contents.

96. AITKEN, JANE (1764-1832). Philadelphia printer and bookbinder
    Papers, 1801-14. 147 pieces.
    Papers concerning her printing business in Philadelphia, including an inventory of the printing house; letters, chiefly to and from John Vaughan, about her father Robert Aitken's estate and her own financial troubles; letters and memoranda about her and her father's account with APS. Table of contents (4 pp.).

97. ALEXANDER, CALEB (1775-1828). Clergyman, author, principal of Onondaga, N.Y., Academy. Appleton
    A grammatical institute of the Latin language intended for the use of Latin schools in the United States. 1 vol.

With a covering letter from the author to Isaiah Thomas, 1793; the manuscript was published by Thomas at Worcester, Mass., 1794.

Presented by Isaiah Thomas, 1794.

98. ALEXANDER, WILLIAM, Earl of Stirling (1726-83). Astronomer, member of New Jersey Council; major general, Continental Army. APS 1770. *DAB*

Variation of the compass.

Written at Basking Ridge, N.J., March 27, 1773, this essay appeals to APS to collect and publish astronomical observations; it was sent to APS, where it was duly read in May, 1773.

99. ALLEN, HARRISON (1841-97). Physician, surgeon, anatomist. APS 1866. *DAB*

Papers, 1861-97. 3 vols.

Two volumes contain genealogical data on the Allen family; one volume is a scrapbook of miscellaneous material on Allen and his family; and there are 9 diplomas and certificates of membership in learned societies, military associations, etc.

Presented by Mrs. Robert P. Esty, 1952.

100. AMERICAN COUNCIL OF LEARNED SOCIETIES

Correspondence, 1926-27. 174 pieces.

Relating to the Committee on Research in the Native American Languages and its publications. Correspondents include:

Edward C. Armstrong	Waldo G. Leland
Leonard Bloomfield	Robert M. Lester
Franz Boas	Fang-Kuei Li
R. W. Bryan	Adrien G. Morice
James McKeen Cattell	William A. Oldfather
Pliny Earle Goddard	Gladys A. Reichard
Charles H. Haskins	Edward Sapir
J. W. Hewitt	E. H. Sturtevant
Melville Jacobs	John R. Swanton
Roland G. Keat	Walter F. Willcox
Alfred L. Kroeber	

Presented by Waldo G. Leland, 1956.

101. AMERICAN COUNCIL OF LEARNED SOCIETIES. COMMITTEE ON NATIVE AMERICAN LANGUAGES

Franz Boas Collection of Materials for American Linguistics, 1927-42. *ca.* 600 bundles.

Materials collected by the Committee, formed 1927, and of which Boas was chairman, and Manuel J. Andrade, Jaime de Angulo, Roland B. Dixon, Pliny E. Goddard, Berard Haile, John P. Harrington, Harry Hoijer, Melville Jacobs, Diamond Jenness, Alfred V. Kidder, Alfred L. Kroeber, Truman Michelson, Frans M. Olbrechts, Gladys A. Reichard, Frank G. Speck, Edgar H. Sturtevant, Morris Swadesh, and John R. Swanton were members. C. F. Voegelin and Zellig S. Harris prepared an index to the collection (*Language* 21, 3, suppl. [1945]), arranging the materials by language and listing much miscellaneous non-linguistic material; much of the latter is data on folklore, mythology, and general ethnology, but it includes some correspondence, notably George Hunt's with Boas, 1895-1931. Table of contents (234 pp.), fuller than Voegelin and Harris' index.

Presented by American Council of Learned Societies, 1945.

102. AMERICAN INDIAN ETHNOLOGY AND LINGUISTICS

Miscellaneous studies.

The Library contains a number of recent scholarly studies of American Indian ethnology and linguistics. Some are theses prepared for advanced degrees, others are reports of field work; most investigations were undertaken with support from the Phillips Fund of APS. In form these studies include typescript, typed carbons, photostats, and mimeographed copies. A few have been published in whole or in part; more have been the basis for the authors' published works; most are fully described in Freeman's *Guide to Manuscripts Relating to the American Indian.* . . . Almost all were presented by the authors. They are listed here by author and title.

Charles Marius Barbeau: The Cayuga dialect of the Iroquois, 1964. 28 pp.

——: The Gwenhoot of Alaska, 1959-60. 664 pp., illus.

——: Haida carvers in argillite, 1954. *ca.* 530 pp.

——: Huron word list. 108 pp.

——: Huron-Wyandot traditional narratives in native texts and translations, 1911-12. 258 pp. and copies.

——: Notes on Onondaga and Tuscarora, with Mohawk suffixes by Charles Cooke, 1951. 132 pp.

——: Raven-clan outlaws of the North Pacific Coast. 447 pp.

——: Temlarh'am: the land of plenty on the North Pacific Coast, 1959. 808 pp.

——: Wolf-clan invaders from the northern plateaux among the Tsimsyans, 1962. 402 pp.

Robert A. Black: A content analysis of Hopi Indian chants. Ph.D. thesis, Indiana University, 1964. *ca.* 500 pp.

——: Report on a study to determine the stylistic changes of meaningful words in Hopi song-texts, as compared with words in spoken Hopi, 1960. 2 pp., with 10 reels of recordings.

Mrs. Jane Esther Willets Ettawageshik: Correlated changes in Ottawa kinship and social organization. M.A. thesis, University of Pennsylvania, 1948.

Ray Fadden: Iroquois past and present in the state of New York, 1949.

Raymond D. Fogelson: The Cherokee ball game: a study in southeastern archaeology. Ph.D. thesis, University of Pennsylvania, 1962.

——: Report on field work among the Cherokee, principally a study of the ball game, 1960. 13 pp. and transcriptions.

Jacques C. B. Forbes: Materials on Papiamento, the native language of the Netherlands Antilles, 1963. Manuscripts, photographs, tapes, slides, and printed materials.

Paul L. Garvin: Wichita paradigms, 1962. 544 pp.

Eugene Gordon: Miscellaneous notes of Penobscot words, 1956. 83 pp.

Kenneth Hale: Lexical variability in Pima-Papago, 1961. 16 pp.

——: Pima-Papago recording transcriptions, 1961-62. 340 pp.

Gertrude Prokosch Kurath: Ceremonial songs of the Tonawanda Seneca longhouse: tonal and rhythmic patterns and ritual functions, 1936. 50 pp. and musical scores.

——: Seneca music and dance style; songs and ceremonies of Coldspring longhouse, 1951. *ca.* 200 pp.

—— and Mrs. Jane Esther Willets Ettawageshik: Religious customs of modern Michigan Algonquians, 1955. *ca.* 500 pp.

Joel Maring: Acoma Keresan dance songs. 228 pp.

Donald Olson: Cheyenne texts, collected in Norman, Okla., 1964. 99 pp., and tapes.

Paul M. Postal: Some syntactic rules in Mohawk. Ph.D. thesis, Yale University, 1962. 1 vol.

Zdeněk Salzmann: Linguistic studies of the Northern Arapaho, 1961. 61 pp.

Nicholas N. Smith: Malecite words pertaining to natural history, collected primarily from Peter L. Paul, New Brunswick, Canada, 1960. 61 pp.

William C. Sturtevant: Report on research on the ethnography of the Oklahoma Seneca-Cayuga, 1963. 7 pp.

Hiroko Sue: Materials on the Hare Indians, Fort Good Hope, N.W.T., Canada, 1962-64. *ca.* 1500 pp., recordings and film.

——: Report on ethnological field research at Fort Good Hope, N.W.T., Canada, 1961. 62 pp.

Oswald Werner: The Navaho ethnomedical domain: prolegomena to a componential semantic analysis, 1964. 34 pp.

——: A typological comparison of four trader Navaho speakers. Ph.D. thesis, Indiana University, 1963. 173 pp.

John Witthoft: A Cherokee economic botany from western North Carolina: Man and nature in the southern Appalachians, 1953. 244 pp.

103. AMERICAN INSTITUTE OF ARCHITECTS. PHILADELPHIA CHAPTER

Records, 1869-1910. 7 vols.

Minutes, 1869-1908; minutes of the Executive Committee, 1903-10; minutes of the Education Committee, 1870-73; minutes of the Admission Committee, 1870-73; and receipt book, 1888-1904.

Deposited by the Chapter, 1965.

104. AMERICAN PHYSICAL SOCIETY AND THE AMERICAN PHILOSOPHICAL SOCIETY. JOINT COMMITTEE ON THE HISTORY OF THEORETICAL PHYSICS IN THE TWENTIETH CENTURY

Archive for the History of Quantum Physics. *ca.* 200 manuscripts, 7 file-cabinet drawers of working papers (correspondence, notes, etc.) and transcriptions of taped interviews, 107 reels of taped recordings of interviews, and 107 reels of film.

Primary source materials for the history of quantum physics in the twentieth century, collected under the auspices of the APS and the American Physical Society, with a grant from the National Science Foundation. The collection includes original manuscripts of Sir Charles Galton Darwin on radiation, quanta, etc., with correspondence with Niels H. D. Bohr, Max Born, Oskar Klein, Henry G. J. Moseley, Erwin Schrödinger, etc. (presented by Lady Darwin); and also original manuscripts of John Hasbrouck Van Vleck on quantum physics, including correspondence with Raymond T. Birge, Gerhard H. Dieke, Paul A. M. Dirac, Edwin C. Kemble, Robert S. Mulliken, etc. (presented by Professor Van Vleck). The working papers contain correspondence with famous figures in physics, with some memoirs, photographs, lectures, etc. Also in the working papers are typed transcriptions of interviews with selected physicists. On microfilm are manuscripts of Niels Henrik David Bohr and his scientific correspondence, and index (27 reels from Niels Bohr Archives, Universitets Institut for Teoretisk Fysik, Copenhagen). Among the physicists whose correspondence and/or other manuscripts are on microfilm are:

Max Abraham	Niels H. D. Bohr
Edoardo Amaldi	Max Born
Edward N. da Costa Andrade	Gregory Breit
Ernst Back	Louis de Broglie
Edmond Bauer	Sir John D. Cockcroft
Jean Becquerel	Arthur H. Compton
Carl Benedicks	Dirk Coster
Arnold Berliner	Sir Charles G. Darwin
Raymond T. Birge	Peter J. W. Debye
Patrick M. S. Blackett	Gerhard H. Dieke

Paul A. M. Dirac
Sir Arthur S. Eddington
Paul Ehrenfest
Albert Einstein
Enrico Fermi
Adriaan D. Fokker
Alfred Fowler
James Franck
Walther Gerlach
Samuel A. Goudsmit
Fritz Haber
Werner Heisenberg
David Hilbert
Frédéric Joliot
Pascual Jordan
Heike Kamerlingh-Onnes
Peter Kapitza
Heinrich Kayser
Edwin C. Kemble
Oskar Klein
Hendrik A. Kramers
Rudolf Ladenburg
Paul Langevin
Max von Laue
Philipp Lenard
Fritz London

John C. McLennan
Lise Meitner
Gustav Mie
Robert A. Millikan
Robert S. Mulliken
Johann von Neumann
Yoshio Nishina
J. Robert Oppenheimer
Friedrich Paschen
Wolfgang Pauli
Linus Pauling
Max Planck
Leon Rosenfeld
Svein Rosseland
Heinrich Rubens
Ernest Rutherford
Karl Scheel
Erwin Schrödinger
Arnold Sommerfeld
Sir Joseph J. Thomson
George E. Uhlenbeck
John H. Van Vleck
Woldemar Voigt
Emil Warburg
Victor F. Weisskopf
Pieter Zeeman

The collection is described and analyzed in *Sources for the History of Quantum Physics: An Inventory and Report,* by Thomas S. Kuhn, John L. Heilbron, Paul Forman, and Lini Allen, APS *Memoirs* (in press).

105. AMOSS, HAROLD LINDSAY (1886-1956). Physician

Papers, 1918-22. *ca.* 2,000 pieces.

Mostly on medical service of the United States Army, 1918-19, immunology, meningitis, poliomyelitis, etc. Correspondents include:

American Red Cross
Stanhope Bayne-Jones
H. K. Beckwith
Alan M. Chesney
Rufus Cole
George W. Corner
Simon Flexner
Harry E. Fosdick
Victor G. Heiser
Arthur P. Hitchens
Edward H. Hume
George F. Kunz
Sir Arbuthnot Lane
Lederle Laboratory
Robert W. Lovett

Thomas McCrae
James B. Murphy
Hideyo Noguchi
Peter K. Olitsky
Sir William Osler
George M. Piersol
Frederick C. Robbins
John D. Rockefeller, Jr.
Peyton Rous
Theobald Smith
Anna L. Van Der Osten
Byron L. West
William H. Woglom
Hans Zinsser

List of correspondents (11 pp.).
Presented by the Rockefeller Institute, 1964.

106. ANCONA, MIRELLA LEVI D' (1919–   )
Florentine book-illumination of the Renaissance, 1956. Typed.

Material collected for, but not published in d'Ancona's *Miniatura e miniatori a Firenze del XIV al XVI secolo. Documenti per la storia della miniatura* (Florence, 1962). The study was made with the assistance of an APS grant.
Presented by the author, 1962.

107. ANDREANI, Count PAOLO (1763-1832). Aeronaut, traveler. APS 1792
Journals, 1783?-91. In Italian. Film. 1 reel.

Manuscripts in possession of Count Antonio Sormanni Verri, Milan. Include a fragment of a diary kept on a trip to Britain, 1783?; journal of a voyage from Milan to Paris, 1784; journal of a trip through New York state (including visits to Albany, the reservations of the Six Nations, Saratoga, and the Shaker community at New Lebanon); also typed transcriptions of the journal of 1790 and of a journal from Philadelphia to Quebec, 1791.

108. ANDREWS, MRS. EMMA B. (d. 1922)
A journal on the Bedawin, 1889-1912. 2 vols. Typed, carbon.

Kept during 17 trips up the Nile on expeditions of her relative Theodore M. David (1837-1915) of New York and Newport, R.I., who excavated the Valley of the Kings at Thebes, the journal contains a daily account of the social and personal life on the expeditions and of passages to and from Egypt, together with accounts of associations with such Egyptologists as Friederich Wilhelm von Bissing, Howard Carter, Gaston Maspero, Percy Edward Newberry, A. H. Sayce, and Arthur Weigall, and with Bernard Berenson.
Presented by Herbert E. Winlock, 1944.

109. ANGUIANO, RAMÓN DE. Spanish general
Descripción geografica del reyno de Guatemala, 1818. 1 vol.

A report on the geography, resources, and population of Central America.

110. ANNEMOURS, CHARLES FRANÇOIS ADRIEN LE PAULNIER, Chevalier d'. French
consul for Virginia and Maryland. APS 1783
Mémoire sur le district du Ouachita dans la province de la Louisianne, 1803. 1 vol.

Presented by Thomas Jefferson, 1805.

111. ANONYMOUS
État indépendant du Congo.

Address on the Congo Free State and its inhabitants.

112. ARAUJO, ANTONIO DE. Jesuit priest
Catecismo brasilico da doutrina Christãa, 1686. 1 vol.

Manuscript copy of a printed work; includes poems, statement of Christian doctrine with Portuguese translation, three catechetical dialogues.

113. L'ATHÉNÉE DE PARIS
Letters, 1792-1853. 227 pieces.

Letters of French scientists, collected for autographic value, on education, natural history, physics, chemistry, and other topics; practically all pertain to lectures at the Athénée; and many are addressed to André Marie Ampère. Table of contents (5 pp.).

114. AUDUBON, JOHN JAMES (1785-1851). Artist and naturalist. APS 1831. *DAB*
Papers, 1821-45. 200 pieces.

Chiefly letters on personal affairs, ornithology, and publications, mostly to his wife Lucy and his son Victor. Many contain descriptions of the sections of the United States where the artist was then traveling to solicit subscriptions for his publications. Other correspondents include John James Abert, John Bachman, William Cooper, Richard Harlan, and Thomas McCulloch, Jr. There is also a fragment of an unpublished journal, New Orleans, 1821. Eighty of the letters are printed in Howard Corning, ed., *Letters of John James Audubon, 1826-1840* (Boston, 1930). Table of contents (4 pp.).

115. AYER, EDWARD EVERETT (1841-1927). Business man, bibliophile. *DAB*
Reminiscences of the Far West, and other trips, 1861-1918. 1 vol. Typed, carbon.

A long account of a journey from Harvard, Ill., to the Nevada mines and to San Francisco, and of military service in the Southwest, 1860-64; shorter accounts of 12 trips by train and automobile in the western and eastern states, Mexico, and Europe, 1881-1918. The original manuscript is in Newberry Library, Chicago.
Presented by Lessing J. Rosenwald, 1961.

116. AZAMBUJA, JACOB FREDERICO TORLADE PEREIRA DE. Portuguese chargé d'affaires in the United States, 1829-34
Memoria sobre o valor das moedas, 1833. 1 vol.

Dedicated to APS; with the letter of presentation by the author.
Presented by the author, 1833.

117. BABBAGE, CHARLES (1792-1871). Mathematician, inventor. *DNB*
Selected correspondence, 1827-71. Film. 1 reel.

From British Museum. Included are letters from the following Americans:

John H. Alexander	Henry W. Howgate
Alexander D. Bache	George W. Hughes
Clement C. Biddle	Elias Loomis
Henry I. Bowditch	Matthew F. Maury
Nathaniel Bowditch	John Pickering
William Ellery Channing	Theodore Sedgwick
Edward Everett	Benjamin Silliman, Sr.
George W. Featherstonhaugh	Benjamin Silliman, Jr.
Benjamin A. Gould	Charles Sumner
Asa Gray	Daniel Vaughan
Joseph Henry	William Vaughan

118. BACHE, ALBERT DABADIE. United States naval officer
Diaries, 1862, 1867-69. 3 vols.

The first diary was kept during the American Civil War, when Bache was captain's clerk on the U.S.S. *Hartford;* the second and third were kept while Bache was an assistant paymaster on the U.S.S. *Iroquois,* of the Asiatic Squadron.

119. BACHE, ALEXANDER DALLAS (1806-67). Physicist, president of Girard College, superintendent of United States Coast and Geodetic Survey. APS 1829. *DAB*
Papers, 1837-63. *ca.* 70 pieces.

Correspondence about engineering, education, science, much of it related to the work of the Coast and Geodetic Survey. Correspondents include:

Louis Agassiz	John McAllister Schofield
Charles Babbage	William H. Seward
William P. Fessenden	Jared Sparks
Cornelius Van Wyck Lawrence	Alan Stevenson
Maria Mitchell	David Stevenson
Andrews Norton	Robert Stevenson
Alonzo Potter	Tench Tilghman
Samuel B. Ruggles	Marshall P. Wilder

120. BACHE, BENJAMIN FRANKLIN (1769-98). Journalist, printer. *DAB*
Diary, 1782-85. 1 vol. Copy.

A record of a schoolboy's life in Switzerland, with comments on his life in Passy with his grandfather. Entries for 1784 were printed by Bernard Faÿ, "Paris, à la fin de l'ancien régime, vu par un petit garçon de Philadelphie," *Franco-American Review* **1**, (1936-37): p. 317.

121. ——
Papers, 1779-87. *ca.* 50 pieces.

Letters of a dutiful child to his parents Richard Bache and Sarah Franklin Bache, and to his grandfather Benjamin Franklin; also letters to William Jones, Robert Frazer, and Margaret H. Markoe, his fiancée; also photostats of letters to Robert Alexander of Virginia, from the originals in University of Virginia Library.

122. BACHE, THOMAS HEWSON (1826-1912). Philadelphia physician. APS 1887
Diary, 1862. 1 vol.

Kept during service as a surgeon in the American Civil War, from Cape Hatteras up the Mississippi to Vicksburg, and then home to Philadelphia.

123. BACHE FAMILY
Papers, 1770-1852. *ca.* 50 pieces.

Correspondence on a variety of topics of members of the family of Richard and Sarah Franklin Bache, with some references to Benjamin Franklin and to his estate. Correspondents include:

Benjamin Franklin Bache	Mrs. Mary Stevenson Hewson
Mrs. Catherine Wistar Bache	Mrs. Mary Eddy Hosack
Theophylact Bache	William Livingston
William Bache	Thomas Mann Randolph
William Franklin	Caspar Wistar
William Temple Franklin	

124. BANCKER, CHARLES NICOLL (1778?-1869). Merchant, financier. APS 1825. *Proc.* 11 (1869)
Papers, 1791-1864. 2 boxes.

Letters to and from Bancker and other members of his family, on education, business, and personal topics. Other correspondents include Samuel Hazard, H. M. McIlvaine, James C. Montgomery, and John T. Montgomery. Table of contents (6 pp.).

125. BANCKER, JAMES A. Philadelphia and New York merchant.
Letters, 1842-49. 46 pieces.

Written from China to his family, these letters contain descriptions of the social life of the Americans and English in China, of Hong Kong after the British acquisition of that place, and of anti-British riots in Canton. A long letter describes the outward voyage from New York to Canton; several letters give an account of a visit to the Philippines; and there is a partial journal of Bancker's return home through the Red Sea.

Presented by Miss Sarah B. Mortimer, 1962.

126. BANKS, SIR JOSEPH (1743-1820). Naturalist, president of the Royal Society. APS 1787. *DNB*

Papers. Film. 45 reels.

Films have been made of Banks papers in the following depositories:
National Library, Canberra. Typed guide.
Royal Geographical Society of Australasia, Adelaide.
Sutro Library, San Francisco.
Mitchell Library, Sydney.
Alexander Turnbull Library, Wellington.
In addition, all Banks manuscripts in APS have been filmed and a table of contents prepared.

127. BARBEAU, CHARLES MARIUS (1883–). Canadian anthropologist

Calendar of Indian captivities and allied documents. 1 vol. Typed.

Presented by Charles Marius Barbeau, 1954-55.

128. ——

Checklist of American Indian antiquities found in European institutions. Photostat.

The repositories include British Museum, Ashmolean Museum, Musée de l'Homme, Bibliothèque Nationale, Paris, and Musée du Louvre.

Presented by Charles Marius Barbeau, 1958.

129. BARKER, ANNA E. Matron, Macdougall Methodist Orphanage, Morley, Northwest Territory, Canada

List of words in the Mountain Stoney dialect. Typed, photostat.

A list of about 500 words collected from a branch of the Sioux Indians at their reservation 40 miles west of Calgary, 1883-86. Original owned by Lucile Yerdon, Fort Plain, N.Y., 1948.

Presented by Charles Marius Barbeau, 1950.

130. BARTLETT, HARLEY HARRIS (1886-1960), collector. APS 1929. *Year Book* 1961

Collection of Batak writings. *ca.* 600 bamboo sticks.

Writings in the Batak language, incised on sticks and bark, collected in Sumatra in 1917 and 1927. For an account of the language, see Bartlett's "A Batak and Malay Chant on Rice Cultivation, with introductory notes on bilingualism and acculturation in Indonesia," APS *Proc.* 96 (1952): p. 629.

Presented by Dr. Bartlett, 1960.

131. BARTON, BENJAMIN SMITH (1766-1815). Physician and naturalist. APS 1789. *DAB*

Journals and notebooks, 1785-1806. Photostats and transcripts.

Photostats of journals and notebooks of Barton's survey of the boundary of western Pennsylvania and Ohio, 1785; commonplace book, 1789; journey through New York to

Niagara Falls, 1797; and Pennsylvania journal, 1798—all in possession of Historical Society of Pennsylvania; with transcripts and notes by Waldo L. McAtee.
Presented by Waldo L. McAtee, 1955.

132. ——
Papers, 1790-94. 17 pieces.
Principally letters to Thomas Pennant, with one essay (74 pp.) on animals of North America, and some notes on birds and fish. Among the topics discussed are: APS, Indians, coal in Pennsylvania and Virginia; William Bartram, mammoth, and yellow fever.

133. ——
A comparative vocabulary of Indian languages. 1 vol.
Extracted from Barton's *New Views of the Origin of the Tribes and Nations of America* (Philadelphia, 1797), with additions by Peter S. Du Ponceau, including a review of Barton's book in *Göttingische Anzeigen von gelehrten Sachen,* June 17, 1799.
Presented by Peter S. Du Ponceau, 1840.

134. BARTRAM, JOHN (1699-1777). Botanist. Original member APS. *DAB*
Correspondence. 719 pp. Typed.
Compiled by Edward E. Wildman and Francis D. West, chiefly from original letters in the Historical Society of Pennsylvania and other depositories, 1956.
Deposited by Edward E. Wildman, 1956.

135. ——
Journal to South Carolina, Georgia, and Florida, 1765. Film.
From Historical Society of Pennsylvania.

136. ——
Papers. Film.
From College of Physicians of Philadelphia and New-York Historical Society.

137. JOHN BARTRAM ASSOCIATION
Papers, 1929-32. 1 box.
Correspondence, chiefly of Francis W. Pennell, concerning the observance of the bicentennial anniversary of the founding of the first botanical garden in the American colonies by John Bartram, and concerning the publication resulting from this observance. Table of contents (4 pp.).
Deposited by the John Bartram Association, 1952.

138. BARTRAM, WILLIAM (1739-1823). Traveler, naturalist. APS 1768. *DAB*
Diary, 1802-22. Film. 1 reel.
From Academy of Natural Sciences of Philadelphia. Record of weather; appearances of birds, flowers, insects, etc.

139. BARUS, CARL (1856-1935). Physicist. APS 1903. *DAB; Year Book* 1937
Autobiography. Typed. Film. 1 reel.
From Brown University Library.

140. BEAUCHAMP, W. M. (fl. 1907)
Sketches of Onondagas of note. 1 reel.

From Onondaga Historical Association, Syracuse, N.Y. Another compilation on the same reel contains names of Iroquois other than Onondagas. The names are taken from treaties, delegations, other documents, and are often accompanied by English translations of the names as well as biographical data.

141. BECCARIA, GIOVANNI BATTISTA (1716-81). Professor of experimental physics, University of Turin. Hoefer

Papers. 3 boxes. In Italian, French, and Latin.

Contains letters to Sir Joseph Banks, Laura Bassi, Gian Francesco Cigna, Benjamin Franklin, and others on electricity, meteorology, phosphorescence, lightning, aurora borealis, earthquakes, and other scientific subjects; also journals of meteorological observations; notes of Eandi's biography of Beccaria. Described and evaluated by Antonio Pace, "The Manuscripts of Giambatista Beccaria, Correspondent of Benjamin Franklin," APS *Proc.* 96 (1952): p. 406.

142. BELDEN, LOUISE C.

Humphry Marshall: American Quaker botanist. Film.

Master's thesis, University of Delaware, 1958.

143. BELMAR, FRANCISCO (1859-?). Mexican linguist

Writings on Mexican languages, 1895-1902. 3 vols.

Consists of a short, elementary text for teaching Mixe to Spanish speakers, entitled *Curso de lengua mixe;* an exposition of Mexican languages, *Las lenguas habladas por los indigenos de la Republica Mexicana,* with special reference to their relations with California languages, prepared for, but not delivered at, International Congress of Americanists, 11th session (1895); and an address on the Indian tribes of the state of Oaxaca and their languages (in English), printed in part in the *Proceedings* of International Congress of Americanists, 13th session (1902), p. 193.

144. BERGMANN, MAX (1886-1944). Biochemist

Papers, *ca.* 1930-1945. 15 boxes.

Letters, reports, addresses and lectures relating to biochemistry and other scientific topics, the Rockefeller Institute, refugee scientists, professional associations, etc. Among the correspondents are:

Lawrence W. Bass	Irving Langmuir
George W. Beadle	Otto Loewi
Franz Boas	Duncan A. MacInnes
James McKeen Cattell	John H. Northrop
Jaques Cattell	Winthrop J. V. Osterhout
Alfred E. Cohn	William J. Robbins
H. D. Dakin	Peyton Rous
René J. Dubos	Fred M. Uber
Albert Einstein	Harold C. Urey
Simon Flexner	Donald D. Van Slyke
Paul Gyorgy	Selman A. Waksman
Karl Landsteiner	Warren Weaver

Table of contents (11 pp.).
Presented by the Rockefeller Institute, 1964.

145. BERKHOFER, ROBERT FREDERICK, JR.

Protestant missionaries to the American Indians, 1787 to 1862. Film. 1 reel.

Doctoral dissertation, Cornell University, 1960.

146. BERNY, PIERRE JEAN PAUL (1722-79). Sketcher and calligrapher. Hoefer
L'Œil du maître, ou essai sur le ministère, 1778. 1 vol.

The essay is dedicated to Benjamin Franklin. In his letter sending it to Franklin,
the author calls it "le fruit de la fréquentation de nombre de Cours où j'ai résidé depuis
la paix dernière." Apparently Franklin never acknowledged its receipt.

147. BIDDLE, NICHOLAS (1786-1844). Scholar, statesman, financier. APS 1813. *DAB*
Notes of queries to William Clark, with replies, 1810. 2 vols.

The notes were taken during Biddle's visit to Clark in Virginia in 1810; they relate
to the Lewis and Clark expedition. The second volume is in a notebook containing
Lewis' Journal of the river trip. Printed in Donald D. Jackson, ed., *Letters of the Lewis
and Clark Expedition* (Urbana, Ill., 1962), p. 497.

Deposited by Edward and Charles J. Biddle, 1915; presented by Charles J. Biddle,
1949.

148. BILLINGS, WILLIAM (fl. 1790). Ship captain
Journals of the Ship *Apollo*, 1789-91. 2 vols.

Record of two voyages (to Corunna, 1789-90, and to Oporto, 1791, and return to
Philadelphia), with observations of differences in temperature between air and water,
especially when passing the Gulf Stream or any land or banks.

Presented by William Billings, 1791, 1792.

149. BLAKESLEE, ALBERT FRANCIS (1874-1954). Botanist. APS 1924. *Year Book* 1954
Papers, 1904-54. *ca.* 15,000 pieces.

Mostly concerned with Blakeslee's studies on beans and blood groups, colchicine,
Datura, embryo cultures, and horticulture; many letters relate to the support and direction of the Smith College Genetics Experiment Station, which he headed; other letters
are with and about the Carnegie Institution of Washington, *Biological Abstracts*, American Association for the Advancement of Science, American Philosophical Society, Institut
de France, University of Connecticut; also travel letters from Germany, and miscellaneous lectures. Principal correspondents include:

John Theodore Bucholz   James H. Hyde
Vannevar Bush   William J. Robbins
Ralph E. Cleland   George Harrison Shull
Charles B. Davenport   Edmund W. Sinnott
Bradley M. Davis   Selman A. Waksman
John E. Flinn   E. B. Wilson

Table of contents (75 pp.).

Presented by Smith College Genetics Experiment Station and the Genetics Society
of America, 1959.

150. BLODGET, LORIN (1823-1901). Statistician, climatologist, publicist. APS 1872.
DAB
Observers and correspondents of the Smithsonian Institution, 1854. 1 vol.

A list of names and addresses, with specialties. The "British provinces" of North
America, as well as "California & Panama," are included.

151. BOAS, FRANZ (1858-1942). Anthropologist. APS 1903. *Year Book* 1942
Correspondence, 1862-1942. *ca.* 10,000 pieces.

Family correspondence, including letters to and from his parents, wife, and children; professional correspondence (with abstracts of many letters in non-English languages), on anthropology, teaching and research at Columbia University, scientific societies, publications, etc.; correspondence relating to the Germanistic Society and to German National Socialism, the expulsion of European scholars, and efforts to establish them in British and American institutions; diary of his first field trip to the Northwest, 1886; diplomas and certificates of membership. Also a dictionary, texts, notes and papers on the ethnology and language of the Kwakiutl Indians. Principal correspondents include:

Miss H. A. Andrews	Aleš Hrdlička
Martha W. Beckwith	Waldemar Jochelson
Waldemar Bogoras	Frederick P. Keppel
Charles P. Bowditch	Alfred L. Kroeber
Nathaniel L. Britton	Berthold Laufer
Herman C. Bumpus	William J. McGee
Nicholas Murray Butler	Truman Michelson
James McKeen Cattell	Elsie Clews Parsons
E. A. Chavez	Paul Radin
M. E. Crane	Edward Sapir
Roland B. Dixon	H. E. Sargent
G. C. Engerrand	Edward Seler
Frank D. Fackenthal	Karl von den Steinen
Leo J. Frachtenberg	John R. Swanton
George B. Gordon	James A. Teit
George G. Heye	Alfred M. Tozzer
Frederick W. Hodge	Clark Wissler
William H. Holmes	Frederic J. E. Woodbridge

Presented by Mrs. Helene Boas Yampolsky, 1961-62, and Dr. Cecil Yampolsky, 1964.

152. ———

Nootka vocabularies, *ca.* 1900. Film.

From National Museum of Canada, Ottawa.

153. BONAPARTE, CHARLES LUCIEN JULES LAURENT, prince of Canino (1803-57). Naturalist. APS 1824. Larousse

Letters to William Cooper (1798-1864), 1825-57. 75 pieces.

Principally correspondence on natural history and on Bonaparte's publications, especially *American Ornithology* and *Observations on the Nomenclature of Wilson's Ornithology;* with references to American and European men of science and learned societies.

154. ———

Correspondence from American scientists. Film. 1 reel.

From Muséum national d'histoire naturelle, Paris. Correspondents include:

John J. Audubon	William H. Keating
William Cooper	Isaac Lea
James Ellsworth DeKay	Constantine S. Rafinesque
Reuben Haines	Thomas Say
Robert Hare	Jeremiah Van Rensselaer

Table of contents (8 pp.).

155. BOSCOVICH, ROGER JOSEPH (1711-87). Italian mathematician and natural philosopher

Papers. Film. 14 reels. In Italian, Latin, and French.

From University of California, Berkeley. Correspondence, including retained copies of *ca.* 420 letters from Boscovich and *ca.* 1,500 letters to him from Giovanni Battista Beccaria, Felice Fontana, Paolo Frisi, Charles Marie de La Condamine, Joseph Jerome Le Français de Lalande, Joseph Liesganig, Nevil Maskelyne, Charles Morton, Joseph Priestley, and Benedetto Stay; also a travel journal in Europe; also a large number of manuscripts on astronomy, hydrography and hydro-mechanics, mathematics and geometry, mechanics, optics; also a volume of poetry. Table of contents (9 pp.).

156. BOWEN, THOMAS BARTHOLOMEW. Captain, 9th Pennsylvania Regiment

Orderly book, 1780. 1 vol.

Covering the period October 12–November 11, 1780, in New Jersey, this contains regimental and divisional orders, returns of arms and equipment, lists of officers with their duties, records of courts-martial, etc.

157. BRECK, SAMUEL (1771-1862). Philadelphia merchant. APS 1838. *DAB*

Historical sketch of the Continental bills of credit, from the year 1775 to 1781, with specimens thereof, 1840. 1 vol., including 153 specimens.

Although the author states that this was read to APS July 3, 1840, it differs markedly from the paper abstracted in APS *Proc.* 1 (1840): pp. 248-251. Breck read a second paper May 26, 1843, abstracted in APS *Proc.* 3 (1843): pp. 57-64. A revised version of the two papers, incorporating material in the manuscript, was printed in APS Historical and Literary Committee *Trans.* 3 (1843): pp. 1-40.

Presented by the author, 1856.

158. ———

Recollections of my acquaintance and association with deceased members of the American Philosophical Society, 1862. 1 vol.

Short sketches of

John Quincy Adams	Duc de La Rochefoucauld-Liancourt
Joel Barlow	Philippe Letombe
William Bingham	Louis Philippe
J. P. Brissot de Warville	Robert Morris
Marquis de Chastellux	John Penn
William Cobbett	Condy Raguet
J. Hector St. John de Crèvecœur	Benjamin Rush
Alexander Hamilton	Marquis de Talleyrand-Périgord
Edward A. Holyoke	Comte de Volney
Henry Knox	George Washington
Marquis de Lafayette	

159. BREWER, JOSEPH

The relation of the English Baptists with New England in the seventeenth century. Film.

Thesis for B.D. degree, University of Leeds, 1953.

160. BRILLON DE JOUY, MME ANNE LOUISE BOYVIN D'HARDANCOURT (1744-1824). Parisian hostess, friend of Franklin

Musical compositions. 26 pieces.

Principally by Mme Brillon, these compositions include marches ("La Marche des Insurgents"), sonatas, songs, etc. Some were played at APS, April 19, 1956, under the direction of Henry S. Drinker. For the program, with notes by Gilbert Chinard, see APS *Proc.* 100 (1956): p. 331.

161. ――――

Plays. 7 pieces. In French.

Comedies and tragedies, possibly not all by Mme Brillon, entitled: "La mort de Sénèque"; "Charles le mauvais, roi de Navarre; ou, La clémence du roi Jean"; "Charles premier, roi d'Angleterre"; "Marguerite d'Anjou, reine d'Angleterre"; "Molière aux enfer"; "Le songe, opéra comique"; and "Le bienfaisant maladroit; ou, plus de bruit que de besogne."

162. BRYCE, JAMES, VISCOUNT BRYCE (1838-1922). British ambassador to the United States, 1907-13. APS 1895. *DNB*

Personal reminiscences of Charles Darwin and of the reception of the "Origin of Species," 1909. Typed.

Corrected typescript of an address to APS commemorating the centenary of Darwin's birth and the fiftieth anniversary of the publication of the *Origin of Species,* April 23, 1909. Printed in APS *Proc.* 48 (1909): p. iii.

163. BURD, JAMES (1726-93). Merchant, soldier, farmer

Burd-Shippen Papers, 1708-92. 6 boxes, 3 vols.

Relating principally to the French and Indian War, 1754-63, in which Colonel Burd commanded at Fort Augusta and elsewhere, this collection contains letters (*ca.* 120) to Burd from Edward Shippen of Lancaster, Henry Bouquet, John Hambright, Lynford Lardner, Samuel Miles, William Trent, Walter Stirling, Daniel Wister, and others, on personal and business matters. Also receipts (*ca.* 450) to Burd for rents, washing, paint for the Six Nations, portage, glazing, repairs for wagons and boats, fabrics, horses, corn, beans, hay, beer, soap, etc.; receipts for wages, clothing, rum, bounty money, washing, barbering, etc., paid for Burd's company. Also miscellaneous invoices, receipts, bills of exchange, promissory notes, memoranda (*ca.* 400 pieces, 3 vols.) relating to Burd's company and his store, including such topics as victualling the troops at Fort Hunter and Fort Augusta, medical care, cutting the road to the Ohio, discipline, ordnance, enlistments, muster rolls, and returns. Persons mentioned include:

George Croghan	Dennis McCormick
Caleb Graydon	Hugh Mercer
David Hall	John Morgan
James Hamilton	Lewis Ourry
John Harris	Richard Peters
Samuel Hunter	James Tilghman

Also meteorological observations, 1747; rules of the Shippensburg, Pa., Library Company, 1753; and a copy of a journal kept at the siege of Fort William Henry, August 2-10, 1757, sent to Burd (printed in I. Minis Hays, "The siege of Fort William Henry," APS *Proc.* 37 [1898]: p. 143). Table of contents (36 pp.).

164. ――――

Business records and accounts, 1747-68. 7 vols.

1. Account book, Philadelphia, 1747-48. 1 vol. Notes of materials in stock (tammys, prunellos, florettas, serpentines, inkpots, knives, rugs, razors, etc.); records of sales. At

the end a member of the Burd family at Shippensburg, Pa., has copied legal forms, "Rules for Health," recipes and prescriptions, etc., *ca.* 1811-16.

2. Sale book, Book C, Philadelphia, 1747-48. 1 vol. Record of sales. The volume also includes the ledger of Joseph Burd of Tinian, Dauphin County, Pa., 1810, with notes, receipts, memoranda.

3. Day ledger, Philadelphia, 1747-49. 1 vol. Record of purchases; customers include: William Biddle, Mrs. Breintnall, Edward Shippen, Joseph Shippen, Dr. William Shippen, and Charles Stedman.

4. Account book, Philadelphia, 1749-51. 1 vol. Accounts, profit and loss statements, records of shipments.

5. Account book, Shippensburg, Pa., 1752-53, and Philadelphia, 1750-56. 1 vol. Sales of beer, malt, hops, wood, barrels; also of rugs, blankets, gunpowder, cambric, etc. Customers include: William Allen, James Benezet, Alexander Graydon, Edward Shippen, Joseph Shippen, Robert Smith.

6. Account book and index, 1765-68. Lancaster, Pa., 2 vols. Among the customers are the suppliers for Fort Augusta.

165. BURR, CHARLES H. Philadelphia lawyer

The treaty-making power of the United States and the methods of its enforcement as affecting the police powers of the states, 1912. Typed.

This essay won the Henry M. Phillips Prize of APS, 1912; and is printed in APS *Proc.* **51** (1912): p. 27.

166. BUXTORF, JOHANN (1564-1629). German Hebrew scholar. Hoefer

Hebrew grammar. 1 vol.

A manuscript translation made by Jonas Altamont Phillips, 1824.
Presented by Henry Phillips, Jr., 1890.

167. BYRD, WILLIAM (1674-1744). Virginia planter, official, writer. *DAB*

Histories of the dividing line betwixt Virginia and North Carolina, 1728. 2 vols.

History of the dividing line and Secret history of the line. Another version of the History and the manuscript of the Secret history are published in Louis B. Wright, ed., *The Prose Works of William Byrd of Westover* (Cambridge, Mass., 1966).
Presented by Mrs. E. C. Izard, 1815.

168. CAKCHIQUEL LANGUAGE TEXTS

The library has several volumes of grammars, vocabularies, sermons and other religious writings in the Cakchiquel language of Central America. Several have been studied, notably by Daniel G. Brinton in APS *Proc.* **21** (1884): p. 345, and Nora B. Thompson, "Algunos manuscutos guatemaltecos en Filadelfia," *Anales de la Sociedad de Geografía e Historia* **23** (1948), Nos. 1-2: p. 3; and all have been described by John F. Freeman, "Manuscript Sources on Latin American Indians," APS *Proc.* **106** (1962): p. 530, and in Freeman's *Guide to Manuscripts relating to the American Indian* (1966).
The Cakchiquel texts are:

Thomas Coto, Vocabulario de la lengua Cakchiquel y Guatimalteca, *ca.* 1700. 1 vol.

Francisco Maldonado, Arte, pronunciación y ortographia de la lengua . . . cakchiquel, *ca.* 1650? 1 vol.

Antonio del Saz, Manual de pláticas de todos los sacramentos para la administración de estos naturales con otras cossas importantes [1664]. 1 vol.

Francisco de Varela, Calepino de la lengua Cakchíquel [1699]. 1 vol.

Doctrina christiana, 1692? 1 vol.

Sermons, catechism, religious discourses, and grammar; the latter was translated by Daniel G. Brinton in APS *Proc.* **21** (1884): p. 345.

Sermon predicable en el domingo di septuagessima, 1727. 1 vol.

Sermons for holy days, the above being the title of the first.

Uae nima vutz rij theologi aindox ubinaam nima [1553, 1605]. 1 vol.

Sermons, with notes and birth records made by later missionaries.

Uae rugotzlem Sant Andros apostol [1605]. 1 vol.

Sermons.

Vocabulario de la lengua Cakchiquel, *ca.* 1675. 1 vol.

Presented by Academia de ciencias de Guatemala, 1836.

169. CANADA. NATIONAL MUSEUM

Catalogue of Indian songs collected by the National Museum, 1911-20. 170 pp. Typed.

Presented by Charles Marius Barbeau, 1951.

170. CANADA. PUBLIC ARCHIVES

Selected materials on Indian affairs. Film. 2 reels.

From Public Archives of Canada, Ottawa. Letters and papers from the Daniel Claus Papers, 1761-96, on Indian affairs at Forts Pitt, Niagara, and Detroit, with letters of Dr. Alexander McKee, Arthur St. Clair, Joseph Chew, Richard Butler, Joseph Brant, and John Graves Simcoe; from the papers of Brigadier Robert Monckton, 1760-61, appointments, returns, reports, bills and receipts, and letters relating to Forts Pitt, Bedford, and Niagara, with letters of James Burd, Horatio Gates, Henry Bouquet, Lewis Ourry, Sir John St. Clair, Thomas Hutchins, John Stanwix, and Lord Amherst; excerpts from Minutes of the Commissioners of Indian Affairs at Albany, 1723-46; transcripts from the Public Record Office on Indians, trade, defense, 1698-1767, including names of persons naturalized in British America, 1740-61, and accounts of Lt. Col. Harry Gordon, 1756-61, 1764-67; also letters of Duquesne to Contrecœur, 1752-53, from Université Laval, Quebec.

171. CANNON, WALTER BRADFORD (1871-1945). Physiologist. APS 1908. *Year Book* 1945

Correspondence with William W. Keen, 1905-28. 6 boxes.

Letters to and from Keen, principally about anti-vivisection, but also concerning medicine and surgery, neurology, tuberculosis, typhoid vaccination, treatment of shock, evolution, APS, the Mayo Clinic, American Medical Association, University of Minnesota, League of Nations, Keen's *Surgery*, University of Pennsylvania, Joseph Lister, Woodrow Wilson, William H. Taft, Edward W. Bok, S. Weir Mitchell, and others.

Presented by Walter B. Bradford, 1942.

172. CAREY, MATHEW (1760-1839). Printer, publisher, economist. APS 1821. *DAB*

Accounts, 1787-95. Film. 3 reels.

From American Antiquarian Society, Worcester, Mass.

173. ——

Letter books, 1788-94. Film. 1 reel.

From Historical Society of Pennsylvania. Correspondents include:

Jeremy Belknap   Tench Coxe
Bishop John Carroll   Timothy Dwight

Benjamin Franklin	Jedediah Morse
William Goddard	Isaiah Thomas
Ebenezer Hazard	Noah Webster
Thomas Jefferson	

174. CARPENTER, EDMUND SNOW (1918–). Archaeologist

The ancient mounds of Pennsylvania, 1941-48. 313 pp. Typed.

A report to APS summarizing archaeological data on Pennsylvania tumuli in manuscripts in APS Library; illustrated with photographs. The particular site reports on which this is based are:

1. McFate site, Crawford Co., by Harry L. Schoff.
2. Phillips site burials, Somerset Co.
3. Identification of faunal remains from southwestern Pennsylvania, by Raymond M. Gilmore and others.
4. Skeletal remains from Fayette and Somerset Cos., by Thomas D. Stewart.
5. Archaeological survey of Somerset Co., by Frank C. Cresson.
6. Brock mound, Lycoming Co.
7. Excavation of the village area near the burial mound on the H. G. Brock property, Muncy, Pa.
8. Cornplanter Run mounds, Warren Co.; Johnson mound, Chautauqua Co., N.Y.; Miller Jacobs, Hooks Run mounds and Frank Logan site, Cornplanter Reservation; Dwight Jimerson's site, Chautauqua Co., N.Y.
9. Irvine mound group, Warren Co., by Harry A. Schoff, Donald A. Cadzow, and Ross P. Wright.
10. Nelson mound, Crawford Co., by Harry L. Schoff.
11. Book mound, Beale township, Juniata Co.
12. Erie site, by Donald A. Cadzow. Published as Bulletin IV, Pennsylvania Historical Commission, 1938.
13. Crall mound.
14. Spartansburg mounds, Crawford Co.
15. Upper Allegheny Valley Survey report, by Edmund S. Carpenter.
16. Guyasutha mound, O'Hara township; Oakmont mound.
17. Williams mound, Warren Co.
18. Clemson's mound, Dauphin Co.
19. McKee's Rocks mound, near Pittsburgh.
20. Skeletal remains from Sugar Run mounds, Warren Co., by Thomas D. Stewart.
21. Photographs from Sugar Run mound group.
22. Field notes, southwestern Pennsylvania, by C. S. Fisher.
23. Kipp Island site, Seneca Co., N.Y.; Wheatland mound, Monroe Co., N.Y.; burial mound on Eagle Bluff, Cayuga Co., N.Y.; by H. L. Schoff.
24. Vandalia mound, Cattaraugus Co., N.Y.
25. 28th Street site, Erie, Pa.; Wesleyville site, Erie Co.
26. Pennsylvania Historical Commission, Archaeological reports, 1929, by Dorothy P. Skinner, Junius Bird, and others.
27. Profiles of Sugar Run mound site, Warren Co.
28. Photographs of sites and artifacts, Somerset and Fayette Cos.
29. Field drawings from Sick site, South Towanda, Bradford Co., excavated by John Witthoft, 1948.

Many of the reports are illustrated by photographs and maps. Most individual reports were prepared under the auspices of the Works Progress Administration.

Presented by Edmund S. Carpenter, 1948-49.

175. CARPENTERS COMPANY OF THE CITY AND COUNTY OF PHILADELPHIA

Papers, 1683-1952. 95 vols. and *ca.* 70 pieces.

The papers include: minutes, 1794, 1802-1942; minutes of the Managing Committee and Committee of Seven, 1791-1950; rough minutes of the Managing Committee, 1819-57; minutes of the Wardens, 1769-1919 (with some gaps); roll of members, 1841-75; price books, 1786, *ca.* 1804, 1827, 1852; Price Book Committee minutes, 1786-91, 1827-97; price book of the Second Carpenters Company, 1784; cash books, 1889-1952; treasurer's account, 1874-1907; ledgers, 1801-96; record of certificates granted to measurers of carpenters' work, 1827-89; account book, 1763-1834; minutes of the Building Committee, 1810-11; minutes of the Committee on fitting up the Old Hall, 1857; minutes of the Committees of Accounts and Rents, 1780-84; minutes of the Library Committee, 1853-89; receipts for books and library record of borrowers, 1846-90; by-laws and rules and regulations and standing resolutions, *ca.* 1866-69; minutes of the Friendship Carpenters Company, 1770-75; account of the Friendship Carpenters Company, 1769-99; rules and regulations of the Friendship Carpenters Company and specifications for building, 1769; relief given to 12 widows, 1818; scrapbook, 1887-92; "Antiques, Curiosities, and Memorabilia," 1683-1855; autographs, pictures, etc., relating to the Centennial Anniversary, 1874; Trustees' minute book, 1895-1941; book of "Dementtions" of carpenter's work by Samuel Jones, 1784; real estate record, 1905-1918; receipt books, 1795-1918; and other materials. The whole collection has been filmed by APS. The Library also has Ann L. Goldman, "The Carpenters' Company of Philadelphia and the beginnings of modern capitalism," 1965. 1 vol. Typed, carbon. Table of contents (6 pp.).

Deposited by the Carpenters Company, 1964.

176. CARSON, JOSEPH, collector

History of the Medical Department of the University of Pennsylvania. Extra-illustrated copy. Film. 1 reel.

From College of Physicians of Philadelphia. The copy of this work in the College of Physicians of Philadelphia library is illustrated with hundreds of letters, prints, and other illustrative material. From these have been selected for filming letters of APS members, persons prominent in scientific activities in early America, and some others, including:

Francis Alison, Sr.	John Fothergill
John Bard	William Hewson
Benjamin Smith Barton	James McClurg
Thomas Bond, Sr.	Peter Middleton
John Clayton	Samuel L. Mitchill
Cadwalader Colden	Thomas Nuttall
Peter Collinson	Joseph Priestley
Thomas Cooper	David Ramsay
William Currie	William Smith
William Darlington	Caspar Wistar

177. CASTLE, WILLIAM ERNEST (1867-1962). Geneticist. APS 1910. *Year Book* 1962

Papers, 1936-62. 20 pieces.

Principally letters to Leslie C. Dunn on genetics and other scientific topics, with several of autobiographical character.

Presented by L. C. Dunn, 1963.

178. CENTRAL AMERICA. ANTHROPOLOGY

Manuscripts on Middle American Cultural Anthropology. Film. 26 reels.

From University of Chicago. Field notes and reports, diaries of expeditions, texts, grammars, dictionaries of Indian languages, theses and research papers. Scholars whose work is represented include:

Manuel J. Andrade	Juan de Dios Rosales
Malcolm Carr	Eugene E. Doll

Virginia Drew	Ernest Noyes
Antonio Gouband Carrera	Robert Redfield
Calixta Guiteras Holmes	Betty W. Starr
Harold H. Key	Sol Tax
Howard F. Kline	Melvin M. Tumin
Jeanne Lepine	Benjamin Lee Whorf
Jackson Steward Lincoln	Charles Wisdom

Table of contents (18 pp.).

179. CERCLE DES PHILADELPHES, Cap-François
    Collection, 1784-87. 8 pieces. In French.
    Materials by and relating to Louis Narcisse Baudry de Lozières, member and president of the Society.

180. CHALMERS, GEORGE, collector
    Papers relating to Indian affairs, 1750-75. Film. 1 reel.
    From New York Public Library. Correspondence, intelligence reports, records of treaties, etc., principally concerning the Indians of the Ohio Valley; writers include Thomas Cresap, Thomas Hutchins, and Sir William Johnson. On the same reel are similar papers from the Schuyler papers, 1710-97.

181. CHEROKEE NATION
    Record book, 1902-03. 1 vol.
    The record book of a mutual aid group, in the Sequoyan syllabary.
    Presented by Raymond D. Fogelson, 1960.

182. CHEYNEY, EDWARD POTTS (1861-1947). Historian. APS 1904. *Year Book* 1947
    Studies in freedom of inquiry and expression, 1938. 1 vol. Typed, carbon.
    Chapters by Cheyney, Max Ascoli, Witt Bowden, Edward Y. Hartshorne, John M. Mecklin, Philip E. Mosley, Edward A. Shils, and Bernhard J. Stern on various aspects of the subject; the essays were edited by Cheyney and published in *Annals* of the American Academy of Political and Social Science, **200** (1938). Included are 13 letters about the manuscript to and from Edwin G. Conklin, Walter B. Cannon, and Roy F. Nichols, 1936-38.
    Presented by Edwin G. Conklin.

183. CLARK, RAYMOND P., JR.
    Introduction and guide to American magazines, 1741-69. Film. 1 reel.
    Master's thesis, University of Tennessee, 1949. An analysis of the contents of the magazines, including at least one newspaper called a "magazine."

184. CLARK, WILLIAM (1770-1838). Explorer, Indian agent, governor of Missouri
        Territory. *DAB*
    Diary, August 25–September 22, 1808. 1 vol.
    Kept on an expedition to make a treaty with the Osage Indians; printed in Kate L. Gregg, *Westward with Dragoons* (Fulton, Mo., 1937).
    Presented by Charles J. Biddle, 1949.

185. ———
    Journal, January 6-10, 1806. 1 vol.
    With notes of distances covered and draft of suggestion for routes for the fur trade.

Compare with the more formal report printed in Reuben G. Thwaites, ed., *Original Journals of the Lewis and Clark Expedition, 1804-1806* (New York, 1904-05) 3: p. 316. Presented by Charles J. Biddle, 1949.

186. CLEAVELAND, PARKER (1780-1858). Mineralogist, geologist. APS 1818. *DAB*

Letters. Film. 1 reel.

From Bowdoin College Library, Brunswick, Maine. Principal correspondents include:

Alexandre T. Brongniart	James Hall
Thomas Cooper	Edward Hitchcock
John Redman Coxe	William Maclure
Amos Eaton	Benjamin Silliman, Sr.
George Gibbs	John Torrey
Robert Gilmor	Benjamin Vaughan

Table of contents (3 pp.).

187. CLYMER, GEORGE (1739-1813). Merchant, signer of the Declaration of Independence. APS 1786. *DAB*

Papers, 1785-1848. 27 pieces.

Legal papers, including deeds, patents, articles of agreement, power of attorney; also some letters from Clymer and John Read to Samuel A. Law. Persons mentioned include Henry Drinker, Tench Francis, Samuel Meredith, and Thomas Meredith. Presented by Arthur Bloch, 1952.

188. CLYMER, L.

Letters, 1779-98. 7 pieces

Letters, principally from Trenton, N.J., to Samuel Meredith of Philadelphia, with comments on the American Revolution, Benjamin Rush, inoculation, Lafayette, taxes, politics, and business.

189. COARD, ROBERT L.

From Benjamin Franklin to Henry Adams: a study of American autobiography. Film. 1 reel.

Doctoral dissertation, University of Illinois, 1952.

190. COATES, MARGARET, and others

Receipt book, 1770-73. 1 vol.

Receipt book of Margaret Coates, Beulah Coates, and Alice Langdale, executors of the estate of Mary Coates; contains receipts for payments by Thomas Bond, Samuel Coates, Benjamin Rush, Amos Strettell, and others.

191. COATES, SAMUEL (1748-1830). Philadelphia merchant and philanthropist. *DAB*

Account and memoranda books, 1785-1830. 5 vols. and 1 reel.

Memorandum book, 1785-1825 (1 reel, film from Pennsylvania Hospital); account book of the estate of Deborah Morris, 1793-1817 (1 vol.), containing a copy of her will, inventory, records of income and disbursements by the executors; day book, 1796-1816 (1 vol.), containing notes of payments and sales, of wills written, mortgages arranged, rentals agreed to, notes signed, etc.; receipt book, 1803-30 (1 vol.), containing signed receipts for purchase of hickory wood, flour, ham, ships stores, oil, varnish, liquors, gravestones, chairs, milk, "cyder," and for payments of taxes, wages, "painting his house," etc., vendors including Zaccheus Collins, John Syng Dorsey, Peter S. Du Ponceau, Christian Febiger, Isaac Hopper, Rebecca Jones, and Ann Moore (presented by Arthur Bloch, 1953); and bank books, 1788-98 (2 vols.), being a record of checks, bills of exchange, notes, gold, silver, and currency "sent to Bank [of North America]."

192. COATES, THOMAS (1659-1719). Philadelphia merchant
Memorandum book, 1678-98. 1 vol.
Principally a record of payments for paper, hay, stockings, butter, silks, coats, nails, flax, etc., with a few journal entries; bound with the *British Merlin*, almanac, for 1683.

193. COLBERT MAULEVRIER, EDOUARD CHARLES VICTURNIEN, comte de (1758-1820). Naval officer
Journal d'un voyage, 1798. Film. 1 reel.
From manuscripts in possession of M. le comte Paul de Leusse. Edited by Gilbert Chinard and published as *Voyage dans l'intérieur des États-Unis et au Canada* (Baltimore, 1935).

194. COLERIDGE, SAMUEL TAYLOR (1772-1834). English poet and philosopher. *DNB*
Marginalia. Film. 5 reels.
From British Museum and other libraries. Marginal notes and jottings from his books; miscellaneous notes on philosophy and philosophers; his Complete System of Logic in the hand of John Henry Green; some letters to Thomas Poole. Table of contents (6 pp.).

195. COLLEGE OF PHYSICIANS OF PHILADELPHIA
Miscellaneous letters. Film.
From College of Physicians of Philadelphia. A small selection of letters of men of science, including Benjamin Smith Barton, William P. C. Barton, William Darlington, Benjamin Silliman, Sr., Robert Hare, Joseph Leidy, Samuel G. Morton, Robert M. Patterson, and others.

196. COLLINS, FRANK SHIPLEY (1848-1920). American botanist. *DAB*
Papers, 1872-1919. *ca.* 1,800 pieces, 4 scrapbooks with 488 mounted specimens of algae.
Letters and copies of letters on botanical subjects, principally algae, many on the identification of species and on the sale and exchange of mounted specimens. Correspondents include:

E. Boruet	T. Reinbold
Mme A. Weber von Bosse	Herbert M. Richards
Cora Huidekoper Clarke	Benjamin Lincoln Robinson
William J. Crozier	L. Kolderup Rosenvinge
Bradley Moore Davis	DeAlton Saunders
Willie Fischer	Camille Sauvageau
Lucy F. Gillette	Jacob R. Schramm
Frederick O. Grover	R. E. Schuh
Ferdinand Hauch	William A. Terry
Tracy E. Haven	George W. Traill
Thomas W. Higginson	Edgar R. Transeau
William Deans Hoyt	George Stephen West
J. E. Humphrey	K. Yendo
Johann Nordal	

Table of contents (26 pp.).

197. COLLINS, ZACCHEUS (*ca.* 1764-1831). Merchant, botanist. APS 1804.

Botanical correspondence, 1805-27. Film. 1 reel.

From Academy of Natural Sciences of Philadelphia. Principal correspondents are:

William Baldwin	Eli Ives
William P. C. Barton	Frederick A. Muhlenberg
Jacob Bigelow	Gotthilf H. E. Muhlenberg
Isaac Cleaver	Thomas Nuttall
Caspar W. Eddy	H. Steinhauer
Stephen Elliott	John Torrey

There is an index and table of contents in the manuscript.

198. COLLINSON, PETER (1694-1768). London merchant and naturalist. *DNB*

Collinson-Bartram Papers, 1732-73. 36 pieces.

Principally letters to Collinson about seeds, plants, and gardens from seedsmen and owners of country estates, including Cadwalader Colden, Josiah Hanbury, Lord and Lady Petre, the Duke of Norfolk, the Duke of Richmond, Sir Hans Sloane, and Daniel Solander. There are also several letters of John Bartram to William Bartram and Philip Miller. Table of contents.

Deposited by the John Bartram Association, 1952.

199. ——

Papers. Film. 1 reel.

From Linnean Society, London. Letters and drafts of replies, memoranda, lists of plants and shrubs, observations on natural history, diary notes, extracts from reading, recipes, etc.; also "Catalogue of Books given to the [Friends] Publick School of Philadelphia" by Collinson, 1749. Correspondents include:

Joseph Breintnall	John Kearsley, Sr.
William Bull, Jr.	Carl Linnaeus
Arthur Dobbs	Robert Hunter Morris
John Fothergill	Israel Pemberton
Alexander Garden	Giles Rainsford
J. G. Gmelin	Sir Charles Wager
Stephen Hales	Edward Wright
Henry Hollyday	

Table of contents (15 pp.).

200. CONDORCET, MARIE JEAN ANTOINE NICOLAS DE CARITAT, marquis de (1743-94). Mathematician, *philosophe*, secretary of the Académie des Sciences. APS 1775. Hoefer

Sur l'utilité des académies, 1785. 1 vol. Draft. In French.

Laid in is the report of the committee appointed to consider this manuscript, extracted from the minutes of the Académie des Sciences, May 12, 1785.

201. CONFERENCE ON SCIENCE MANUSCRIPTS

Records, 1958-64. 1 box.

Correspondence, papers, accounts, etc., about a conference at Washington, D.C., May 5-6, 1960, to discuss the need, feasibility, and methods of collecting, preserving, and studying the papers of scientists. Nathan Reingold was chairman of the Conference. The papers read at the Conference are printed in *Isis*, 53, 1 (1962).

Presented by Dr. Reingold, 1965.

202. COOKE, CHARLES (1870-1958). Canadian ethnologist
Iroquois personal names, 1900-50. 1332 pp. Typed.
Alphabetical list of about 6,200 Iroquoian names.
Presented by Charles Marius Barbeau, 1951.

203. COPE, EDWARD DRINKER (1840-97). Paleontologist. APS 1866. *DAB;* APS
Proc. Memorial Volume 1 (1900)
Field diaries, 1872-74, 1876-77, 1879, 1881-85, 1892. Film.
From American Museum of Natural History, New York. Notes kept on paleonto-
logical expeditions to the American West; with one journal of a trip to Paris.

204. CORNPLANTER, JESSE. Seneca Indian
Indian songs in Seneca dialect in syllables. And other rituals, 1916-51. 1 vol.
Typed.
Songs transcribed by Cornplanter from manuscripts of his father Edward Corn-
planter and of George Pierce, and also from memory, with 4 letters between Jesse
Cornplanter and William N. Fenton.
Presented by William N. Fenton, 1951.

205. CORRÊA DA SERRA, JOSÉ FRANCESCO (1750-1823). Portuguese naturalist and
diplomat. APS 1812. Appleton
Papers, 1772-1827. 2 boxes.
About 200 transcripts and photocopies of letters, made by Richard B. Davis for
"The Abbé Correa in America," APS *Trans.* 45, 2 (1955). Correspondents include:

John Quincy Adams	Gotthilf H. E. Muhlenberg
Thomas Cooper	George Ord
Edward J. Corrêa da Serra	William Rawle
Peter S. Du Ponceau	Richard Rush
Alexander von Humboldt	Fulwar Skipwith
Thomas Jefferson	Sir James Edward Smith
Carl Linnaeus	John Vaughan
James Madison	Robert Walsh
James Monroe	Caspar Wistar

Table of contents (3 pp.).
Presented by Richard B. Davis, 1958.

206. ———
Miscellaneous letters. Film. 1 reel.
Letters to and from Corrêa da Serra, collected by Richard Beale Davis from several
libraries, including British Museum, Library of Congress, University of Virginia, Duke
University, Linnean Society of London, Historical Society of Pennsylvania, Bibliotheca
Nacional, Rio de Janeiro, and National Archives, Washington.

207. COXE, JOHN REDMAN (1773-1864). Philadelphia physician, teacher, and editor. APS 1799. *DAB*
Observations & remarks tending to explain certain parts of the sacred scrip-
tures, 1812-13. 1 vol.
Contains also some newspaper clippings and a manuscript obituary of Julian Halliday Coxe (1833-34), infant son of Daniel T. Coxe.

208. CRAMER, FREDERICK HENRY (1906-54). Professor of history, Mount Holyoke College

Astrology in Roman law and politics, 1954(?).

This is volume 2, lacking chapter 1, of a scholarly study of which the first volume was published as APS *Memoirs* 37 (1954).
Presented by Mrs. Cramer, 1956, 1958.

209. CUMMINGS, HUBERTIS MAURICE (1884-1963). Historian

Edward Shippen of Lancaster, 1936. 36 pp. Typed.

Biographical sketch, without bibliography or citations.
Presented by the author, *ca.* 1936.

210. CUTLER, MANASSEH (1742-1823). Clergyman, colonizer, botanist. APS 1785. *DAB*

Letters, 1777-90. Film.

From Northwestern University Library, Evanston, Ill. Letters from Jeremy Belknap, Aaron Dexter, Ezra Stiles, Samuel Vaughan, Jr., and others; with drafts of some of Cutler's letters.

211. DALE, RICHARD (1756-1826). Naval officer. *DAB*

Miscellaneous letters and papers, 1780-1845. Film. 1 reel.

From the Estate of Edward C. Dale, 1947. The collection contains letters of Commodore Dale to the Secretary of the Navy, William Bainbridge, Samuel Barron, William Eaton, David Humphreys, Rufus King, British, Algerian, and Tripolitanian officials, 1801-02; also a miscellaneous collection of letters of Charles Biddle, James Biddle, Mahlon Dickerson, John Paul Jones, John Y. Mason, Oliver H. Perry, Edward Preble, Benjamin Stoddert, Thomas Truxtun, and others, 1780-1845; and Dale's journal on a voyage to Canton, 1787-88. Table of contents.

212. DARLINGTON, WILLIAM (1782-1863). Physician and naturalist. APS 1823. *DAB*; APS *Proc.* 9 (1864)

Letters and papers, 1777-1863. Film. 1 reel.

From Free Library of Philadelphia. Miscellaneous letters and drafts of letters; genealogical notes, medical essays, copies of letters and essays sent to newspapers and magazines; bills and receipts; invitations; military and other commissions; biographical memoir of General John Lacey, 1823; also papers, principally official, of his son Lieut. B. S. B. Darlington, U.S.N.

213. ———

Selected letters, 1836-57. Film.

From New-York Historical Society. A few letters to Darlington from, among others, Spencer F. Baird, Robert Carr, Edward D. Ingraham, Moses Marshall, George Ord, John Jay Smith, and John F. Watson; also from Joseph Johnson, enclosing a sketch of the life of Stephen Elliott (1771-1830). Table of contents (9 pp.).

214. DARRACH, CHARLES GOBRECHT. Civil engineer, Philadelphia

Topography of the earth, 1914. Blueprint of typed copy.

The author claims that studies in paleontology, biology, and topography "practically eliminate the Darwinian hypothesis from serious consideration in the study of nature." The essay, which is illustrated by maps, is "dedicated to the memory of Henry Pemberton, Member American Philosophical Society."
Presented by the author, 1915.

215. DARWIN, CHARLES ROBERT (1809-82). Naturalist, author of *Origin of Species.*
APS 1869. *DNB*

Letters, 1837-82. *ca.* 700 pieces.

Chiefly correspondence between Darwin and other scientists on scientific topics, notably natural selection, the theory of evolution, the controversy caused by *Origin of Species,* and coral islands. Correspondents include:

James Scott Bowerbank
William Buckland
George Busk
Thomas Campbell Eyton
Sir William Henry Flower
David Forbes
Sir Michael Foster
Asa Gray
John Edward Gray
Albert C. L. G. Günther
John Thomas Gulick
Albany Hancock
John Stevens Henslow
John Maurice Herbert
Sir Joseph Dalton Hooker
Leonard Horner
Alexander von Humboldt
Thomas Henry Huxley
Edwin Lankester

Joseph Leidy
Sir John W. Lubbock
Sir Charles Lyell
Henri Milne-Edwards
Sir Roderick Impey Murchison
William Ogle
Daniel Oliver
Sir Richard Owen
John Phillips
Jean Louis Armand de
    Quatrefages de Bréau
Sir William Ramsay
George John Romanes
Philip Lutley Sclater
George Henry Kendrick
    Thwaites
Alfred Russel Wallace
Benjamin D. Walsh
Jeffries Wyman

The collection includes photostats of 18 letters from Walsh to Darwin in the Chicago Museum of Natural History, and photostats of Darwin manuscripts in possession of Dr. Robert M. Stecher, Cleveland, Ohio.

216. ――――

Miscellaneous correspondence, 1836-82. Films.

From Down House, Kent: Correspondence with his family, Sir William J. Hooker, Sir John W. Lubbock, William Ogle, Daniel Oliver, John Tyndall, and Sir William Ramsay, 1836-82 (1 reel). Table of contents (13 pp.).

From the collection of Dr. Robert M. Stecher, Cleveland, Ohio (1961): Letters to J. Brodie-Innes, W. H. Bates, Lady Dorothy Nevill, and others (1846-82); also letters to his wife and son and letters and papers about him (1 reel).

From New York Botanical Garden; from Burgerbibliothek, Berne; from Medizin-historische Institut, Zurich; from University of Basel Library; from Bibliothèque Publique et Universitaire, Geneva; and other sources: Letters from Darwin to G. H. K. Thwaites, William B. Tegetmeier, Albany Hancock, Richard Owen, Bernhard Studer, Auguste H. Forel, J. Moulinie, A. Bohrn, Karl Christoph Vogt, François Joseph Pictet de la Rive, and others.

217. DARWIN, SIR FRANCIS GALTON (1848-1925). Botanist. APS 1909. *DNB*

Letters, 1869-1912. 27 pieces.

Principally letters to Charles Edward Sayle and on musical programs; letters to Thomas Roscoe Rede Stebbing about the Linnean Society, the Royal Society, and the publication of Charles Darwin's papers; also a letter of Charles Darwin to Stebbings and several letters of Francis Darwin to other persons.

218. DAVENPORT, CHARLES BENEDICT (1866-1944). Biologist; director, Department of Genetics, Carnegie Institution of Washington. APS 1907. *Year Book* 1944

Papers, 1874-1944. 175 transfer cases, 12 file drawers.

Diaries, student notebooks, and family correspondence; papers relating to the founding of the Station for Experimental Evolution of the Carnegie Institution, 1904, and of the Eugenics Record Office, 1905 (later combined as Department of Genetics); correspondence with Albert F. Blakeslee, George H. Shull (as editor of the journal *Genetics*), and Milislav Demerec. Other correspondents include:

William E. Castle	Theodore Roosevelt
John H. Finley	Elihu Root
Irving Fisher	Vilhjalmur Stefansson
C. B. S. Hodson	John H. Stokes
William T. Hornaday	Oscar W. Underwood
William C. Redfield	

Presented by Carnegie Institution of Washington, 1965.

219. DAVID LIBRARY OF THE AMERICAN REVOLUTION

Collection. Film. 1 reel.

From David Library of the American Revolution, Washington Crossing State Park, Pa. A miscellaneous collection of autograph letters of public figures of the American Revolutionary period, with some printed materials, mostly dated during the years of the war. Except for Washington, Lafayette, and Robert Morris, most persons are represented with only a single letter or document. There is an "Epitre à Franklin" in the collection. An alphabetical index of writers precedes the manuscripts.

220. DAVY, SIR HUMPHRY (1778-1829). English natural philosopher. APS 1810. *DNB*

Correspondence, 1803-22. 34 pieces.

Chiefly correspondence with Alexander John Gaspard Marcet on chemistry, with references to Sir Joseph Banks, John Eric Berger, Johan Jakob Berzelius, Jean Baptiste Biot, and others; a few letters to and from John Bostock, Thomas Cooper, and Giovanni Fabroni.

221. DAWES, MRS. ELIZABETH F., collector

Miscellaneous documents of American history, 1681-1921. 70 items. 1 packet.

Principally of Pennsylvania interest, 1757-1809, including letters to Richard I. Manning from John C. Calhoun, Marquis de Lafayette, George McDuffie, and William Wirt; also letters of Clement C. Biddle, James Buchanan, Francis J. Grund, James Madison, Timothy Pickering, and William H. Seward; also several musical scores, and 19 canceled checks drawn by Ticknor & Fields, Boston, to the order of various American authors, 1861-71. Table of contents (3 pp.).

222. DAY, GORDON M., compiler

Wampanoag material supplied by Chief Wild Horse. Film. 1 reel.

From Dartmouth College Library. Word lists, phrases, and sentences, with English equivalents.

223. DEANE, SIDNEY NORTON (1878-1943)

A New England pioneer among the Oneida Indians. Film.

From manuscript in possession of Benjamin D. Meritt, Princeton, N.J., 1962. Sketch of the life of James Dean (1748-1823) of Westmoreland, N.Y.; with a version of the Oneida creation myth.

224. DEERING, FRANK C., collector
Collection of Indian captivities. Photostat, typed.
A list of titles, with analyses by Charles Marius Barbeau.
Presented by Charles Marius Barbeau, 1950-53.

225. DE LAGUNA, FREDERICA. Anthropologist
Notes on recordings of songs and dances. 1960. Film. 1 reel.
From manuscript in possession of Miss de Laguna, Bryn Mawr College. The recordings were made at Copper River, Alaska.

226. DE LAGUNA, FREDERICA, and CATHARINE McCLELLAN. Anthropologists
Field notebooks, 1950-60. Film. 5 reels.
From manuscripts in possession of Miss de Laguna, Bryn Mawr College. Ethnological notes on the Tlinglit of Yakutat and Angoon, and of the Copper River Atna Athabaskans of Chitina, Copper Center, and Christochina, Alaska.

227. DELAWARE. NEWCASTLE
Charter, 1724. 32 pp.
Sir William Keith's copy of the royal charter issued by George I.
Presented by Dr. and Mrs. George Logan, 1817.

228. DOBBS, ARTHUR (1689-1765). Governor of North Carolina. *DAB*
Letters to the Earl of Loudoun, 1756-57. Film.
From Henry E. Huntington Library and Art Gallery, San Marino, Calif. Table of contents.

229. DOBLAZ, GONZALO DE (1744-1809). Adventurer and official.
Memoria histórica, política y económica de esta provincia de misiones de Indios Guaranis, 1785. 1 vol.
An account of Spanish policy toward the Guarani Indians in Spanish mission settlements, especially after the suppression of the Jesuits; prepared for Felix de Azara, commandant of Paraguay. Printed from a variant manuscript in Pedro de Angelis, *Colección de obras y documentos relativos a la historia antigua y moderna de las provincias del Río de la Plata* (Buenos Aires, 1836).
Presented by Joel R. Poinsett, 1820.

230. DODGE, BERNARD OGILVIE (1872-1960). Botanist, plant pathologist
Papers, 1908-61. 44 pieces.
Contains letters to Dodge from Charles H. Peck, William G. Farlow, David R. Goddard, Robert A. Harper, and H. Rehm; certificates and diplomas of learned societies; and letters and data about Dodge addressed to William J. Robbins, who used them in preparing his memoir of Dodge for the *Biographical Memoirs* of the National Academy of Sciences.
Presented by William J. Robbins, 1963.

231. DONALDSON, HENRY HERBERT (1857-1938). Neurologist. APS 1906. *DAB; Year Book* 1938
Diaries and papers, 1869-1938. 50 vols.

Diaries, 1890-1938, containing brief records of professional work and family events (49 vols.); also autobiography entitled "Memories for my boys," 1930, referring to his childhood and to his professional career and mentioning Franz Boas, William Comstock, Livingston Farrand, William W. Keen, S. Weir Mitchell, Elihu Root, and W. T. Sedgwick and also APS, University of Chicago, Johns Hopkins University, Yale University, and Wistar Institute (1 vol.); also a few miscellaneous papers, 1869-1932, chiefly letters to and from members of his family, and also Poultney Bigelow, Simon Henry Gage, and S. B. Van Ingen; two essays ("The Days of Man" and "A Venetian Night"); genealogical data; verses dedicated to his wife; extracts of letters to supplement his diaries.

Presented by Mrs. Donaldson, 1939-40.

232. DUANE, WILLIAM J. (1780-1865). Lawyer, Secretary of the Treasury. *DAB*

Memoirs. Film.

From manuscripts in possession of Morris Duane, Philadelphia, 1963. A biographical sketch illustrated with pictures and letters of, among others:

John Quincy Adams	Andrew Jackson
Nicholas Biddle	Amos Kendall
Henry Clay	James Madison
Thomas P. Cope	Thomas McKean
George M. Dallas	Robert Morris
John Fothergill	David Rittenhouse
John C. Frémont	John Sergeant
Stephen Girard	John Witherspoon
Joseph Hopkinson	Levi Woodbury

233. DUANE FAMILY

Papers, 1770-1933. *ca.* 120 pieces.

Principally social letters among members of the family, including Mrs. Deborah Bache Duane, Charles William Duane, Russell Duane, William J. Duane, William Duane (1760-1835), and William Duane (1807-82); also letters and papers of Roland S. Morris, including letters to his sister Mrs. Russell Duane, 1896-1933. Other letters refer to Benjamin Franklin, education, Japan, the election of Woodrow Wilson as president of the United States, wills, estates, and legal matters. Other correspondents include:

Alexander Viets Griswold Allen	George W. Moore
Alexander D. Bache	William Ford Nichols
Phillips Brooks	William H. Odenheimer
George W. Curtis	James Parton
John Dickinson	William Stevens Perry
John Fries Frazer	Alonzo Potter
George Angier Gordon	Henry R. Schoolcraft
Josiah G. Holland	Jared Sparks
William R. Huntington	William Bacon Stevens
Charles J. Ingersoll	Samuel J. Tilden
Brantz Mayer	John Vaughan
Daniel Merriman	Daniel Webster

Table of contents (3 pp.).

Presented by Morris Duane, 1957, and Samuel Moyerman, 1953.

234. DUHAMEL DU MONCEAU, HENRI LOUIS (1700-82). French agronomist and botanist. Hoefer

Papers, 1716-89. 17 boxes, 25 folders. In French.

Principally on botany and agriculture, this collection includes many manuscripts on trees, shrubs, and plants of different species, copies of botanical essays by others, essays on fruit trees, etc., by Auguste Denis Fougeroux de Bondaroy (1732-89), notes and drafts for the latter's revision of Duhamel's *Traité des Arbes et Arbustes.* Also miscellaneous essays, sketches, and memoranda on bones of birds and animals, electricity, poisons, steam engines, ventilation, temperature and air pressure, mathematics, paleontology ("Observations sur les os d'éléphante fossile"), chemistry, metallurgy, entomology, architecture, taxidermy ("Méthode pour empailler les oiseaux"); lists of plants; notes on England, Canada, Mexico, China; notes of reading in Pliny, John Evelyn, Alexander Russell, William Derham, and others. Also a translation of Jethro Tull's *Horse-Hoeing Husbandry,* with additions and revisions by Duhamel du Monceau. Also an alphabetical catalogue of Duhamel's gardens, prepared by Fougeroux de Bondaroy. Also correspondence (*ca.* 170 pieces) with, among others, Duc d'Ayen, Duc de Noailles, Louis J. M. Daubenton, Mathurin Jacques Brisson, Jean François Gauthier, Comte de La Galissonière, Chrétien Guillaume de Lamoignon de Malesherbes, Emerich Vattel. The collection has been described in part by Gilbert Chinard, "Recently Acquired Botanical Documents," APS *Proc.* **101** (1957): p. 508; and by Joseph Ewan, "Fougeroux de Bondaroy (1732-1789) and his Projected Revision of Duhamel du Monceau's *Traité* (1755) on Trees and Shrubs. I. An Analytical Guide to Persons, Gardens, and Works mentioned in the Manuscripts," APS *Proc.* **103** (1959): p. 807. Table of contents (15 pp.).

235. Dumas, Jean Baptiste André (1800-84). Chemist. APS 1860. Larousse

La Vie de J.-B. Dumas, 1800-1884, par son petit fils, le Général J.-B. Dumas, 1924. 1 vol. Mimeographed.

Presented by the author, 1925.

236. No item.

237. Dunbar, William (1749-1810). Planter and scientist. APS 1800. *DAB*

Journal of a geometrical survey . . . [to] the hot springs, 1804-05. 1 vol.

Printed in Thomas Jefferson, *Documents Relating to the Purchase and Exploration of Louisiana . . .* II. *The Exploration of the Red, the Black, and the Washita Rivers, by William Dunbar* (Boston, 1904).

Presented by Daniel Parker, 1817.

238. Dunglison, Robley (1798-1869). Physician, teacher, writer. APS 1832. *DAB*

Autobiographical ana. Film. 4 reels.

From College of Physicians of Philadelphia. Edited by Samuel X. Radbill and published in APS *Trans.,* n.s., **53**, 8 (1963).

239. Dupaix, Guillermo

Viages sobre las antiqüedades mejicanas, 1805-07. 2 vols.

Accounts of three archaeological expeditions, 1805-07; 1 volume of sketches. Printed in Viscount Kingsborough, *Antiquities of Mexico* (London, 1831) **5.**

Presented by Joel R. Poinsett, 1830.

240. Du Ponceau, Peter Stephen (1760-1844). Lawyer, author, philologist. APS 1791. *DAB*

Papers, 1786-1842. 9 pieces.

Letters on law, business, Indian languages, APS, etc., to and from Edward S. Burd, Samuel Coates, Albert Gallatin, and William Tilghman.

241. ——

Commonplace book, 1820. 1 vol.

Notes on the colonial history of Pennsylvania, with emphasis on William Penn and his family, the Society of Friends, James Logan, and the charters granted by Penn; with some notes on the study of languages and definition of words.

Bequeathed by the author, 1844.

242. ――――

Notebooks on philology, 9 vols.

Principally on American Indian languages, with some notes on the languages of the Tartars, Arabs, Greeks, Polynesians, and others.

Bequeathed by the author, 1844.

243. ――――

Essai de solution du problème philologique proposé en l'année 1823 par la commission de l'Institut de France. 1 vol.

The commission was charged with offering a prize on linguistics, under the will of Count Volney. Formerly, this essay was thought to have been by Baron Nicolas Massias (1764-1848), who won the Volney prize in 1828.

Bequeathed by the author, 1844.

244. ――――

Indian vocabularies, 1820-44. 1 vol.

The first 23 pages of the volume are the Continuance Docket of the Court of Common Pleas, Philadelphia County, 1783-86. Cases noted are those involving Stephen Dutilh, Samuel Garrigues, John Girard, John Holker, Charles J. de Longchamps, and Claude P. Raguet.

Bequeathed by the author, 1844.

245. ――――

Sea terms in different languages. 1 vol.

Bequeathed by the author, 1844.

246. ――――

Letters to Albert Gallatin, 1801-43. Film.

From New-York Historical Society. Table of contents.

247. ――――

Letters to John Heckewelder, 1816-22. Film.

From State Historical Society of Wisconsin. Mostly on Indian linguistics.

248. DU PONT DE NEMOURS FAMILY

Papers relating to the American Philosophical Society, 1800-94. *ca.* 50 pieces. Photostats.

Correspondents include:

Augustin P. de Candolle	Thomas Jefferson
José F. Corrêa da Serra	J. P. Lesley
Eleuthère I. du Pont	Joseph Philippe Letombe
Henry A. du Pont	François André Michaux
Pierre S. du Pont de Nemours	James Monroe
Victor Marie du Pont	Henry Phillips
Philippe Nicolas Harmand	William Strickland
Thomas C. James	John Vaughan

From the originals in the Eleutherian Mills-Hagley Historical Library.

249. DUPRÉ, AUGUSTIN (1748-1833). French medalist

Drawings and matrices of medals relating to the American Revolution and the United States. 16 pieces.

The drawings are described and reproduced in Carl Zigrosser, "Medallic Sketches of Augustin Dupré in American Collections," APS *Proc.* 101 (1957): p. 535.

250. EAST INDIA COMPANY

Instructions for observing the Transit of Venus, 1761. Film. 1 reel.

Also the results of inquiries concerning Bencoolen, Batavia, and St. Helena as sites for taking observations of the Transit, June 6, 1761, with notes on locations, personnel, etc. Also letters of Lord Macclesfield, Charles Mason, Jeremiah Dixon; and a bill from John Bird for astronomical equipment.

251. EDWARDS, BENJAMIN (fl. 1820-30)

Letters, 1819-27. 6 pieces.

Addressed to his father about Major Stephen H. Long's Rocky Mountain expedition, 1819-20, of which the writer was a member.

252. ELKINS, WILSON H.

British policy in its relations to the commerce and navigation of the United States of America from 1794 to 1807. Film. 1 reel.

Doctoral thesis, Oxford University, n.d.

253. EYTON, THOMAS CAMPBELL (1809-80). English naturalist. *DNB*

Correspondence, 1836-74. *ca.* 325 pieces.

Letters on subjects in natural history, especially birds and mollusks, from men of science, including:

Robert Ball	Albert Carl Ludwig Gotthilf
Thomas Bell	Günther
Edward Blyth	John Stevens Henslow
Charles Robert Bree	Sir William Jackson Hooker
Francis Trevelyan Buckland	Thomas Henry Huxley
August Leopold Crelle	Sir William Jardine
Hugh Cuming	William Allport Leighton
Charles Robert Darwin	Sir Richard Owen
Sir Philip de Malpas Grey Egerton	Robert Patterson (1802-72)
William Henry Flower	Philip Lutley Sclater
Edward Forbes	Earl of Derby
John Gould	Hugh Edwin Strickland
George Robert Gray	Alfred Russel Wallace
John Edward Gray	William Yarnell

This collection was made for its value as a group of autograph letters.

254. FABRONI, GIOVANNI VALENTINO MATTIA (1752-1822). Italian scientist; director of the Mint, Florence. Hoefer

Papers, 1652-1875. In Italian, French, Latin, English.

Letters from, and drafts of letters to, scientists, artists, musicians, soldiers, political figures, court personages throughout Europe, especially Italy and France, not only on personal and social affairs, but also on agriculture, botany, geology, natural history, coinage, museum management, politics, weights and measures, current affairs. Also diaries, 1778-80 (5 vols.), of a visit to England, with sketches of machines, locks, bridges, tools, etc., notes on persons, quotations from useful publications, descriptions of manufacturing processes. Among the correspondents are:

Giovanni Aldini
Carlo Amoretti
Jacques Laurent Anisson Duperon
Sir Joseph Banks
Carlo Botta
Roger Joseph Boscovich
Luigi Gaspard Brugnatelli
Jacques A. C. Charles
Antoine Court de Gébelin
Lorenz Crell
Georges L. C. F. D. Cuvier
Vicenzo Dandolo
Jean Darcet
Sir Humphry Davy
Joseph Philippe François Deleuze
Francesco Favi
Felice Fontana
George Forster
Johann Reinhold Forster
Giorgio Gallerio
Stefano Gallini
Henri Grégoire
Gabriel Grimaldi
Frederick Augustus Hervey, Earl of
    Bristol and Bishop of Derry
Alexander von Humboldt
Wilhelm von Humboldt
Jan Ingenhousz
Angelica Kauffmann
Richard Kirwan

Bernard G. E. de la Ville,
    comte de Lacépède
Marquis de Lafayette
Joseph Jerome le Français
    de Lalande
François A. F. de La Roche-
    foucauld-Liancourt
Mme Lavoisier
Filippo Mazzei
Jean Hyacinthe Magellan
Thomas Penrose
Jan Potocki
Joseph Priestley
Giuseppe Raddi
Rudolph E. Raspe
Luigi Sacco
Giorgio Santi
William Saunders
Gaetano Savi
James Smithson
Daniel Solander
Ottaviano Targioni-Tozzetti
Abbé Alexandre H. Tessier
Arsène Thiebaut
Karl Peter Thunberg
Antonio M. Vassalli-Eandi
Giambattista Venturi
Josiah Wedgwood
John Whitehurst

Tables of contents (51 pp.).

255. FEATHERSTONHAUGH, GEORGE WILLIAM (1780-1866). Geologist, traveler. APS 1809. *DNB*

Papers, 1809-26. 15 pieces. Photostats.

Letters, chiefly relating to APS, from Peter S. Du Ponceau, John Vaughan, and James Mease. From originals in possession of Mrs. Duane Featherstonhaugh, Duanesburg, N.Y., 1961.

256. FEINS, CLAIRE K.

Dr. David Hosack at Hyde Park: a report for the Vanderbilt Mansion National Historic Site at Hyde Park. Film.

A historical study prepared for the National Park Service.

257. FERMI, ENRICO (1901-54). Physicist. APS 1939. *Year Book* 1955

Letters to Enrico Perisco, 1918-26. Copies.

Several letters and postal cards on scientific and personal matters, with a long letter about Fermi's career from Adolfo Amidei to Emilio Segrè, 1958.

Presented by Emilio Segrè, 1965.

258. FIELDS, HAROLD B.

The influence of Peter Muhlenberg in Virginia, 1772-76. Film.
Master's thesis, University of Chicago, 1929.

259. FITZPATRICK, FRANKLIN E.

Irish immigration into New York from 1860 to 1880. Film.
Doctoral dissertation, Catholic University of America, 1948.

260. FLEXNER, SIMON (1863-1946). Physician, pathologist, administrator. APS
    1901. *Year Book* 1946

Papers, 1891-1946. *ca.* 200,000 pieces.

A great collection, chiefly correspondence, of letters, diaries, drafts of articles and
addresses, etc., of a man who studied medicine at the Johns Hopkins University, was professor of pathology at the University of Pennsylvania, and was director of the Rockefeller
Institute for Medical Research; the manuscripts record or reflect almost every movement
in the organization of medical science in the first half of the twentieth century and are
rich in social, cultural, and educational history. There is a large amount of correspondence among members of the Flexner and Thomas families, including Abraham Flexner,
director of the Institute for Advanced Study, and M. Carey Thomas, dean and president
of Bryn Mawr College; also several boxes of letters from William H. Welch, one box of
letters of Abraham Flexner to Franklin P. Mall, 1910-16; materials for and letters about
Flexner's life of Welch; biographical data on Simon Flexner. A random sampling of
correspondents shows the names of:

Hugh Cairns	Albert B. Sabin
Walter B. Cannon	Ronald S. Saddington
Edwin G. Conklin	Edward B. Shaw
William T. Councilman	Richard E. Shope
Frederick S. Lee	Theobald Smith
Sir William B. Leishman	Wilhelm Spielmeyer
Jacques Loeb	Walter B. Stewart
Peter K. Olitsky	Joseph Stokes, Jr.
Henry Fairfield Osborn	Donald D. Van Slyke
Anna L. von der Osten	Oswald Veblen
Louis Pasteur Vallery-Radot	

Presented by the Rockefeller Institute and James Thomas Flexner, 1964.

261. FORT AUGUSTA, PENNSYLVANIA. QUARTERMASTER

Account books, 1753-65. 8 vols.

Record of personal expenses, 1753-65, including entries made at Harris' Ferry,
1760, and at Fort Augusta, 1761-63 (1 vol.); ledgers, 1757-64, with lists of soldiers
with payments for wages (4 vols.); record of rations issued to Mr. Hunter's mess,
Colonel Burd's company, and Mr. Graydon's mess, 1761-63 (1 vol.); day books, 1762-63
(2 vols.). All the volumes contain records of purchases of beef, venison, bread, corn,
sugar, rum, butter, salt, etc., of payments for washing, tobacco, playing cards, tea,
lemons, thread, combs; and for purchases of medicines, shoes, clothing, etc. Probably
originally among the Burd and Burd-Shippen papers.

262. FORT PITT, PENNSYLVANIA. QUARTERMASTER

Cash book, July 12–December 10, 1760. 1 vol.

Receipts of payments by Horatio Gates, Robert Monckton, Sir John St. Clair, and others; expenditures for oats, candles, hire of horses and drivers, tobacco, rum, express riders, etc.

263. FOTHERGILL, JOHN (1712-80). English Quaker physician and naturalist. APS 1770. *DNB*

Letters to Charles Alston, 1737-50. 15 pieces. Photoprints.

Letters to the professor of botany at Edinburgh University on medicine, botany, and science in general. From the originals in Edinburgh University Library.

Presented by Mrs. Betsy Copping Corner, 1961.

264. CHARLES PEMBERTON FOX FAMILY

Legal papers, 1686-1881. 2 packages.

About 100 deeds to properties in or near Philadelphia and in Luzerne County, Pa., between Charles P., George, Joseph, and Samuel M. Fox, and other members of the family on the one hand, and Mary Ball, Edward Shippen Burd, George Clymer, Gavin Hamilton, Henry Hill, John Lukens, Samuel Micklé, Israel Pemberton, Samuel Pleasants, Samuel Rhoads, Jr., Robert Strettell, William Wallace, Nicholas Waln, and others on the other hand. Also mortgages, leases, and correspondence relating to these properties (31 pieces); letters to Dr. George Fox, 1792-98, from Gouverneur Morris, Robert Morris, N. Cantwell Jones, Thomas Eddy, and others; and from William Constable and Sir Robert Herries & Co. (17 pieces) relating to investments of William Temple Franklin.

265. FOX, GEORGE (1759-1828). Philadelphia physician and man of affairs. APS 1784.

Letter book, 1786-97. 1 vol.

Principally business correspondence with his friend William Temple Franklin or about Franklin's lands and investments in America. Other correspondents include:

Robert Barclay	John Kelly
William Constable	Robert Millegan
William Cooper	Gouverneur Morris
Edward Hand	Matthew Pearce
Thomas Hartley	George Read
Sir Robert Herries & Co.	Cornelius Schenk
Jesse Higgins	John Williamson
N. Cantwell Jones	

266. FRANKLIN, BENJAMIN (1706-90). Printer, scientist, politician, diplomat, philosopher. APS 1743. *DAB*

Papers.

The Society owns more than half the known surviving manuscripts of Benjamin Franklin, and it has—or soon will have—microfilm, photostat, or other copies of the remainder. The manuscript "Franklin Papers" include letters and drafts of letters to and from Franklin and members of his family, manuscript and printed enclosures, bills, receipts, account books, shop books, diaries, post office records, calling cards, memoranda, and reports of every description. The contents of the collection are so numerous, so varied in form and content, and come from so many different sources that they can be treated here only in general terms.

By far the largest group—upwards of 11,000 pieces—was presented to the Society in 1840 by Charles Pemberton Fox and his sister Mary Fox of Philadelphia. These they had inherited from their father Dr. George Fox, with whom William Temple Franklin deposited them in 1790 and to whom he bequeathed them in 1823. Once in a while thereafter someone gave the Society a Franklin letter or transcript, but for nearly a century the Fox gift was essentially the whole of the Society's Franklin manuscripts. In

1936 the Society purchased a collection of about 1,100 pieces from Franklin Bache, a descendant. By this action the Society committed itself to a policy of augmenting its Franklin holdings. Thereafter it acquired by purchase, gift, or deposit hundreds of manuscripts in single pieces or small lots. In addition, it collected, though not systematically, microfilms, photostats, facsimiles, prints, transcripts, and copies of several thousand more documents of Franklin interest in private and institutional collections throughout the world. The Society has, for example, a film of the Library of Congress Franklin collection.

Significant groups of Franklin manuscripts, mostly letters, acquired since 1936, are:

1. Letters to Richard Jackson, agent of Pennsylvania in London. Edited by Carl Van Doren, *Letters and Papers of Benjamin Franklin and Richard Jackson, 1753-1785*, APS *Memoirs* 24 (Philadelphia, 1947).

2. Letters to Mme Brillon de Jouy.

3. Letters to Catharine Ray Greene. Edited by William G. Roelker, *Benjamin Franklin and Catharine Ray Greene: Their Correspondence, 1755-1790*, APS *Memoirs* 26 (Philadelphia, 1949).

4. Letters to and from Mary Stevenson Hewson, many of which were presented by James S. Bradford and Miss Frances M. Bradford, 1956. Described by Whitfield J. Bell, Jr.," 'All Clear Sunshine': New Letters of Franklin and Mary Stevenson Hewson," APS *Proc.* **100** (1956): p. 521.

5. Letters of Jane Mecom. Edited by Carl Van Doren, *The Letters of Benjamin Franklin and Jane Mecom*, APS *Memoirs* 27 (Philadelphia, 1950).

A few individual documents and small groups of related documents have been studied in short articles in the Society's *Proceedings*, especially in the years between 1945 and 1960; and Franklin's account books, Ledgers A & B and Ledger D, have been analyzed and descriped by George Simpson Eddy in two privately printed monographs, 1928 and 1929.

The Franklin papers in the Society in 1908—principally the Fox gift—were carefully calendared in the five volumes of I. Minis Hays, ed., *Calendar of the Papers of Benjamin Franklin in the American Philosophical Society* (Philadelphia, 1908). Unfortunately, when the manuscripts were sorted, arranged, and bound in the nineteenth century, enclosures and covering letters were separated and little effort was spent in dating undated documents or identifying the authors of unsigned communications; and most of these deficiencies were preserved in Hays' *Calendar*. The papers that the Society has acquired since 1908, whether manuscript or copy, including a few letters transferred to the Franklin collection from the Archives, are catalogued chronologically and by recipient in card files in the Library. Furthermore, the Society is sponsor, with Yale University, of *The Papers of Benjamin Franklin* (New Haven, 1959–   ), and as each volume of this work appears photostats, prints, transcripts, or copies of every manuscript found by the editors which is not in the Society's collection are to be deposited there. Ultimately, therefore, the Society should have the manuscript or some kind of copy of every known Franklin paper. See William E. Lingelbach, "Benjamin Franklin's Papers and the American Philosophical Society," APS *Proc.* **99** (1955): p. 359, and "Benjamin Franklin and the American Philosophical Society in 1956," *ibid.* **100** (1956): p. 354.

267. FRANKLIN, JAMES, JR. (*ca.* 1730-62). Printer of Newport, R.I.

Accounts, 1753-62. Film. 1 reel.

From Newport Historical Society. Includes a book of accounts with customers, a day book, miscellaneous bills and receipts of himself and his estate.

268. FRANKLIN, WILLIAM (1731?-1813). Governor of New Jersey. APS 1768. *DAB*

Papers, 1760-1813. 1 box.

A small collection of miscellaneous manuscripts and photostat copies of letters and documents, including his will and testamentary papers. Addressees include Sarah Franklin Bache, Aaron Burr, William Temple Franklin, Joseph Galloway, John Hughes, and William Trent.

269. ——

Letters. Film.

From Yale University Library. Principally to Sarah Franklin Bache, Joseph Galloway, and William Strahan.

270. FRANKLIN, WILLIAM TEMPLE (1760-1823). Secretary of Benjamin Franklin. APS 1786. Appleton

Correspondence, 1775-1819. 9 vols., 1 box.

There are 8 vols. of letters addressed to Franklin, 1775-90; they are calendared in I. Minis Hays, ed., *Calendar of the Papers of Benjamin Franklin in the American Philosophical Society* (Philadelphia, 1908). Also a box of personal correspondence, principally to George Fox on business matters; but including letters to Henry Drinker, Jean Baptiste Le Roy, James Monroe, Solomon Ridgway, Thomas Ruston, Fulwar Skipwith, and Jonathan Williams. Some of these are transcripts and photostats. Also a diary of engagements, January 1–September 18, 1785 (1 vol.).

Presented by Charles Pemberton Fox, 1840 (part).

271. FRASER, THOMAS E.

Rough record of circumstances &c. on Mount Hamilton during the construction of the Lick Observatory, 1880-84. Film. 1 reel.

From Lick Observatory, University of California. Daily record of the superintendent of construction.

272. FRAZER, JOHN FRIES (1812-72). Philadelphia scientist, teacher, editor. APS 1842. *DAB;* APS *Proc.* 13 (1873)

Papers, 1834-71. *ca.* 650 pieces.

Consists principally of correspondence with Alexander Dallas Bache, Louis Agassiz, Joseph Henry, and Titian R. Peale on general scientific topics; although with Bache personal and family matters were discussed. Other correspondents include:

John Henry Alexander	Isaac I. Hayes
George Allen	John L. Le Conte
Frederick A. P. Barnard	Charles D. Meigs
James Curtis Booth	Samuel G. Morton
Alexis Caswell	Benjamin Peirce
George Davidson	William B. Reed
William H. Emory	Solomon W. Roberts
Frederick Fraley	Henry D. Rogers
Wolcott Gibbs	Lewis M. Rutherford
Benjamin Apthorp Gould	Charles F. Schaeffer
Arnold H. Guyot	Charles M. Wetherill
Samuel S. Haldeman	

Topics discussed in the letters include: University of Pennsylvania, boiler explosions, education, National Academy of Sciences, the Smithsonian Institution, fossils, magnetism, solar eclipses, APS, weights and measures, Coast and Geodetic Survey, scientific instruments, American Civil War, electricity, United States Mint, Franklin Institute, scientists of the period, natural history, publications, etc.

273. FRAZER, PERSIFOR (1844-1909). Geologist, mineralogist. APS 1872. *DAB*

Papers, 1884. 150 pieces.

Correspondence, principally from British scientists, on the 1884 meeting of the American Association for the Advancement of Science in Philadelphia. Table of contents (4 pp.).

274. FRAZER, ROBERT. Philadelphia lawyer

Papers, 1814. 18 pieces, including 2 maps.

Letters to Thomas Clarke, Isaac Roberdeau, and Jonathan Williams, Jr., about the defense of Philadelphia against possible British attack.

275. FREEHAUFF, DANIEL. Astronomer of Allentown, Pa.

Astronomical calculations, 1778 and 1779. 2 vols.

Calculations of an eclipse of the sun, June 24, 1778, and of the moon, May 29, 1779, adjusted to the meridian of Philadelphia; with drawings. Also a duplicate, incomplete, of the calculations for the sun, and a duplicate of the calculations for the moon. An apparently personal reference in the text suggests that Freehauff was a native of Germany.

Presented by George Vaux, 1834.

276. GABB, WILLIAM MORE (1839-78). Paleontologist. APS 1869. *DAB*

On the Indian tribes and languages of Costa Rica, 1875. 114 pp. (incomplete).

Printed in full in APS *Proc.* 14 (1875): p. 483.

277. GAGER, WILLIAM (1555-1622). English dramatist. *DNB*

Latin plays. 1 package.

The text of his dramatic works, edited by C. F. Tucker Brooke ([1883-1946], APS 1938). The introduction to the manuscript, "The Life and Times of William Gager (1555-1622)," was printed in APS *Proc.* 95 (1951): p. 401.

Presented by Mrs. Brooke, 1951.

278. GARDINER, MRS. EMMA HALLOWELL

Penobscot Indian vocabulary, 1821. 1 vol. In Penobscot and English.

Presented by the author, 1821.

279. GARY, ANNE THOMAS

The political and economic relations of English and American Quakers (1750-1785). Film. 1 reel.

Doctoral thesis, Oxford University, 1935.

280. GAUBIUS, HIERONYMUS DAVID (1705-80). Physician and medical teacher. Hoefer

Annotationes in *Praxin et Aphorismos* Boerhaavi, 1738-39. 3 vols.

Lectures on Boerhaave's *Praxis medica* (1728).

Presented by Dr. Nathaniel Chapman, 1815.

281. GAULD, GEORGE (*ca.* 1732-82). English surveyor. APS 1774

A general description of the sea-coasts, harbours, lakes, rivers &c. of the province of West Florida, 1769. 1 vol.

Contains also an extract of a letter from Dr. John Lorimer to Gauld, 1772, and a sketch of the Middle and Yellow Rivers of West Florida by Lieut. Thomas Hutchins. Endorsed: "This long uninteresting Paper can hardly obtain a Place in the Transactions of a Philosophical Society. It should however be preserved in the Files for the Use of Historians or map makers."

Presented by the author, 1773.

282. GAVER, DON ANTONIO DE (fl. 1742-73). Spanish military engineer

Relación general . . . de las plazas de Oran y Mazalquivir, 1773. 2 vols.

Descriptions of several fortified towns in North Africa (Oran, Mazalquivir, Ceuta, and Mellila), their populations, government, notable events, etc., with brief notes on the viceroys, captains-general, governors, and other officers; and a history of Oran, 1505-41. The volumes contain other manuscripts of historical interest, including a brief description of the kingdom of Tlmecen in North Africa, a synopsis of the Franco-Spanish treaty of 1761, and two poems by Don Sebastian Fernandez de Medrano.

Presented by Joel R. Poinsett, 1820.

283. GENTH, FREDERICK AUGUSTUS (1820-93). Chemist. APS 1854. *DAB; APS Proc.* **40** (1901)

Complete catalogue of the collection of minerals. 1 vol. Typed, carbon.

Arranged according to Edward S. Dana, *Descriptive Mineralogy* (6th ed., 1892).

284. GÉRARD DE RAYNEVAL, JOSEPH MATHIAS (1746-1812). French author. APS 1779. Hoefer

On the freedom of the seas. 3 vols.

Translated as an exercise, but not intended for publication, by Peter S. Du Ponceau from the author's *De la liberté des mers* (2 vols., Paris, 1811).

Presented by Peter S. Du Ponceau, 1840.

285. GILLESPIE, JOHN DOUGLAS

Miscellaneous collection on the American Indian, 1949-61. *ca.* 365 pieces, 75 photographs, etc.

Pertaining principally to the Cherokees of North Carolina and their language, this collection includes Indian studies and correspondence by Gillespie, notes on Indian dances and linguistics, bibliographies, publications of the Archaeological Society of Brigham Young University, newspaper clippings, etc.

Presented by John D. Gillespie, in honor of Frank G. Speck, 1962.

286. GIRARD, STEPHEN (1750-1831). Merchant, banker, philanthropist. *DAB*

Papers, 1769-1831. Film. *ca.* 600 reels.

From Board of Trustees of the Estate of Stephen Girard, deceased. The complete archives of one of the largest mercantile and financial operations in the United States of his day, the collection includes correspondence, with translations of letters in French (139 reels); bank records, account books, ledgers, cash books, journals, etc.; papers, documents, and records of trading voyages, arranged by vessel and date; records of Girard's country house, "The Place"; records of real estate, rents, etc.; prices current in ports of the world. There is a card index of correspondents (14 reels). Table of contents (14 pp.).

287. GLAUERT, EARL T. Historian

The introduction of the scientific enlightenment to New Spain, 1958. Typed.

A short survey. See the author's report on his research in *Year Book* 1958: p. 462.

288. GLEMONA, BASILE DE (fl. 18th century). Italian missionary, Chinese scholar. Hoefer

Dictionarium linguae sinensis. 1 vol. In Chinese and French.

One of many manuscript copies of the work made in the eighteenth and early nineteenth centuries, this was understood to have been the work of "a native of Macao." Published, from another manuscript, as the work of Chrétien Louis Joseph de Guignes, under the title *Dictionnaire chinois, français et latin* (Paris, 1813).

Presented by John Vaughan, 1817.

289. GLIDDON, GEORGE ROBINS (1809-57). Archaeologist, Egyptologist. Appleton
Analecta hieroglyphia, 1839-41. 1 vol. Copy.

Compiled in Egypt, where Gliddon lived for 23 years, and copied from his original manuscripts for Samuel G. Morton by Edward M. Kern, Philadelphia, 1842. With drawings and illustrations.

Deposited by the Academy of Natural Sciences of Philadelphia, 1952.

290. GOODSPEED, ARTHUR W. (1860-1943). Physicist, radiologist. APS 1896. *Year
Book* 1943
Scrapbook. Film. 1 reel.

From the original in possession of Arthur W. Goodspeed, Jr., Springfield, Pa., 1962. Diplomas, certificates of membership, invitations, programs, some letters (including a few of APS interest); family photographs; historical sketch of the Goodspeed family in America; obituary notices.

291. GRANIER DE CASSAGNAC, BERNARD ADOLPHE (1806-80). French historian and
publicist. Larousse
History of the noble and ennobled classes. 1 vol.

Translated by Benjamin E. Green from the author's *Histoire des classes nobles et des classes anoblies* (1840).

Presented by C. E. McCalla.

292. GRAY, ASA (1810-88). Botanist. APS 1848. *DAB*
Papers, 1838-87. 72 pieces.

Principally letters to Charles Edwin Bessey on botanical matters, including publications, in the United States and Europe; with a few letters to Moncure D. Conway, Charles G. Ridgely, Benjamin Silliman, Jr., William Vrolik, and Henry A. Ward. Table of contents (3 pp.).

293. GRAY, JOHN EDWARD (1800-75). English naturalist. *DNB*
Letters, 1783-1884. 487 pieces; also autographs and address sheets.

Principally letters to Gray on aspects of natural history from, among others:

Sir Henry Wentworth Acland	Thomas Bland
Louis Agassiz	Charles L. J. L. Bonaparte
Sir George B. Airy	Joseph Bonomi
George James Allman	Nicholas Robert Bouchard-
William Andrews	Chantereaux
Charles C. Babington	William Lisle Bowles
Spencer Fullerton Baird	William John Broderip
Antoine Jerome Balard	Joshua Brookes
Charles Spence Bate	William Buckland
Miles Joseph Berkeley	George Busk
Henri Marie Ducrotay de Blainville	Hugh Cuming

James Dwight Dana	Jan van der Hoeven
Charles Robert Darwin	Sir William Jardine
Paul Belloni Du Chaillu	Jean-Jacques Lefevre
André Marie Constant Duméril	Matthew Fontaine Maury
Michael Faraday	Samuel George Morton
Asa Fitch	Johannes Müller
Sir William Henry Flower	Thomas Nuttall
Edward Forbes	Louis Georg Karl Pfeiffer
Sir Francis Galton	Sir Robert H. Schomburgk
Isidore Geoffroy Saint-Hilaire	Johann J. S. Steenstrup
Jacob Green	Achille Valenciennes
Joseph Henry	Jens Jacob Asmussen Worsaee

Table of contents (10 pp.).

294. GREAT BRITAIN. BOARD OF TRADE

Papers on the West Indies, 1707-09. 24 pieces.

Miscellaneous documents relating to appointments, money acts, defense, etc., mostly addressed to Charles Spencer, Earl of Sunderland, Secretary of State for the Southern Department.

Presented by Arthur Bloch, 1952.

295. GREENE, NATHANAEL (1742-86). Major general, Continental Army. *DAB*

Papers, 1778-80. 12 vols.

Letters to and from General Greene and other papers on the conduct of the office of Quartermaster-General of the Continental Army, which Greene held; also proceedings of a court of inquiry into the conduct of Capt. John Bancker, barrackmaster of New York. Calendared in: *Calendar of the Correspondence Relating to the American Revolution of . . . Major-General Nathanael Greene* (Philadelphia, 1900).

Presented by Robert Desilver, 1820.

296. GREENWOOD, ARTHUR M., and CHARLES MARIUS BARBEAU

Time Stone Farm and the collections of an old New England homestead, 1948. 392 pp. Typed, carbon.

Catalogue and notes of the collection of Dr. and Mrs. Greenwood of Marlborough, Mass., with bibliographical references. Indian captivities make up a large portion of the collection.

Presented by Charles Marius Barbeau, 1949.

297. GREGG, DAVID M.

Three Pennsylvania statesmen of the olden times. Film. 1 reel.

From manuscript in possession of Paul A. W. Wallace. Biographical accounts, prepared in 1932, of Joseph Hiester, Frederick A. Muhlenberg, and Andrew Gregg; with genealogical tables.

298. GREW, THEOPHILUS (d. 1759). Schoolmaster, mathematician, almanac-maker.

Tables of the sun & moon fitted to the meridian of Philadelphia, 1746-61. 1 vol.

A book of calculations, including problems in the elements of astronomy, the calculation of eclipses at Philadelphia, Halley's tables of the sun and moon, etc.

Presented by Charles Smith, 1804.

299. GRIFFITH, HIRAM H.

Thermometrical log of a trip of the brig *Harriet*, 1847-48. 1 vol.

The voyage was from Norfolk to Granada, Guadeloupe, Mobile, and Philadelphia.

300. GUATEMALA. ARCHIVO NACIONAL

Selected documents on the history of Guatemala, 1568-1806. Film. 2 reels.

From Archivo Nacional, Guatemala City. Miscellaneous documents selected by Troy S. Floyd. Table of contents.

301. GULICK, JOHN THOMAS (1832-1923). Missionary, naturalist, author. *DAB*

Papers, 1853-98. *ca.* 100 pieces.

Correspondence on natural history and evolution, and especially on his collection and study of shells from Japan and the Pacific islands. Principal correspondents include: Louis Agassiz, Charles Robert Darwin, Sir William Henry Flower, Alpheus Hyatt, George Newbold Lawrence, George J. Romanes, Alfred R. Wallace, and the Linnean Society of London. Many of the letters were printed in Addison Gulick, *Evolutionist and Missionary: John Thomas Gulick, Portrayed Through Documents and Discussions* (Chicago, 1932). Table of contents (5 pp.).

Presented by Addison Gulick, 1960-61.

302. ———

Correspondence with George J. Romanes, 1887-93. Film. 1 reel.

From typed copies in Academy of Natural Sciences of Philadelphia. Some of the letters on this film are transcripts of letters in manuscript collection No. 301; the manuscripts of other letters are in the Linnean Society of London.

303. HAINES & TWELLS. Philadelphia brewers

Account book, 1767-70. 1 vol.

In addition to the College of Philadelphia, the city prison, and uncounted widows, the firm's customers included:

Anthony Benezet	Lynford Lardner
Owen Biddle	Archibald McCall
Thomas Bond	Timothy Matlack
Benjamin Chew	Reese Meredith
Lewis Farmer	William Moore
Paul Fooks	John Morgan
John Foxcroft	Lewis Nicola
Benjamin Franklin	James Pemberton
David Franks	Daniel Roberdeau
James Hamilton	Hugh Roberts
Francis Hopkinson	Philip Syng
Henry Keppele	Stephen Watts
Ebenezer Kinnersley	Thomas Willing

304. HALDEMAN, SAMUEL STEHMAN (1812-80). Scientist, philologist. APS 1844. *DAB; APS Proc.* **19** (1881)

Letters, 1859-75. 7 pieces.

Addressed to S. J. Sedgwick on personal affairs, scientific topics, publications, and Negroes.

305. HALL, DAVID (1714-72). Printer and bookseller. APS 1768. *DAB*

Papers, 1745-75. 10 vols. and *ca.* 100 pieces.

Receipt book, 1771-76. 1 vol.

in Salem County, N.J., Historical Society, containing principally business correspondence with Benjamin Franklin, William Strahan, and the stationers Bloss & Johnson,
London, Johnson & Unwin, London, and Hamilton & Balfour, Edinburgh; also accounts
current, 1748-68 (2 vols.), of which one contains Franklin and Hall's account for printing done for the province of Pennsylvania, 1756-67; also an index volume to the
accounts; record of bills of exchange remitted to London, 1745-52 (1 vol.); 79 letters
from William Strahan to Hall, 1745-75; and a receipt book, 1771-76. Table of contents
(10 pp.).

306. ⸻

Receipt book, 1771-76. 1 vol.

Receipts for payments by Hall for paper and other printing supplies, 1771-72;
continued by his son William, 1772-76; with typed index of names. Payments made to,
among others, the following:

Thomas Affleck	Benjamin Loxley
Daniel Benezet	Thomas Potts
Nathaniel Falconer	Benjamin Randolph
Deborah Franklin	Henry Sheetz
Rebecca Grace	Enoch Story
John Keppele	

307. HALL & SELLERS. Printers

Shop book, 1767-69. 1 vol.

A daily record of purchases of books, paper, quills, ink, and other stationer's supplies by, among others:

Thomas Barton	Caleb Johnson (of Lancaster)
James Biddle	Thomas Penn
Thomas Coombe, Jr.	Richard Peters, Sr.
John Dickinson	John Redman
Jacob Duché, Jr.	Provost William Smith
Paul Fooks	Charles Thomson
Benjamin Franklin	Trustees of the Academy of
George Glentworth	Philadelphia
Thomas Graeme	Union Library Company

308. HAMILTON, ANDREW III (*ca.* 1707-47). Merchant

House building account, 1737-41. Film.

From manuscript in possession of Arnold Nicholson, Philadelphia, 1961.

309. HANEY, JOHN LOUIS (1877-1959). Professor of English, 1900-20, and president, 1920-43, Central High School, Philadelphia. APS 1929. *Year Book*
1960

Papers, 1887-1959. 36 vols.

Diary, 1887-1959 (29 vols.); list of books read, 1887-1904 (2 vols.); scrapbooks
relating to Haney, his family, friends, and Central High School (2 vols.); autobiography
entitled "Days of My Years," 1954, in original and revised drafts; etc.

Presented and bequeathed by the author, 1958-60.

310. HARE, ROBERT (1781-1858). Chemist. APS 1803. *DAB*

Papers, 1764-1859. *ca.* 500 letters, 348 scrolls, 3 vols.

Letters on personal and business matters; drafts of letters to editors of journals on such varied topics as fish guano, slaughterhouses, paper money, and the meaning of the term "Yankee annexations." The scrolls are drafts of letters, essays, and lectures, which Hare composed on ordinary sheets of paper, then pasted end to end, and rolled up. Essay and lecture topics include: chemistry, storms, slavery, currency, fire-fighting, capital punishment, railroads, Smithsonian Institution, Michael Faraday, religion and spiritualism, riots in Philadelphia, epidemics, underwater blasting, and Ralph W. Emerson; some scrolls contain verse. The collection also contains an account book of Hare and his wife, 1806-29, and Samuel Powel, Jr.'s "Short notes on a course of antiquities at Rome, 1764." Correspondents include:

Alexander D. Bache	Thomas S. Kirkbride
Franklin Bache	Joseph Henry
William Ellery Channing	Matthew F. Maury
Robley Dunglison	Charles Partridge
Michael Faraday	Benjamin Silliman
John Fisher	Benjamin Silliman, Jr.
Richard Fisher	Petty Vaughan
John Kintzing Kane	William Vaughan

Table of contents (13 pp.).

311. HARVEY, EDMUND NEWTON (1887-1959). Physiologist. APS 1929. *Year Book 1959*

Papers, 1923-59. 9 boxes, 19 notebooks.

Consisting of correspondence, notes, memoranda, extracts from publications, reprints, drafts of essays, poems, magazine and newspaper articles, comic strips, popular songs, etc., on bioluminescence, collected principally 1945-59 for his *History of Luminescence from the Earliest Times until 1900* (APS *Memoirs* 44, 1957). Other topics are chemistry, military medicine, natural history, professional associations, etc. There are 24 letters to Talbot Howe Waterman about the chapter "Light Production," which Harvey wrote for Waterman's *Physiology of crustacea* (New York, 1960-61). Other correspondence is with persons in Princeton and other universities, the National Institutes of Health, and the United States Department of Agriculture. The notebooks contain reports to the United States Office of Scientific Research and Development on wound ballistics, bubble formation, decompression sickness, etc.

Presented by Princeton University, 1964, and Talbot Howe Waterman, 1961.

312. HARVEY, JACOB. New York merchant

Papers, 1808-47. Film. 3 reels.

From manuscripts in possession of Mr. and Mrs. Daniel M. Feins. Include correspondence, commonplace book, journal of a trip to Canada, 1820, journal of a tour to the West, 1820-21. Harvey was a son-in-law of David Hosack. Table of contents.

313. HARVEY, WILLIAM HENRY (1811-66)

Papers, 1848-65. Film. 1 reel.

From manuscripts in possession of Miss Georgina Biddle. Principally correspondence with members of his family. Table of contents (3 pp.).

314. HAUPT, LEWIS MUHLENBERG (1844-1937). Civil engineer; member, Isthmian Canal Commission. APS 1878. Appleton; *Year Book* 1937

Papers, 1890-1940. *ca.* 40 pieces.

Copies of letters, printed and mimeographed reports relating principally to break-waters at Aransas Pass, Texas, and Manasquan Inlet, N.J.; 12 blueprints and 7 drawings of devices for reclaiming beaches.

Presented by Miss B. M. Haupt, 1940, 1957.

315. HAWKINS, BENJAMIN (1754-1818). Indian agent, United States senator. *DAB*

Sketch of the Creek country in the years 1798 and 1799. 1 vol.

Printed from another manuscript in Georgia Historical Society, *Collections* **3,** 1 (1848).

Presented by Thomas Jefferson, 1816.

316. ——

Letter book, 1798-99. Film. 1 reel.

From National Park Service. Chiefly official correspondence.

317. ——

Journal of occurrences in the Creek agency . . . 1802. Film. 1 reel.

From Library Company of Philadelphia. Account of the negotiation of an Indian treaty at Fort Wilkinson.

318. HAYES, PATRICK. Philadelphia sea captain and merchant

Letters, 1796-1840. Film. 1 reel.

From manuscripts in possession of W. Horace Hepburn, Jr., Philadelphia. Principally on shipping and mercantile affairs; with some letters of members of his family. Table of contents (6 pp.).

319. HAYRE, CHARLOTTE RUTH WRIGHT

Samuel Jackson Pratt, novelist and poet, 1747-1814. Film.

Doctoral dissertation, University of Pennsylvania, 1953. Pratt met Benjamin Franklin in Paris, using the name Courtney Melmoth.

320. HAYS, ISAAC MINIS (1847-1925). Physician, editor, librarian of APS. APS 1886. APS *Proc.* **65** (1926)

A note on the history of the Jefferson manuscript draught of the Declaration of Independence in the Library of the American Philosophical Society, 1898. 1 vol.

Accompanying this reprint from APS *Proc.* **37** (1898): p. 88, are facsimiles of the Jefferson draft; 3 letters from Richard Henry Lee, Jr., to John Vaughan, 1836, 1840; a letter from Isaac Leet to Vaughan, 1840; a note on the manuscript by Vaughan; two letters between Vaughan and George Combe, 1841; and other notes.

321. HAZARD, EBENEZER (1744-1817). Editor; postmaster-general, United States. APS 1781. *DAB*

Papers, 1767-1813. 1 vol.

Miscellaneous material relating to postal affairs, including Hazard's appointments in the service; certificates of membership in APS, New-York Historical Society, American Academy of Arts and Sciences, and other institutions; letters from Richard Bache, George Clinton, Benjamin Franklin, John Hancock, Samuel Huntington, Thomas Jefferson, Timothy Matlack, Samuel Miller, George Washington, and others. One manuscript is endorsed: "My Covenant with the most high God"—which is Hazard's reaffirmation of the vows made for him by his parents at the time of his baptism.

322. HECKEWELDER, JOHN GOTTLIEB ERNESTUS (1743-1823). Moravian missionary.
    APS 1797. *DAB*

    Communications to the Historical and Literary Committee, 1816-21. 1 vol.

    Notes, letters, and essays on the history, manners, and languages of the American Indians, sent to the Committee or to members of the APS. Many refer to the Lenni Lenape, Indian writing, translations of English into Indian tongues.

323. ——

    Letters to Peter Stephen Du Ponceau, 1816-22. 1 box.
    Chiefly on Indian languages.
    Presented by Peter S. Du Ponceau, 1840.

324. ——

    Meteorological observations, 1802-14. 1 vol.

    Observations of 1802-10 made by Heckewelder at Gnadenhütten, Pa.; these are a continuation of those for 1800 made by him there and published in *Philadelphia Medical and Physical Journal* 1, 2 (1805): p. 134. Observations of 1810-14 were made by George G. Miller at Beersheba, Ohio. The volume also contains a meteorological record made at Fairfield, Upper Canada, by C. F. Dencke, September 1-7, 1800, which was printed in *Philadelphia Medical and Physical Journal*, cited above, p. 142.

325. ——

    Notes, amendments, and additions to his Account of the Indians, 1820. 1 vol.

    The "Account of the History, Manners, and Customs of the Indian Nations . . ." was printed in the *Transactions* of the Historical and Literary Committee of APS, 1819.
    Presented by the author, 1820.

326. ——

    Names which the Lenni Lenape . . . had given to rivers, streams, places, &c., 1822. 1 vol.

    Prepared for publication by Peter S. Du Ponceau and printed in APS *Trans.*, n.s., 4 (1834): pp. 351-396.
    Presented by the author, 1822.

327. ——

    Letters and manuscripts, 1741-1822. Film. 1 reel.

    From Archives of the Moravian Church, Bethlehem, Pa. Letters, reports, journals of travel, etc., relating to Indians, Moravian missions and communities at Salem, N.C., Gnadenhütten, Muskingum, Fairfield in Upper Canada, and Bethlehem; also personal correspondence and an autobiography. Correspondents include John Ettwein, George Henry Loskiel, Nathaniel Seidel, Abraham Steiner, and David Zeisberger. Table of contents (10 pp.).

328. ——

    Journal of travels among the Indians, 1793. Film.
    From Historical Society of Pennsylvania.

329. ——

    Miscellaneous letters and papers. Film.
    From Massachusetts Historical Society and Harvard University Library. Tables of contents (2 pp.).

330. ——

English, Algonkian, and Delaware comparative vocabulary. 1 vol.

331. ——

Names of various trees, shrubs, and plants in the language of the Lenape. 1 vol.

With their Latin and botanical names, prepared by C. F. Kampmann.

Presented by Peter S. Du Ponceau, 1840.

332. HEIBERG, BENJAMIN

Forelaesninger over Fødselsvidenskaben, 1802. 1 vol.

Lecture on obstetrics, recorded by one Fenger.

333. HENRY, MATTHEW S.

Correspondence on Indian names, 1854-60. 1 vol.

A volume of letters from John Henry Alexander, Edward Ballard, P. W. Leland, Usher Parsons, Sebastian Ferris Streeter, and others on Indian names of the eastern United States. Also a letter to J. Francis Fisher and others of the Historical Society of Pennsylvania, in response to a circular appeal, on Indian names of Northampton County, Pa., 1854.

334. ——

English–Lenni Lenape and Lenni Lenape–English dictionary, 1859-60. 1 vol., with 7 maps.

Presented by the author, 1860.

335. HERALDRY

Books of heraldry. 2 vols.

One volume, an incomplete manuscript, contains an alphabetical list of family names, with some colored sketches of coats of arms; the other volume contains descriptions of coats of arms, including Benjamin Franklin's, with a note and a map relating to the Mason and Dixon survey, taken from the *Philosophical Transactions*. The Franklin inscription in this second volume is a forgery.

Presented by Mrs. Arthur Bloch, 1954 (second volume).

336. HEWITT, JOHN NAPOLEON BRINTON (1859-1937). Iroquois Indian and ethnologist.

Myths, legends, ethnological notes, historical information *in re* the Tuscaroras of New York State, 1883-90.

Collected by Hewitt and Albert Samuel Gatschet; copied from materials in the Bureau of American Ethnology.

Presented by Anthony F. C. Wallace, 1949.

337. HEWSON FAMILY

Papers, 1761-1836. 30 pieces.

Letters of William Hewson, Mary Stevenson Hewson, Thomas Tickell Hewson, chiefly to members of the family on personal affairs; transcript of a draft of William Hewson's account of his quarrel with Dr. William Hunter; letter of Barbeu Dubourg to Mary Stevenson Hewson. Table of contents (2 pp.).

Presented by Miss Frances Bradford, 1961, and Mrs. Hendrik Booraem, 1962.

338. ――――
Family papers. Film. 1 reel.

From manuscripts in possession of Mrs. Addinell Hewson. Letters of Mary Steven-son Hewson to her mother-in-law, sister-in-law, and children, their letters to her, espe-cially letters from Thomas Tickell Hewson in London and Edinburgh; letters and papers of William Hewson, including letters from Anthony Fothergill, John Morgan, and Wil-liams Smibert; letters about Mary Stevenson Hewson's estate. There are many references to Benjamin Franklin, Benjamin Franklin Bache, Jonathan Williams, John Hawkesworth, and others. Included is a list of the entire collection of Mrs. Addinell Hewson, only part of which is on the film. Table of contents (13 pp.).

339. HISTORY OF SCIENCE SOCIETY
Records and papers, 1939-50. *ca.* 1,500 pieces.

Official records, reports and correspondence of the Society, kept by successive secretaries, including materials on meetings, programs, publications, officers, *Isis, Osiris,* etc. Among the correspondents are John F. Fulton, Marjorie Nicolson, George Sarton, Richard H. Shryock, and Henry R. Viets.
Presented by the Society, 1965.

340. HOOKER, SIR JOSEPH DALTON (1817-1911). English botanist and traveler. APS 1869. *DNB*
Letters to Sir Henry Cole, 1867-69. 6 pieces.

Principally on business matters, with some reference to publications.

341. HOPKINSON, FRANCIS (1737-91). Author, musician, statesman. APS 1768. *DAB*
Miscellaneous works. 5 vols.

A collection of his prose writings, prepared by him for publication. These volumes are numbered 1-4 and 6; volume 5, missing here, contains his verse. Printed in Hopkin-son's *Miscellaneous Essays and Occasional Writings* (3 vols., Philadelphia, 1792).
Presented by Joseph Hopkinson, 1832.

342. ――――
Notebook, 1784-91.

Memoranda of personal expenses; 5 leaves only.

343. ――――
Poems. 12 pieces.

Some of these are printed in Hopkinson's *Miscellaneous Essays and Occasional Writings* (Philadelphia, 1792) 3.

344. HORSFIELD, TIMOTHY (1708-73). Justice of the peace, Bethlehem, Pa.
Papers, 1733-71. 2 vols.

Principally relating to the Indian affairs of Pennsylvania, especially the war in 1756, this collection contains letters and documents by and to, among others:

George Croghan
William Denny
Benjamin Franklin
James Hamilton
Robert Hunter Morris
William Parsons
Richard Peters

James Read
Edward Shippen (of Lancaster)
Augustus Gottlieb Spangenberg
Teedyuscung
Conrad Weiser
David Zeisberger

Presented by Joseph Horsfield, 1818.

345. HORSMANDEN, DANIEL (1694-1778). Chief justice of New York. APS 1744. *DAB*

Selected papers relating to the Six Nations, 1734-47. Film.

From New-York Historical Society. Letters, papers, documents selected from the Horsmanden papers.

346. HOSACK, DAVID (1769-1835). New York physician and horticulturist. APS 1810. *DAB*

Materials for a biography. *ca.* 300 pieces.

Photostats, transcripts, notes, etc., collected by Mrs. Christine C. Robbins for her biography of *David Hosack: Citizen of New York*, APS *Memoirs* 62 (Philadelphia, 1964). Correspondents include: Sir Joseph Banks, Peter S. Du Ponceau, Amos Eaton, Thomas Parke, John Torrey, and John Vaughan.

Presented by Mrs. Robbins, 1963, 1965.

347. ——

Letters and papers. Film.

From Columbia University Library, Linnean Society of London (1 reel), New York Academy of Medicine (2 reels), New York Botanical Garden, New-York Historical Society, New York Public Library (1 reel), Rutgers University Library, University of Pennsylvania Library (1 reel), Yale University Library, John Hampton Barnes, Jr., West Chester, Pa., 1957, and Miss Georgina Biddle. Miscellaneous Hosack letters, papers, lectures, essays, etc. Table of contents (7 pp.).

348. HUMBOLDT, ALEXANDER VON (1769-1859). Naturalist. APS 1804. Hoefer

Papers, 1801-59. 2 boxes.

Miscellaneous letters and papers relating to explorations in South America, travels in North America, scientific investigations, publications, etc. Correspondents include:

William Buckland	Edmé François Jomard
Athanase L. C. Coqueral	Sir Charles Lyell
José Francesco Corrêa da Serra	André Michaux
Peter S. Du Ponceau	Henry William Pickersgill
Friedrich Wilhelm IV	Sir Edward Sabine
Mme Emma Gaggiotti-Richards	Hermann Rudolph Alfred von
Louis Charles Galunsky	Schlaginteweit-Sakülünski
Isidore Geoffroy Saint-Hilaire	Gustav Friedrich Waagen
Leonard Horner	Karl Ludwig Willdenow
Thomas Jefferson	John Vaughan

Table of contents (9 pp.). See also Helmut de Terra, "Alexander von Humboldt's Correspondence with Jefferson, Madison, and Gallatin," APS *Proc.* 103 (1959): p. 783, and "Studies of the Documentation of Alexander von Humboldt," *ibid.* 102 (1958): pp. 136, 560.

349. ——

Miscellaneous correspondence. Film.

From Deutsche Akademie der Wissenschaften, Berlin (correspondence with Friedrich Wilhelm Bissell); National Archives, Washington (with Matthew F. Maury); Bibliothèque Universitaire, Zurich (with Paulus Usteri); from Royal Society, London; Bibliothèque Nationale, Geneva, Göttingen University Library, British Museum, Massachusetts Historical Society, Library of Congress (1 reel), Westdeutsche Bibliotek, Marburg (2 reels), Deutsche Staatsbibliotek, Berlin, and other depositories; also manuscripts in possession of Frau von Heinz, Schloss Tegal (correspondence with Johann G. Galli).

Other correspondents include Charles Babbage, George Bancroft, Sir Charles Blagden, Robert Brown, William Buckland, Sir John F. W. Herschel, Oscar Lieber, and Thomas Young. Table of contents (5 pp.).

350. HUME, DAVID (1711-76). Historian and philosopher. *DNB*
    Manuscripts. Film. 4 reels.

    From Royal Society of Edinburgh. For the contents of this collection, see J. Y. T. Greig and Harold Benyon, eds., "Calendar of Hume MSS. in the Possession of the Royal Society of Edinburgh," Royal Society, *Proceedings* **52** (1932).

351. HUNTER, ALEXANDER. Paymaster, Pennsylvania Provincial troops
    Receipt book, 1763-64. 1 vol.

    Signed receipts for rations received by the officers for troops at Fort Augusta, November 16, 1763–November 19, 1764.

352. HUNTER, GEORGE (1755-1824). Apothecary, physician, traveler, and explorer
    Journals, 1796-1809. 4 vols.

    Record of travel from Philadelphia to Kentucky, 1796; to Kentucky with his son George H. Hunter, 1802; to Louisiana and up the Red River, 1804-05; and to Upper Louisiana, 1809, with notes on natural history and meteorological observations. The Red River journal was copied as "Journal up the Red and Washita Rivers with William Dunbar" (manuscript, 1 vol., in APS), from which extracts were printed in Thomas Jefferson, *Message . . . Communicating Discoveries Made in Exploring the Missouri* (New York, 1806), and which is described by Isaac J. Cox, "An Early Explorer of the Louisiana Purchase," APS *Library Bulletin* 1946: p. 73. The remainder of the journals was edited by John F. McDermott and published in APS *Trans.*, n.s., **53**, 4 (1963).

    Presented by Daniel Parker and Bishop William White, 1817 (Red and Washita Rivers journal).

353. HUNTER, THOMAS MARSHALL
    Medical service for the Yankee soldier. Typed, carbon.
    Doctoral dissertation, University of Maryland, 1952.

354. HUNTER, WILLIAM (d. 1761). Printer of Williamsburg, Va.
    Journal, 1750-52. Xerox copy.

    From University of Virginia Library. A daily record of sales of books, stationery, advertising, printing, binding, etc., and of household and shop expenses.

355. HUTCHINSON, JAMES (1752-93). Philadelphia physician. APS 1779. *DAB*
    Papers, 1771-1928. 106 pieces.

    Letters between Hutchinson and Israel Pemberton his uncle, written from London, where Hutchinson was a student of medicine; 12 tickets of admission to medical lectures in Philadelphia and London, including William Hunter's, with 3 unused cards of admission to Hutchinson's own lectures; Hutchinson's marriage certificate; genealogical data on the Hutchinson, Hare, and Pemberton families; stock certificates of the McKean and Elk Land and Improvement Company, 1857-72. Correspondents include, in addition to Pemberton:

Charles F. A. le Paulnier	Clement Biddle
d'Annemours	Charles Caldwell
Benjamin F. Bache	Thomas Corbyn
Sir Joseph Banks	Andrew Ellicott
Isaac Bartram	John Ewing

John Fothergill	John Coakley Lettsom
Nathanael Greene	Charles Pettit
Joseph Hiester	Benjamin Rush
Charles H. Hutchinson	John Townsend

Table of contents (3 pp.).

Presented by S. Pemberton Hutchinson, 1962.

356. HUXLEY, THOMAS HENRY (1825-95). Man of science. APS 1869. *DNB*

Letters, 1851-88. *ca.* 80 pieces.

Letters on a variety of topics, such as the age of man, evolution, education, natural history, science, spiritualism, and geology, received from or addressed to, among others:

Sir Henry Cole	Aubrey Lackington Moore
Charles Robert Darwin	Sir James Paget
Thomas Campbell Eyton	William Thomas Quekett
William Ewart Gladstone	The Royal Society
Sir Charles Lyell	Philip Lutley Sclater
Henri Milne-Edwards	Alfred Russel Wallace

357. ———

Papers. Film. 20 reels.

From Imperial College of Science and Technology. For the contents of this collection, see Warren R. Dawson, ed., *The Huxley Papers: A Descriptive Catalogue of the Correspondence, Manuscripts and Miscellaneous Papers . . . in the Imperial College of Science and Technology* (London, 1946).

358. INDEPENDENCE NATIONAL HISTORICAL PARK

Reports on Benjamin Franklin's houses, 1960-61. Typed.

A report on Franklin's house, prepared by M. O. Anderson, John D. R. Platt, and B. Bruce Powell, 1960, and another report on the same subject, prepared by Dennis C. Kurjack, Martin I. Yoelson, William M. Campbell, and Richard Tyler, 1961; report on Franklin's "tenant houses," prepared by James F. O'Gorman, 1960.

Deposited by the United States National Park Service, 1961.

359. INGENHOUSZ, JAN (1730-99). Physician, naturalist. APS 1786

Letter book, 1774-93. Film.

From Stedelijk Archief, Breda, The Netherlands. Principal correspondents include Achille Guillaume le Begue de Presle, Francis Coffyn, Peter Elmsley, Abbé Felice Fontana, Benjamin Franklin, Nikolaas Joseph Jacquin, Sir John Pringle, Richard Huck-Saunders, Friedrich Theodor Schubert, Samuel Wharton, and Jonathan Williams. Index of correspondents (8 pp.).

360. JACKSON, HALLIDAY (1771-1835). Pennsylvania Quaker missionary to the Indians

Some account of my journey to the Seneca Nation of Indians, and residence amongst that people, 1798-99. 1 vol.

Another, differently worded copy of this journal was edited by Anthony F. C. Wallace and published in *Pennsylvania History* 19 (1952): pp. 117, 325.

361. ———

Journals, 1805-06. Film. 1 reel.

From Friends Historical Library, Swarthmore College. Contains drafts of his *Civilization of the Indian Natives* (Philadelphia, 1830). Described by George S. Snyderman,

"Halliday Jackson's Journal of a Visit Paid to the Indians of New York (1806)," APS *Proc.* **101** (1957): p. 565.

362. ——

Journal, 1814. Film.

From Chester County Historical Society, West Chester, Pa. Account of a visit to the Indians of New York state.

363. JACOBS, MICHAEL (1801-71). Pennsylvania Lutheran clergyman and educator. *DAB*

Meteorological observations made for the Franklin Institute, 1839-65.

Observations made at Gettysburg, Pa. The entries for January, 1860–September, 1865 are duplicates. One series was made under the direction of the Smithsonian Institution and are on the printed forms supplied by that institution.

Presented by Lutheran Theological Seminary, Mount Airy, Pa., 1958.

364. JAMES, EDWIN (1797-1861). Explorer, naturalist, physician. APS 1833. *DAB*

Conjugation of the verb *to hear* in its various forms in the Chippeway language, *ca.* 1833. 1 vol.

Printed forms, with manuscript notes by Peter S. Du Ponceau.
Presented by Peter S. Du Ponceau, 1839.

365. ——

Some account of the Menomonies, with a specimen of an attempt to form a dictionary of their language, 1827. 1 vol.

Presented by the author, 1827.

366. JEFFERSON, THOMAS (1743-1826). President of APS and of the United States. APS 1780. *DAB*

Papers, 1775-1825. 5 boxes.

Several hundred miscellaneous letters and writings, much on science and linguistics. Correspondents include:

Franklin Bache	Charles Willson Peale
Peter S. Du Ponceau	Edmund Pendleton
John W. Eppes	David Rittenhouse
William Fleming	Benjamin Rush
Robert Fulton	William Thornton
Louis Hue Girardin	John Vaughan
Jan Ingenhousz	Bushrod Washington
Richard Henry Lee	George Washington
James Mease	Jonathan Williams
Samuel L. Mitchill	Caspar Wistar
Robert Patterson	

367. ——

Chronological series of facts relating to Louisiana; its limits and bounds, 1804. 1 vol.

Sent to APS in a letter to Peter S. Du Ponceau, December 30, 1817; read in the Historical and Literary Committee, 1818; and printed in Thomas Jefferson, *Documents Relating to the Purchase and Exploration of Louisiana* (New York, 1904).

368. ——

Comparative vocabularies of several Indian languages, 1802-08. 1 vol.

Presented by Thomas Jefferson, 1817.

369. ——

Papers. Film. 101 reels.

From Library of Congress. These include 5 reels of indexes. In addition, there is a film of Jefferson manuscripts in the Henry E. Huntington Library (1 reel), and also a film (51 reels) of the control files (alphabetical, chronological, bibliographical, and source) prepared by the editors of *The Papers of Thomas Jefferson,* Princeton University, for their use, and published on film, 1957.

370. JENNINGS, GEORGE NELSON (1833-1903). Physician of Tonica, Ill., and Covina, Calif.

Autobiography, 1897. 1 vol.

Includes quotations from journals, especially one of a trip to California, 1872; with a short sketch of his later years by his daughter Helen Jennings Barrett, 1937, and genealogical notes. Mentions his son Herbert S. Jennings.

Presented by Miss Carolyn Jennings, 1957.

371. JENNINGS, HEBRERT SPENCER (1868-1947). Naturalist and geneticist. APS 1907. *Year Book* 1947

Diary, 1927-42. 13 vols.

Personal and professional activities and travels.

372. ——

Papers, 1893-1947. 9 boxes, 2 vols.

Drafts of lectures on genetics, evolution, population, biology, etc.; miscellaneous writings on biology, protozoa genetics, biometry, evolution and natural selection, paramecium, etc.; 9 notebooks containing letters from France, 1911, tables, formulae, materials on biometric methods, vitalism, Chinese characters, Japanese language; letters from students and colleagues on the twenty-fifth anniversary of his doctorate, 1921 (1 vol.), and letters presented on his seventy-fifth birthday, 1943 (1 vol.); diplomas and certificates of membership. Correspondents include:

Jerome Alexander	Rheinhart Parker Cowles
Herbert Blumer	Wilbur L. Cross
Paul P. Boyd	Lincoln V. Domm
Luther Burbank	Arthur C. Giese
Philip Burnet	Vernon L. Kellogg
Elmer G. Butler	Maynard M. Metcalf
Gary Nathan Calkins	Hjalmar L. Osterud
James McKeen Cattell	Fred E. Pomeroy
Jaques Cattell	Aaron F. Shull
Edmund V. Cowdry	John B. Watson

Table of contents (17 pp.).

Presented by Mrs. Vernon Lynch and Burridge Jennings, 1947-64.

373. JONES, ROBERT STRETTELL (1745-92). Philadelphia merchant. APS 1768

Papers, 1761-79. 6 folders.

Includes college notes on metaphysics and rhetoric, 1761-62; copy of the substance of depositions in the indictment of Jones for treason, 1779; copy of the will of his aunt Ann Strettell, 1771, etc.

Presented by the Estate of Robert Strettell Jones Fisher, 1953.

374. JUSSIEU, ANTOINE LAURENT DE (1748-1836). French botanist. Hoefer

Catalogue des plantes démontrées en 1782 au Jardin du Roi. 1 vol.

List of plants with brief descriptions, used by Jussieu in public lectures in the Jardin du Roi. The plants are arranged according to the classification which Jussieu published in 1789 under the title: *Genera Plantarum Secundum ordines naturales disposita.* The manuscript formerly belonged to Charles Claude Flahaut de la Billarderie, comte d'Angivillier, director-general of the Royal Gardens.

375. KAMPMANN, CHRISTIAN FREDERICK (fl. 1780-1808). Physician

Catalogus plantarum sponte crescentium circa Bethlehem . . . in Pensylvania & Hope . . . in West New Jersey. 1 vol.

The author was a Moravian physician who came to Pennsylvania in 1781; he practiced at Bethlehem, Pa., and Hope, Sussex County, N.J., finally returning to Bethlehem in 1808. He copied this document at the request of John Heckewelder "for the information of the Philosophical Society," and Heckewelder transmitted it to the Society.

Presented by the author.

376. KANY, ROBERT HURD

David Hall: printing partner of Benjamin Franklin. 308 pp. Typed, carbon.

Doctoral dissertation, Pennsylvania State University, 1963.

Presented by the author, 1963.

377. KAYSER, HEINRICH GUSTAV JOHANNES (1853-1940). German physicist and spectroscopist

Erinnerungen aus meinen Leben, 1936. 1 vol. Typed, carbon.

Autobiography of the professor of physics at Bonn, 1894-1920, who mapped a large number of spectra of the elements, in association with Carl David Runge (1856-1927).

Presented by William F. Meggers, 1963.

378. KELSO, HENRY B.

Indian-English dictionary, 1822. 1 vol.

Ojibwa-English vocabulary, Winnebago numerals; family genealogical data, and miscellaneous notes kept at Green Bay, Wis.

379. KEW. ROYAL BOTANIC GARDENS

Correspondence of American botanists. Film. 9 reels.

From Royal Botanic Gardens, Kew. Letters and papers relating to North America, chiefly from the official correspondence of the Gardens and the correspondence of its two directors, Sir William Jackson Hooker and Sir Joseph Dalton Hooker. There are 2 reels of letters from Asa Gray to the Hookers (but other Gray letters are elsewhere in the collection), and a few letters from Americans to William Forsyth, superintendent of the Royal Gardens of St. James' and Kensington, 1787. An index volume is included in the film.

380. KIDDER, ALFRED VINCENT (1885-1963). Archaeologist. APS 1934. *Year Book* 1963

Correspondence with Neil Merton Judd, 1920-62. 68 pieces.

Friendly letters about archaeological research and publications on the United States Southwest (e.g., Chaco Canyon ruins, Bonito pueblo, Pecos del Arroyo), Alfred V. Kidder Award, Sylvanus G. Morley, Earl Morris, Carl Guthe, the National Geographic Society, and family events.
Presented by Neil M. Judd, 1965.

381. KIDDER, HOMER HUNTINGTON, recorder. Mining engineer
Ojibwa myths and halfbreed tales, related by Charles and Charlotte Kobawgam and Jacques Lapique, 1893-95. 1 vol.
Presented by A. V. Kidder, 1953.

382. KINLOCH, FRANCIS (1755-1826). Lawyer, planter, member of the Continental Congress
Letters to Johannes von Müller, 1776-1809. Film.
From Stadtbibliothek, Schaffhausen, Switzerland. Table of contents (4 pp.).

383. ———
Correspondence with Charles Bonnet, 1780-1818. Film.
From Bibliothèque Nationale, Geneva, Switzerland. Table of contents (1 p.).

384. KLETT, JOSEPH F.
Regulation of the medical profession in America, 1780-1860. Film.
Doctoral dissertation, Harvard University, 1964.

385. KRUMEL, DONALD W.
Philadelphia music engraving and publishing, 1800-1820: a study in bibliography and cultural history. Film.
Doctoral dissertation, University of Michigan, 1957.

386. LA HARPE, BÉNARD DE. French officer and explorer
Journal historique concernant l'établissement des Français à la Louisianne, 1699-1723. 1 vol.
Taken from the memoirs of d'Iberville and Bienville; copied from the original in possession of Dr. John Sibley, 1805; translated and published in B. F. French, *Historical Collections of Louisiana*, pt. 3 (New York, 1851).
Presented by William Darby, 1816.

387. LANDSTEINER, KARL (1868-1943). Medical researcher, Nobel laureate. APS 1935. *Year Book* 1943
Biographical data. *ca.* 7,500 pieces.
Correspondence of Dr. George M. Mackenzie with friends and associates of Landsteiner; memoranda of conversations; notes and recollections of Landsteiner by Thomas M. Rivers, 1944-52, and by Max Neuberger; Landsteiner's departmental reports at Rockefeller Institute, 1923-43; correspondence on publications. There is much material on immunology, the study of blood, the Nobel award, 1930, anti-Semitism, the Vienna medical schools, etc. Table of contents (3 pp.).
Presented by the family of Dr. Landsteiner, 1958.

388. LANGSTROTH, LORENZO LORRAINE (1810-95). Apiarist. *DAB*
Papers, 1852-95. *ca.* 180 pieces.
Principally on bees and beekeeping, especially his efforts to win legal recognition

of his invention of the movable-frame beehive; also a fragment of autobiography; newspaper clippings. Correspondents include editors of bee journals, manufacturers and suppliers of materials for apiaries, and Charles P. Coffin, Thomas William Cowan, Charles Dadant, D. A. Jones, Charles V. Muth, and George W. York.

Presented by Miss Anna L. Cowan, 1954.

389. LA ROCHE, RENÉ (1795-1872). Philadelphia physician and epidemiologist. APS 1827. *DAB*

Papers, 1827-1901. 35 pieces.

Passports, 1827; membership certificates; receipts; family letters; 20 letters to La Roche from Thomas Dunn and Ayres P. Merrill on scientific, medical, and personal topics.

Presented by Morris Duane, 1964.

390. LARREY, Baron DOMINIQUE JEAN (1766-1842). Military surgeon. APS 1831. Larousse

Letters, 1818-73. Film.

From Bibliothèque Nationale, Paris. Addressed to him and to his nephew Baron Felix Hippolyte Larrey (1808-95), chiefly from American medical personages. Table of contents.

391. LAW ACADEMY OF PHILADELPHIA

Opinion Book A: Opinions delivered before the Law Academy of Philadelphia by the provost and vice provost, 1820-22. 1 vol.

The opinions are signed by Peter S. Du Ponceau as provost. Founded in 1821, but actually a successor of earlier associations for legal education, and incorporated in 1838, the Law Academy provided students with the experience of moot courts; it also offered systematic instruction until 1850, when a professorship of law was established at the University of Pennsylvania.

392. LEACOCK, JOHN (1729-1802). Philadelphia silversmith

Observations, experiments &c. extracted from the *Philosophical Transactions* respecting farming, gardening, &c., 1768-1800. 1 vol.

Despite the title, few of the extracts are from the *Philosophical Transactions*. This is a commonplace book which contains farm directions, as for curing beef, making compost, draining, grafting, making wine, catching rats; recipes for beer, shoe-blacking, bologna sausage; prescriptions for colds, fevers, toothache, rheumatism; and instructions for engraving, etching, making porcelain. Also a song about the Stamp Act, a "Parody on the Tempest by R. H. Esqr.," and recipes for diet drinks by James Logan and Dr. Cadwalader Evans.

Presented by Mrs. Malcolm G. Sausser, 1953.

393. LE BOULANGER, JEAN BAPTISTE (1664-*ca.* 1724). French missionary priest

French and Miami-Illinois dictionary, *ca.* 1720. Photocopy.

Texts of prayers, catechisms, selections from the Gospels, and a large part of the book of Genesis. From the original in the John Carter Brown Library.

394. LE CONTE, JOHN EATTON (1784-1860). Engineer and naturalist. APS 1851. Appleton

Papers, 1816-77. 1 box.

Primarily papers relating to the work of the United States Army Corps of Topographical Engineers, with special reference to surveys of harbors of the eastern United

States seaboard; some papers and letters relate to natural history and are addressed to John Lawrence Le Conte. Correspondents include Rutherford B. Hayes, Joseph Henry, Daniel Parker, and E. G. Squier.

395. ――――

Entomological drawings. *ca.* 3,700 drawings in 8 vols.

The drawings are in color and in black and white; two in the first volume are by Titian R. Peale, and others may be by John Lawrence Le Conte. Contents of the collection:

Vol.   I: Coleoptera. 654 figures.
Vol.   II: Diptera, Hemiptera, and Lepidoptera. 564 figures.
Vol. III: Coleoptera. 698 figures.
Vol. IV: Coleoptera and Hymenoptera. 228 figures.
Vol.   V: Coleoptera. 657 figures.
Vol. VI: Hymenoptera and Diptera. 234 figures.
Vol. VII: Diptera. 304 figures.
Vol. VIII: Hemiptera, Araneina, Myriopoda. 356 figures.

396. ――――

Correspondence with Thaddeus W. Harris and others. Film.

From Boston Society of Natural History and Museum of Comparative Zoology, Harvard University. Letters to and from Harris, Frederick E. Melsheimer, Levi W. Leonard, Henry McMurtrie, Margaretta Hall Morris, and others, 1829-51, chiefly on topics in natural history.

397. ――――

Observations on the soil and climate of East Florida, 1822. Film.

From National Archives, Washington.

398. LE CONTE, JOHN LAWRENCE (1825-83). Entomologist, physician. APS 1853. *DAB; APS Proc.* **21** (1883)

Papers, 1812-97. 19 boxes.

Generally entomological material, with much information on the description and identification of particular insects, entomological collections, and the study of entomology in Europe and the United States. In addition, there are materials on medicine and hospitals during the American Civil War, on the Corps of Topographical Engineers, United States Army, on natural history in the United States, and on Le Conte's family life. Some letters relate to President Rutherford B. Hayes and the Commissionership of Agriculture, 1877. Letters of John Eatton Le Conte and Joseph Le Conte are included. Among the correspondents are:

Alexander Agassiz	John Fries Frazer
Victor Audubon	Horace H. Furness
Alexander D. Bache	Benjamin Apthorp Gould
Spencer F. Baird	Augustus Radcliffe Grote
Frederick A. P. Barnard	Herman August Hagen
John Shaw Billings	Samuel Stehman Haldeman
Lorin Blodget	James Hall
Henry Cadwalader Chapman	Thaddeus William Harris
Elliott Coues	Ferdinand V. Hayden
James Dwight Dana	Joseph Henry
Anton Dohrin	George Henry Horn
William H. Emory	Henry G. Hubbard

Jean Théodore Lacordaire
Leo Lesquereux
Otis Tufton Mason
F. E. Melsheimer
Thomas C. Mendenhall
George Ord
Carl Robert von Osten-Sachen
Benjamin Peirce

Charles Valentine Riley
Hermann Schaum
Philip Lutley Sclater
Eugene Amandus Schwartz
Lewis Henry Steiner
Henry Ulke
Benjamin Dann Walsh
Charles Wilkes

Table of contents (43 pp.).
Deposited by the Academy of Natural Sciences of Philadelphia, 1954 (part).

399. LE CONTE FAMILY

Papers, 1827-1901. 1 box.

Principally letters from John Lawrence Le Conte, John Eatton Le Conte, Joseph Le Conte and Mrs. Jane Le Conte Harden to Mrs. Matilda Jane Harden Stevens, and also to Sumner Morrison Ramsey, Mrs. Ann Le Conte Stevens and Louis Le Conte, on both family matters and natural history. Table of contents (2 pp.).

400. [LEE, ARTHUR] (1740-92). Physician, lawyer, diplomat. APS 1768. *DAB*

Account of the robbery of the papers of Arthur Lee, American agent at Berlin, June 26, 1777. 1 vol. In German, with French translation.

"They are the proceedings before the criminal Judge, of the Government of Prussia, in relation to the robbery of Dr. Lee's official papers, while Minister at that Court." The episode is described in Richard H. Lee, *Life of Arthur Lee* (Boston, 1829), 1: p. 96.

Presented by Richard H. Lee, 1826.

401. LEE, RICHARD HENRY (1732-94). Statesman. *DAB*

Correspondence. 2 vols.

Letters to Lee from John Adams, Samuel Adams, Thomas Jefferson, Marquis de Lafayette, Arthur Lee, John Page, Mann Page, Benjamin Rush, George Washington, George Wythe, and others; a small number of letters from Lee, with other papers; and 8 letters to Arthur Lee; principally of the period of the American Revolution. Most of the letters were printed in Richard Henry Lee, *Life of Richard Henry Lee* (Philadelphia, 1825), and all are listed in *Calendar of the Correspondence relating to the American Revolution of . . . Hon. Richard Henry Lee, Hon. Arthur Lee . . .* (Philadelphia, 1900), p. 35.

Presented by Richard Henry Lee, 1825.

402. LEGAUX, PETER (1748-1827). Lawyer and farmer. APS 1789.

Journal of the Pennsylvania Vine Company, 1803-27. 4 vols.

Records of expenses, planting and harvesting, and weather.

Presented by William J. Duane (to whom Legaux bequeathed it), 1866.

403. ——

Observations météorologiques faites à Springmill [Pennsylvania]: 1787-1800. With an English translation.

One chart is addressed to Benjamin Franklin, "président de l'État de Pennsylvanie et président de la société phylosophique . . . 1789." All or most of the material was sent to Thomas Jefferson as president of the United States and of the Philosophical Society. Included are extracts from Legaux' journal from Santo Domingo to Philadelphia, 1785.

Presented by the author.

404. ——

Meteorological observations, 1820-21. 1 vol.

Made at Spring Mill, Pa.
Presented by the author, 1822.

405. LEÓN Y GAMA, ANTONIO DE (1735-1802). Mexican archaeologist

An historical and chronological description of two stones found under ground, in the great square of the City of Mexico, in the year 1790, 1792. 1 vol.

Translated by William E. Hulings, with a query by the translator about the possible relation of the Aztecs to the Mound Builders.
Presented by William E. Hulings, 1818.

406. LESLEY, J. PETER (1819-1903). Geologist. APS 1856. *DAB;* APS *Proc.* 37 (1898), 45 (1906)

Papers, 1826-98. 29 boxes.

Contains a large number of letters to and from Lesley and his wife on scientific topics, abolition, educational reform, organized charity, Unitarianism, etc.; among the correspondents are:

Alexander D. Bache	Ferdinand V. Hayden
Spencer F. Baird	Joseph Henry
Horace Bushnell	Thomas Wentworth Higginson
Lydia Maria Child	Clarence King
James Freeman Clarke	Leo Lesquereux
Moncure D. Conway	Sir Charles Lyell
Edward D. Cope	Horace Mann
James D. Dana	Othniel C. Marsh
Edouard Desor	J. Miller McKim
Ralph Waldo Emerson	Sir Roderick Impey Murchison
Austin Flint	Richard Owen
John F. Frazer	Benjamin Peirce
Horace H. Furness	Charles Pickering
Wolcott Gibbs	Henry D. Rogers
Arnold Guyot	Nathaniel S. Shaler
Edward Everett Hale	Charles Sumner
Lucretia Peabody Hale	J. Edgar Thomson
Samuel S. Haldeman	Henry Winsor
James Hall	

The collection also includes a diary, 1874-81 (4 vols.) relating to the Geological Survey of Pennsylvania, 1874-96, with newspaper clippings, letters, extracts from publications, etc., of which the second vol. is a "private" diary; also accounts of the Geological Survey, 1874-96 (4 vols.). Among many miscellaneous notebooks are Lesley's notes of a geological survey of the Pottsville District, 1851 (in the same volume with which is Benjamin Smith Lyman's Levels of survey near Llewellyn, 1862); his notes of a survey at Emigh's Gap; and Alexander McKinley's geological report book, 1839, for the Seven Mountains and Warrior's Ridge, Center County, Pa., with Lesley's final report, 1839-40. In addition there are notebooks containing poems (1 vol.), data on the Flood, ancient heroes, and ancient myths (1 vol.), philological notes (1 vol.), and a dictionary of fossils found in Pennsylvania. Also journals kept on a tour of France, Germany, and Switzerland, 1844-45 (4 vols.); a survey by Benjamin Smith Lyman of Converse and Panolt Leases, Glace Bay, Cape Breton Island (1 vol.); and miscellaneous notes on a wide variety of topics, many abstracted from printed works, on obelisks, the Zend-

Avesta, European place names, Egyptian burial customs, lists of Hawaiian words, notes on Javanese and East Indian words and customs (7 vols.). Table of contents (55 pp.).
Presented by Charles Lesley Ames, 1942.

407. LESUEUR, CHARLES ALEXANDRE (1778-1846). Naturalist, artist

Sketches. Film. 5 reels and 120 colored slides.

From Musée-Bibliothèque, Le Havre, France. For a description of the collection and a list of the drawings as they were in the Musée d'histoire naturelle in Le Havre before World War II, see Waldo G. Leland, "The Lesueur Collection of American Sketches," *Mississippi Valley Historical Review* 10 (1923): p. 53; on the collection as here photographed, see Gilbert Chinard, "The American Sketchbooks of Charles-Alexandre Lesueur," APS *Proc.* 93 (1949): p. 114.

408. LEWIS, JOHN FREDERICK (1860-1932). Lawyer, philanthropist, patron of arts. APS 1909

Papers, 1878-1932. *ca.* 31,000 pieces.

Although most of this large collection consists of papers of Lewis' legal practice, there are important groups which relate to the furnishing and maintenance of his city and country houses and the management of his farm, to the assembling of his outstanding collections of Oriental and medieval illuminated manuscripts and of Babylonian clay tablets (now at the Free Library of Philadelphia), and to institutions with which he was closely associated, such as APS, University of Pennsylvania, Pennsylvania Academy of the Fine Arts. Many letters and papers are about business—mortgages, rents, directorships in banks and insurance companies, investments—and about the social and cultural life of Philadelphia—operas, libraries, museums, music, schools for the handicapped, etc.

409. LEWIS, MERIWETHER (1744-1809). Explorer. APS 1803. *DAB*

Journal, August 30–December 12, 1803. 1 vol.

Journal of the river trip from Pittsburgh to the winter camp of the Lewis and Clark expedition. Of the 126 leaves in this journal, 31 contain questions by Nicholas Biddle, with William Clark's replies, 1810. Printed in Milo M. Quaife, ed., *The Journals of Captain Meriwether Lewis and Sergeant John Ordway, Kept on the Expedition of Western Exploration, 1803-1806* (State Historical Society of Wisconsin, *Collections* 22 [1916]). Biddle's questions printed in Donald Jackson, ed., *Letters of the Lewis and Clark Expedition* (Urbana, Ill., 1962), p. 497.
Presented by Charles J. Biddle, 1949.

410. LEWIS, MERIWETHER (1744-1809), and WILLIAM CLARK (1770-1838). Explorers. *DAB*

Manuscript journal of travels to the source of the Missouri River & across the American continent to the Pacific Ocean, 1804-1806. 18 bound codices and 12 loose-leaved codices.

Arranged, annotated, and indexed by Elliott Coues; interlineations throughout by Nicholas Biddle. Printed in Reuben G. Thwaites, ed., *Original Journals of the Lewis and Clark Expedition, 1804-1806* (New York, 1904-05).
Deposited by Thomas Jefferson, 1817 (part) and by Nicholas Biddle, 1818 (part); presented by Charles J. Biddle, 1949 (part).

411. LIBRARY COMPANY OF PHILADELPHIA

Minutes, 1768-94. Film. 1 reel.

From Library Company of Philadelphia.

412. LINDSAY, JOHN, Earl of Crawford (1702-49). Soldier. *DNB*

Military journals and papers, 1681-1739. 3 vols.

An account of a voyage from England to St. Petersburg, thence by Moscow through Poland until he joined the Russian army (2 vols.); and a journal of the campaign in Hungary, 1737, with a diary, 1738-39 (1 vol.); also 13 short papers on such military topics and geometry and fortification, military discipline, journals and accounts of campaigns under Prince Eugen and others, lists of regiments, and "Un traité touchant les conquêtes qu'on pouroit faire en Amérique sur la maison de Bourbon au cas que la guerre devienne générale et qui seules peuvent rétablir l'équilibre de l'Europe." These documents and journals have been described in Joseph G. Rosengarten, "The Earl of Crawford's Manuscript History in the Library of the American Philosophical Society," APS *Proc.* 42 (1903): p. 397.

Purchased from the library of Benjamin Franklin, 1803.

413. LINGELBACH, WILLIAM EZRA (1871-1962). Historian; librarian of the APS.

APS 1916. *Year Book* 1963

Papers, 1902-63. *ca.* 5,000 pieces.

A large mass of lecture notes, research notes, papers and addresses, memoranda, drafts of letters and papers, with some correspondence, relating to his career at the University of Pennsylvania, where he was professor and dean, and at the APS, where his interests were directed toward Benjamin Franklin; materials on some civic associations, notably the Committee for the Preservation of Cultural Resources, Philadelphia; letters received on his ninetieth birthday, 1961 (film, 1 reel).

From the Lingelbach Family, 1963.

414. LINNAEAN SOCIETY OF LANCASTER COUNTY, PENNSYLVANIA

Minute book, 1862-96. 1 vol.

Contains lists of members from 1862 to 1880, the printed constitution of the Society, newspaper accounts of deceased members, etc. Beginning with February 28, 1874, the minutes are reports of meetings clipped from newspapers, with manuscript additions.

415. LINNEAN SOCIETY OF LONDON

Correspondence of American scientists. Film. 2 reels.

From Linnean Society of London. Letters and papers by or to American scientists or about America, selected from the Society's collections. Included are letters to William Swainson from John Abbott, John J. Audubon, Constantine S. Rafinesque, Isaac Lea, and John E. Le Conte; letters to Sir James Edward Smith from Jacob Bigelow, DeWitt Clinton, J. F. Corrêa da Serra, David Hosack, Theodore Lyman, William Dandridge Peck, Rafinesque, Gotthilf H. E. Muhlenberg; letters to William Darlington; letters to Asa Gray; letters of John Bartram; letters of Peter Collinson to J. F. Gronovius; letters and papers of John Ellis, including letters from Alexander Garden, Samuel Martin, and Bernard Romans; letters to Carl Linnaeus from John Bartram, John Clayton, Cadwalader Colden, Corrêa da Serra, Peter Kalm, Adam Kuhn, James Logan, John Mitchell, and Charles Wrangel. Table of contents (12 pp.).

416. LOGAN, JAMES (1674-1751). Merchant, statesman, scholar. *DAB*

Selections from his correspondence. 4 vols. Copies.

Copied by Mrs. Deborah Norris Logan from original letters and papers in her family, with additions by J. Francis Fisher and Redmond Conyngham. Printed in large part in *Correspondence Between William Penn and James Logan* (Historical Society of Pennsylvania, *Memoirs* 9, 10 [1870-72]). Among the items not included in this work are Logan's letters to Governors George Clarke of New York, Sir William Gooch of

Virginia, and George Thomas of Pennsylvania, 1737-45, on Indian and general colonial policies; extracts from Logan's commercial letter book, 1717; letters on literary topics, book purchases, and his library, including letters to Peter Collinson, Benjamin Franklin, Abraham Redwood, and John Whiston.

Presented by Dr. and Mrs. George Logan, 1817-19, and by Redmond Conyngham and J. Francis Fisher.

417. ——
Letters, while president of the Council, 1736-44. 1 vol. Copy.

Copies by Mrs. Deborah Norris Logan of letters from Logan to the Proprietors of Pennsylvania, the Duke of Newcastle, Ferdinand John Paris, and others, on province business.

418. LONG, WILL WEST, and others
Cherokee medicinal and magical texts, 1928-36. 2 notebooks, 91 pieces.

Recorded in the Sequoyan syllabary. Part of the papers of Will West Long of Big Cove, Qualla Reservation, N.C.
Presented by John Witthoft, 1953.

419. LOOS, JOHN LOUIS
A biography of William Clark, 1770-1813. Film. 1 reel.

Doctoral dissertation, Washington University, St. Louis, 1953.

420. LOZANO, PEDRO (1697-1752). Spanish Jesuit missionary
Diccionario historico-indico, 1748-52. 1 vol.

Volume 3 only (G-L) of a biographical and geographical dictionary of Jesuit and Franciscan missionaries in Spanish America, with citations to printed and manuscript sources.
Presented by Joel R. Poinsett, 1820.

421. LUKENS, JOHN (1720?-89). Surveyor-general of Pennsylvania. APS 1767
Papers, 1760-88. 16 pieces.

Several letters concern Lukens' official position, and there are 10 books of surveys, 1760-75, of lands near the State-House (now Independence) Square, in the Northern Liberties of Philadelphia, and in Lancaster and Berks Counties.

422. LYELL, SIR CHARLES (1797-1875). Geologist. APS 1842. *DNB*
Papers, 1808-74. *ca.* 250 pieces.

Letters on geology, botany, natural history, evolution, natural selection, and other scientific questions, addressed chiefly to Lyell (about 10 are to his father) by, among others:

Louis Agassiz	John Curtis
Charles Babbage	Charles Robert Darwin
John Ball	George Don
Odoardo Beccari	Sir Philip de Malpas Grey
Sir Henry Thomas de la Beche	Egerton
George Bentham	William Henry Fitton
Sir Charles James Bunbury	John Fleming
George Busk	Sir William Henry Flower
William Benjamin Carpenter	Edward Forbes
William Daniel Conybeare	Ernst Haeckel

John Stevens Henslow
Sir John F. W. Herschel
Sir Joseph Dalton Hooker
Sir William Jackson Hooker
Alexander von Humboldt
Thomas Henry Huxley
John Wesley Judd
Sir George Steuart Mackenzie
Gideon Algernon Mantell
Sir Roderick Impey Murchison
Alfred Newton
Thomas Nuttall

Sir Richard Owen
Sir Edward Sabine
Adam Sedgwick
Sir James Edward Smith
James Sowerby
Philip Lutley Sclater
Georg Torchhammer
Dawson Turner
Alfred Russel Wallace
William Whewell
Searles Wood

423. ———

Correspondence. Film. 10 reels.

From University of Edinburgh Library. Incoming correspondence; a sample of two reels gives the following names:

Henry Hicks
Edward Hitchcock
David Milne Home
William Hopkins
Thomas Horsfield
Edward Hull
Thomas Sterry Hunt
Charles T. Jackson
Sir Henry James
Thomas F. Jamieson
John W. Judd
Joseph Bette Jukes

Theodore Lyman
William Whewell
Josiah D. Whitney
Edward Whymper
Sir Gardner Wilkinson
William Crawford Williamson
W. R. Wills
Alexander R. Wollaston
Searles Wood
Samuel P. Woodward
Jeffries Wyman

Table of contents (24 pp.).

424. LYMAN, BENJAMIN SMITH (1835-1920). Geologist and mining engineer. APS 1869. *DAB*

Papers, 1850-1918. *ca.* 18,000 pieces.

Notes, sketches, memoranda, etc., made while Lyman directed the geological survey of Japan, 1873-79, with reports on petroleum resources, copper, coal, iron, and gold mines, mineral springs, and other mineral resources of the Japanese archipelago. Data on the Japanese, Chinese, Ainu, and French languages, and on Japanese manners and customs, wit and humor, gardening, painting, measurements, swords, etc. Notes and data on the life, travels, and publications of Bernard Varenius. Notes collected for Lyman's *Vegetarian Diet and Dishes.* Materials on the geology of New Jersey, Ohio, Pennsylvania, Virginia, Iowa, Colorado, New Mexico, and West Virginia; and on coal and iron fields in those states and elsewhere. Manuscripts of articles on instruments for boring wells, theodolites for mining and civil engineers, other surveying instruments, etc. Also a large number of letters (55 boxes) from and to Lyman, on personal and business affairs.

Deposited by the Academy of Natural Sciences of Philadelphia, 1942.

425. LYON, JOHN (d. 1814). Gardener and seedsman

Botanical journal, 1799-1814. 1 vol.

Pertains to his travels in the eastern part of the United States. Edited by Joseph and Nesta Ewan and printed in APS *Trans.* **53,** 2 (1963).

426. McATEE, WALDO LEE (1883-1962). Zoologist, ornithologist, entomologist
Papers, 1883-1942. 168 letters, 216 autographs.

Correspondence relating chiefly to *The Auk* and to investigations into the stomachs of birds carried on by the United States Biological Survey. Correspondents include: Francis V. Greene, Henry Wetherbee Henshaw, Edgar A. Mearns, Clinton H. Merriam, Frank R. Rathbun, and others; also the Biological Society of Washington and the American Ornithologists' Union. The autograph collection was assembled principally from signatures on mailing instructions for *Auk* and on envelopes addressed to McAtee and others. Table of contents (8 pp.).
Presented by Waldo L. McAtee, 1952.

427. McKENNEY, THOMAS LORRAINE (1785-1859). Superintendent of the Indian Bureau. *DAB*
Sketches of a tour to the Lakes, 1826. 3 vols. Copy.

A record of a journey from Washington, D.C., to Lake Superior, with a description of the character and customs of the Chippewa Indians, an account of the treaty of Fond du Lac negotiated by McKenney and Lewis Cass, and a vocabulary of the Algic or Chippewa language. Illustrated with water color sketches of scenes and persons. Published: *Sketches of a Tour to the Lakes* (Baltimore, 1827).
Presented by Thomas L. McKenney, 1831.

428. MACLURE, WILLIAM (1763-1840). Merchant, geologist. APS 1799. *DAB*
Letters and papers, 1796-1848. Film. 10 reels.

From Workingmen's Institute, New Harmony, Ind. Letters to Maclure; journals of travel in Europe and America; notes and essays; also manuscripts, transcripts, and notes relating to Maclure. Correspondents include:

William Amphlett	Samuel G. Morton
Frances Wright D'Arusmont	Robert Dale Owen
Marmaduke Burroughs	Obadiah Rich
George William Erving	Lucy Say
Mme Marie Duclos Fretageot	Thomas Say
Charles Alexandre Lesueur	John Speakman
Alexander Maclure	

Table of contents (34 pp.).

429. ———
Letters to Benjamin Silliman, 1817-38. Film.
From Yale University Library. Table of contents (2 pp.).

430. MADISON, JAMES (1751-1836). President of the United States. APS 1785. *DAB*
Meteorological journals kept at his plantation, 1784-93, 1798-1902. 3 vols.

Contain also notes on sowing and harvesting, migration of birds, etc. Some notes are in Mrs. Madison's hand.
Presented by Mrs. Dolley Payne Madison, 1839.

431. MAILLET, BENOÎT DE (1656-1738). French diplomat, traveler, author. Hoefer
Nouveau système du monde. 3 vols.

Extract from a manuscript. Purchased at the sale of Benjamin Franklin's library, 1803.

432. MALESHERBES, CHRÉTIEN GUILLAUME DE LAMOIGNON DE (1721-94). French official, horticulturist. Hoefer

Essays on botanical and horticultural topics. Film. 1 reel.

From Muséum d'Histoire Naturelle, Paris.

433. MANDRILLON, JOSEPH (1743-94). French businessman and writer. APS 1785. Hoefer

Recherches philosophiques sur la découverte de l'Amérique, 1783. 1 vol.

Prepared for the Académie des Sciences, Belles Lettres et Arts, Lyon, 1783; printed, with slight changes, in *Le Spectateur américain ou remarques générales sur l'Amérique septentrionale et sur la république des Treize États-Unis* (Amsterdam, 1784).
Presented by the author, 1784.

434. MARCHANT, HENRY (1741-96). Rhode Island jurist, delegate to the Continental Congress. *DAB*

Journal, 1771-72. Typed, carbon.

An account of a voyage from Newport, R.I., to London, with descriptions of Boston, Dover, London, Edinburgh, and other cities; many references to Benjamin Franklin. A microfilm of the entire journal is in Rhode Island Historical Society.
Presented by James Bennett Nolan.

435. MARCOUX, ABBÉ M.

Iroquois grammar and dictionary. Film. 1 reel.

From Mission Iroquoise de Saint-Regis and Mission Caughnawaga, Quebec. The dictionary is both Iroquois-French and French-Iroquois.

436. MARSHALL, JOHN (1755-1835). Chief Justice of the United States. APS 1830. *DAB*

Opinions delivered in the circuit court of the United States, 1803-31. 1 vol.

Manuscript drafts of his opinions.
Presented by John Brockenbrough, Reporter of the court, 1837.

437. MARTIN DE LA BASTIDE, ———

Mémoire sur la possibilité, les avantages, et les moyens d'ouvrir un canal dans l'Amérique septentrionale, pour communiquer de la mer Atlantique, ou du Nord, à la mer Pacifique, ou du Sud, *ca.* 1785. 1 vol.

This copy was secured by Thomas Jefferson, June 30, 1785, and was presented by him to APS Historical and Literary Committee, November 6, 1817. With some changes the memoir was printed: *Mémoire sur un nouveau passage de la mer du nord à la mer du sud* (Paris, 1791).
Presented by Thomas Jefferson, 1817.

438. MARY CANISIUS, SISTER

James A. McMaster [1820-86]: pioneer Catholic journalist. Film.

Master's thesis, Catholic University of America, 1935.

439. MASON, CHARLES (1730-87). Astronomer, surveyor. APS 1768. *DNB*

Journal during the survey of the Pennsylvania-Maryland line, 1763-68. Film.

From National Archives, Washington (film microcopy No. 86).

440. ——
Papers, 1750-1815. Film. 2 reels.
From Royal Observatory, Greenwich. Letters, memoranda, computations, and tables.

441. MASON AND DIXON SURVEY
Minutes and papers, 1745-71. Film and photostats.
Miscellaneous pieces from various sources, including field notes and journals of the surveys, 1761, 1762-63 (film from Hall of Records, Annapolis, Md.), with instructions to Jonathan Hall, Thomas Garnett, John Lukens, and Archibald McLean; papers and documents (films and photostats from Royal Society, British Museum, Historical Society of Pennsylvania, Maryland Historical Society, and others), relating to the Survey, the Transits of Venus, 1761 and 1769, etc., including letters of Charles Mason and Jeremiah Dixon to Nevil Maskelyne.

442. MASSACHUSETTS. ARCHIVES
Selected materials on Indian affairs, 1665-1775. Film. 3 reels.
From Massachusetts Archives. Letters and papers from the official records of the province; many relate to the Six Nations in New York and to French activity and influence among the Indians.

443. MASSENGALE, JEAN M.
An Houdon bust of Franklin, 1964. Film.
On the bust in possession of the Boston Athenaeum.

444. MATLACK, TIMOTHY (1730-1829). Revolutionary soldier, Pennsylvania state official. APS 1780. *DAB*
Account book, 1783-1800. 1 vol.
Contains receipts and expenditures for the Flying Camp, 1783; also business accounts for purchase of bread and candles and for expenses of traveling and lodging, 1785-1800.

445. MAZZEI, FILIPPO (1730-1816). Florentine diplomatic agent, author
Letter book, 1788-92. Film. 2 reels.
From Biblioteca Nazionale Centrale, Florence. Kept principally in Paris, with a diary of events there; also drafts and copies of some of his writings; some correspondence with Virginians (e.g., John Blair, John Banister, Jr., John Page).

446. MEAD, MARGARET (1901–). Anthropologist
An anthropologist at work: writings of Ruth Benedict. Typed.
First working draft of a book published 1959; contains more than the published version, including correspondence of Ruth Benedict with Franz Boas, Reo F. Fortune, and the author.
Presented by the author, 1959.

447. MEDICINE
Formulaire médical, *ca.* 1750. 1 vol.
Prescriptions for various complaints, including epilepsy, hemorrhoids, and ringworm.

448. MENTZEL, CHRISTIAN (1622-1701). German physician, naturalist, philologist.
Larousse

Chinese lexicon. 1 vol.

A translation, with additions, by "J. W.," 1806, from Mentzel's *Sylloge minutiarum lexici latino-sinico-characteristici ex autoribus et lexicis Chinensium eruta* (Nuremberg, 1685).

Bequeathed by Peter S. Du Ponceau, 1844.

449. MERIAM, EBENEZER. New York Indian agent

Papers, 1850-55. 32 pieces.

Letters from two young Christian Onondagas, Thomas La Fort and Jameson L. Thomas, about their efforts to get an education so they might help their tribe; also from Chief David Hill, leader of the Christian Onondagas, asking for financial and political aid when the New York state legislature refused money for a school on the Onondaga reservation and when the Christian and pagan Indians sought to divide the reservation between them.

450. METEOROLOGY

Miscellaneous records, 1748-1822.

In addition to meteorological observations and records listed elsewhere, the Library has various records of different length and value, among them observations by:

William Adair at Lewes, Del., 1773-78. The entry for July 9, 1776, reads: "An Express from Congress. Independence proclaimed at the Head of the Delaware Battalion—July 10 with 3 Cheers."

Samuel Curson in South American waters, 1811.

Reuben Haines at Germantown, Pa., 1820-21.

Samuel Hazard on a voyage from Smyrna to Philadelphia, 1815, with an account of a "falling star," October 26, 1815.

Phineas Pemberton at Philadelphia, 1748-78 (abstracted in APS *Trans.*, n.s., **6** [1839]: p. 395), in Maryland, 1753-54, and elsewhere.

Charles Gotthold Reichel at Nazareth, Pa., 1787-90.

Samuel Williams in New England, 1771-73, with an account of a hurricane at Salisbury, Amesbury, and Haverhill, August 12, 1773.

Presented by the authors and others, various dates.

451. METHODIST EPISCOPAL CHURCH. MISSIONARY SOCIETY

Documents relating to the Oregon Mission, 1835-48. Film. 1 reel.

From Division of National Missions, Board of Missions of the Methodist Church. Contains much on missions to the Indians.

452. MICHAUX, ANDRÉ (1746-1802). French botanist and traveler. *DAB*

Botanical journal in North America, 1787-96. 8 vols. In French.

Printed in APS *Proc.* **26** (1889): p. 1, with an introduction by C. S. Sargent. That portion of the journal covering the travels in Kentucky, 1793-96, was included in Reuben G. Thwaites, *Early Western Travels, 1748-1846*, **3**: p. 27.

Presented by François André Michaux, 1824.

453. ——

Letters and papers, 1783-1885. 6 pieces. In English and French.

Includes letters to his son François André and an act of New Jersey authorizing Michaux to purchase lands in the state to establish a botanical garden.

Presented by François André Michaux, 1824 (in part).

454. ——

Documents on his botanizing in the United States, 1785-1807. Film. 2 reels.

From Bibliothèque Nationale and Archives Nationales, Paris. Letters, reports, lists of plants and trees, official documents, many addressed to the Comte d'Angiviller, concerning Michaux' visit to America to collect specimens for a nursery.

455. MICHAUX, FRANÇOIS ANDRÉ (1770-1855). French botanist, silviculturist, and traveler. APS 1809. *DAB;* APS *Proc.* 6 (1856); APS *Trans.* 11 (1860)

Papers, 1802-1911. *ca.* 300 pieces.

Relating especially to APS business, these papers contain many letters to and from men of science and institutions in Europe on the purchase and shipment of books and on the publications of the Society; many are to or from John Vaughan. Other papers relate to the Michaux bequest to APS to further silviculture in the United States, the Society's developing interest in American forests, the acquisition of books on silviculture by the APS Library, and the planting and care of the Michaux Grove of oaks in Fairmount Park, Philadelphia.

456. ——

Essays, 1820, 1849. Film.

From Muséum d'Histoire Naturelle, Paris. Two essays: on the trees of North America, and on a project of a nursery of foreign trees and plants in the vicinity of Bayonne; with accompanying letters.

457. MIFFLIN, JOHN FISHBOURNE (1759-1813). Philadelphia lawyer. APS 1796

Receipt book, 1800-13. 1 vol.

Receipts for payments of taxes, ground rents, rents, judgments, bills of exchange, settlements of estates, etc. Some are for monies collected for APS and for Major Zebulon Pike's expedition, 1811. The names of Samuel Breck, James Mease, Robert Millegan, and John Vaughan appear.

Presented by Seymour Adelman, 1948.

458. MILES, SAMUEL (1739-1805). Soldier, member of the Pennsylvania Assembly, mayor of Philadelphia. APS 1769. Appleton

Papers, 1776-1802. 16 pieces.

Letters and copies of letters to Sir William Howe, Joseph Reed, David Rittenhouse, George Washington, and others, with a book of accounts, principally on his capture and imprisonment during the Revolutionary War, 1776-78; also an autobiographical sketch, 1802 (published in *American Historical Record* 2 [1873]: p. 49).

459. MILLER, PETER. Philadelphia notary public

Register Book H, 1765-77. 1 vol. In German and English.

Copies of depositions sworn before him; letters of attorney, bonds, receipts, bills of sale, contracts of marriage, etc. There is an index, which lists, among many others, the names of George Glentworth, John Kearsley, Reese Meredith, Frederick Phile, and James Ralph.

460. MILLHAUSER, MILTON

Robert Chambers, evolution, and the early Victorian mind. Film.

Doctoral dissertation, Columbia University, 1951.

461. MINTO, WALTER (1738-96). Mathematician. APS 1789. *DAB*

Papers, 1738-96. Film.

From William L. Clements Library, Ann Arbor, Mich. Letters from Benjamin Rush, diplomas, testimonials, etc.

462. MISCELLANEOUS MANUSCRIPTS COLLECTION

There is no other way to describe the 3,000 manuscript letters, essays, and other papers in 29 boxes in this collection. For the most part they are items which have not fallen readily into existing Library collections, although, from time to time, as individuals come to be represented in the Miscellaneous Manuscripts by a significant number of pieces, these are removed and a separate collection begun under the individual's name. Many of the letters have considerable biographical, historical, or scientific interest. Although the manuscripts date from 1668, three-quarters of the collection is of the period between 1750 and 1850. The manuscripts are arranged chronologically, but each is entered in the general catalogue in the Manuscripts Room. The following names of correspondents have been selected at random:

Louis Agassiz	Simon Newcomb
Sir Joseph Banks	Sir Isaac Newton
Thomas Cooper	Joel R. Poinsett
Elliott Coues	David Rittenhouse
Georges L. C. F. D. Cuvier	Henry R. Schoolcraft
William Darlington	Adam Seybert
Thomas A. Edison	Jared Sparks
Albert Einstein	Herbert Spencer
Edward Everett	Henry Stevens
Frederick A. Genth	Thomas Sully
Asa Gray	Charles Thomson
Warren G. Harding	Anthony Wayne
Sir William J. Hooker	Alexander Winchell

463. MITCHELL, MARIA (1818-89). Astronomer. APS 1869. *DAB*
464. MITCHELL, WILLIAM (1791-1869). Astronomer. *DAB*

Papers. Film. 9 reels.

From Nantucket Maria Mitchell Association, Nantucket, Mass. The manuscripts of father and daughter are not easily separated, and are treated here together. The collection includes William Mitchell's autobiography, his memoir of Judge Walter Folger of Nantucket, astronomical and meteorological observations, lectures, family and other correspondence. Maria Mitchell's papers include many lectures, diaries and accounts of travel in the American South and West, 1854-57, and in Europe, 1857-58, materials on the women's rights movement, newspaper clippings, poems, meteorological and astronomical observations and calculations. Correspondents include:

Sir George B. Airy	Edward Everett Hale
Alexander D. Bache	Joseph Henry
Alvin Clark	Sir John Herschel
James Dwight Dana	Julia Ward Howe
Dorothea Dix	Alexander von Humboldt
Benjamin A. Gould	Matthew F. Maury

There are also some genealogical notes. Included in the film are five items from the Nantucket Atheneum Library. Table of contents (5 pp.).

465. MONTGOMERY FAMILY

Papers, *ca.* 1650-1900. 2 boxes.

Legal papers, correspondence, marriage settlements, genealogical tables, and memoranda of William Montgomerie of Brigend, Scotland, who emigrated to East Jersey, *ca.* 1701; pedigree of Alexander Forbes of Balogie; correspondence of John Burnet, merchant of Edinburgh, London, and New York, and of John Burnet, Jr., of Perth Amboy, N.J., chiefly with their sister and aunt Elizabeth Forbes, to 1755; genealogy of the Montgomery family in the United States, prepared by Thomas H. Montgomery, 1853, and others; copy (seventeenth century) of fundamental documents, accounts, and patents of East Jersey (1 vol.).

Presented by Mrs. H. H. Norton, 1949.

465a. MONTIGNY, ÉTIENNE MIGNOT DE (1714-82). French engineer and geometrician, treasurer of France

Reports on papers read to the Académie royale des sciences, Paris, 1746. 1 vol.

Reports made for the Académie des inscriptions et belles lettres of papers by:

Exupère Joseph Bertin	Charles Marie de La
Pierre Bouger	Condamine
Abbé de la Caille	Pierre Le Monnier
Jacques Cassini	Paul Jacques Malouin
César François Cassini de Thury	Jean Dominique Maraldi
Alexis Claude Clairaut	Vicomte de Morogues
Marquis de Courtivron	Abbé Nollet
Henri Louis Duhamel du Monceau	Henri Pitot
Étienne Louis Geoffroy	René Antoine Ferchault de
Antoine Jussieu	Réaumur

Most of the papers reported on are printed in full in *Histoire de l'Académie royale des sciences* for 1745-47.

466. MONTREAL, SÉMINAIRE DE MONTRÉAL. LES PRÊTRES DE SAINT-SULPICE

Indian manuscripts. Film. 12 reels.

From the Archives of the Order of Saint-Sulpice. Dictionaries, grammars, catechisms, prayers, Bible tales, etc., prepared by French missionaries in New France in Indian languages. Table of contents (2 pp.).

467. MOORE, E. M., collector

Autograph collection, 1816-1917. 153 letters and documents, 24 clipped signatures.

Many letters were addressed to Aubrey Lackington Moore, English writer who tried to reconcile evolution and traditional Christianity. Some discuss scientific questions of the day, but others are merely formal social notes of no significance. Correspondents include:

John Abernethy	William E. H. Lecky
Sir Henry Wentworth Acland	Sir Oliver Lodge
John Couch Adams	Sir John William Lubbock
George Bentham	Sir Richard Owen
Elizabeth Blackwell	Sir James Paget
Charles Edouard Brown-Séquard	Louis Pasteur
Sir Francis G. Darwin	George John Romanes
Charles Robert Leslie Fletcher	William Thomson
Sir William Henry Flower	Sir George Otto Trevelyan
Sir Francis Galton	Sir William Turner
George Grote	Rudolf Ludwig Karl Virchow
Sir William Jackson Hooker	Alfred Russel Wallace
Thomas Henry Huxley	William E. Gladstone

Table of contents (9 pp.).

468. MOORE, IRA. Teacher, surveyor, engineer

Papers, 1848-56. 2 boxes.

Letters from relatives, friends, and former students, chiefly on family affairs, social events, and schools in Maine, Massachusetts, and Connecticut; receipts for personal expenditures; letters of recommendation for teaching positions and from J. P. Lesley for admission to Yale College, where Moore received the Ph.B. degree, 1855. Moore was Lesley's assistant in preparing the Pennsylvania Railroad maps of western Pennsylvania.

469. MORAN, FRANCISCO. Spanish friar

Arte y vocabulario de la lengua Cholti, 1695. 1 vol. Copy. In Spanish and Cholti.

A copy of Moran's "libro grande" (1625-50), including two versions of the grammar, a vocabulary, and confessional materials. The first 3 pages are a narrative of Spanish missions, 1689-92, by Thomas Murillo. The manuscript was described by Daniel G. Brinton in *American Journal of Science*, 2nd ser. **47** (1869): p. 224, and the work was published, in somewhat condensed form, by the Maya Society, Publication No. 9 (Baltimore, 1935).

Presented by the Academia de ciencias de Guatemala, 1836.

470. MORELLET, ABBÉ ANDRÉ (1727-1819). Writer and *philosophe*

Commonplace book. Film. 1 reel.

From British Museum. Quotations, definitions, reflections, and anecdotes arranged alphabetically. There are some otherwise unrecorded anecdotes by Benjamin Franklin.

471. MORGAN, JOHN (1735-89). Philadelphia physician and teacher. *DAB*

Letters, 1763-84. 10 pieces. Photostats.

Nine of the letters are addressed to Sir Alexander Dick of Edinburgh, 1763-68, and relate to Morgan's medical studies, his travels on the Continent, and the founding of the medical department of the College of Philadelphia. The other is to William Smith. The letters to Dick are copies from the originals in possession (1949) of Mrs. Dick-Cunyngham, Prestonfield House, Edinburgh.

472. MORGAN, LEWIS HENRY (1818-81). Ethnologist, anthropologist. *DAB*

Journal and letters. Film. 2 reels.

From University of Rochester Library. Includes a record of letters received from Indians. Table of contents (11 pp.).

473. MORGAN, THOMAS HUNT (1866-1945). Zoologist. APS 1915. *Year Book* 1945

Papers, 1919-45. 31 pieces.

Principally letters to Otto L. Mohr concerning problems and progress in genetics, the Nobel Prize, etc.; with a partial biographical essay on Calvin Blackman Bridges; some account of Mohr and his family under the Nazi occupation of Norway, 1940-45.

Presented by Otto L. Mohr, 1963.

474. MORLEY, SYLVANUS GRISWOLD (1883-1948). Archaeologist. APS 1940. *Year Book* 1948

Diary, 1905-47. 39 vols. Typed.

Beginning with his college life at Harvard, Morley's diaries continue through his earliest travels in Central America, with information on the study of Mayan hieroglyphs, publications, the study of Central American ruins, and the manners and customs of the jungle Indians. Five volumes are devoted to four separate archaeological expeditions:

Copan expedition, 1937; Uxmal expedition, 1941-42; Central American expedition, 1944 (2 vols.); and Guatemala and Honduras expedition, 1947. For a description, see Alfred V. Kidder, "The Diary of Sylvanus G. Morley," APS *Proc.* **103** (1959): p. 778.

Presented by Mrs. Sylvanus G. Morley, 1955.

475. MORTON, SAMUEL GEORGE (1799-1851). Physician, naturalist, anthropologist. APS 1828. *DAB*

Papers, 1819-50. 6 boxes.

Correspondence, chiefly on scientific subjects, including education, medical practice, geology, mineralogy, craniology, paleontology, the Wilkes Expedition, his publications (*Crania Americana* and *Crania Aegyptica*), some as corresponding secretary of the Academy of Natural Sciences, from, among others:

John James Audubon	Thomas Hodgkin
John Bachman	René La Roche
Robert Montgomery Bird	William Maclure
Samuel Breck	Gideon A. Mantell
Alexandre Brongniart	Samuel Latham Mitchill
William Buckland	Thomas Nuttall
Charles Caldwell	Charles Pickering
Parker Cleaveland	Joel R. Poinsett
George Combe	William S. W. Ruschenberger
T. A. Conrad	Mrs. Lucy Way Say
William Cooper	Thomas Say
James E. DeKay	Lewis D. de Schweinitz
Jacob E. Doornik	Henry R. Schoolcraft
Peter S. Du Ponceau	Benjamin Silliman
Amos Eaton	Benjamin Tappan
George W. Featherstonhaugh	John Torrey
Asa Gray	Gerard Troost
Samuel S. Haldeman	James Collins Warren
Richard Harlan	Prince Maximilian de Wied
Samuel P. Hildreth	

Also Morton's "Some Remarks on the infrequency of mixed offspring between the European and Australian races," 1850; Joseph B. Pentland, Notes on the aborigines of Peru; newspaper clippings on Morton's death.

Presented by Arthur V. Morton and Mrs. John Story Jenks, 1943.

476. MUHLENBERG, GOTTHILF HEINRICH ERNST (1753-1815). Lutheran clergyman, botanist. APS 1785. *DAB*

Journals, 1777-1815. 2 vols. In German.

A record of daily occurrences, with many features of a commonplace book, for this contains prescriptions, notes of questions asked candidates for the Lutheran ministry, the plan of a barn, etc. There is also a biographical account of Rev. Henry Melchior Muhlenberg (1711-87).

Presented by Dr. Hiester Muhlenberg, 1954.

477. ——

Letters from Christian Frederick Heinrich Dencke, 1798-1811. 19 pieces. In Latin and German.

On botanical matters, with special reference to descriptions and identifications in Dencke's herbarium.

Presented by Rev. Frederick A. Muhlenberg, 1890.

478. ——

Writings on botany and natural history, 1784-1813. 24 vols.

Written in Latin or German script, in a tiny hand, this great mass of material, probably of considerable significance, has seldom been used and never entirely studied with care. For some information on the manuscripts and their author, see C. Earle Smith, Jr., "Henry Muhlenberg–Botanical Pioneer," APS *Proc.* **106** (1962): p. 443. For convenience, the material is presented here in essentially chronological order.

1. Botanice, 1781. 1 vol. In Latin. Catalogue of plants, with special reference to North American species, identified and described according to a disused system of Linnaeus.

2. Botanisches tagebuch, 1784-85. 1 vol. Journal and daybook, with lists of botanical specimens, meteorological observations, notes of travel, personal and church affairs, etc.

3. Calendarium florae, 1785. 1 vol. Much the same as No. 2 above.

4. Sammlung von beiträgen zur kenntnis der Natur, 1785-1804. 1 vol. A collection of notes and articles on natural history, especially that of Pennsylvania; description of Lancaster, Pa.; observations on agriculture; lists of plants and herbs, etc.

5. Natur-tagebuch, 1786. 1 vol. Diary for January 11–June 20, kept irregularly, with descriptions of plants and grasses, record of purchases, medical recipes, comments on weather, etc.

6. Agricultural journal, 1786. 1 vol. Much the same as No. 2 above.

7. Botanische tagebuch, 1786-90. 1 vol. Much the same as No. 2 above.

8. Nachschrift von Baümen und Stauden, 1787. 1 vol. In German, Latin, and English. Description of trees and shrubs, including red cedar, dogwood, acacia, pine, which he had seen growing wild or cultivated in the vicinity of Lancaster, Pa.

9. "Pflanzen die ich noch nicht nach dem Linné bestimen kann, weitläuftich zu meinem eignem Verbessern beschrieben im Jahr 1788." 1 vol. Descriptions of plants, from herbs and cassia to cryptogamis, which he has seen but plans at a later date to describe more fully.

10. Flora Lancasteriensis: botanisches tagebuch, 1790-99. 1 vol. Much the same as No. 2 above.

11. Monographien von Gewächsen aus Lancaster, 1790. 1 vol.

12. Monographia plantarum Lancastriensis, 1792. 1 vol. In Latin and German. Descriptions of trees, shrubs, and plants, including local names in German, English, and Indian languages. Bound with No. 12 is "Samlungen von dem was Ich aus dem Thierreich habe bemerken können," 1 vol. This contains Muhlenberg's observations of animals, birds, and insects in and near Lancaster; and also a list of the native animals of Vermont.

13. Cryptogama Lancastriensia, 1791. 1 vol. In Latin, German, and English. Botanical notes on ferns, mosses, fungi, lichens, etc., especially those found in the vicinity of Lancaster, Pa.

14. Lichenes Lancastriensis, 1791. 1 vol. In Latin and German.

15. Descriptio plantarum ex aliis partibus Americae septentrionalis, 1792. 1 vol. Notes on herbs, shrubs, and trees from North America.

16. Agrostographia Pensilvanica, 1792. 1 vol. In Latin and German. Descriptions of the grasses of Pennsylvania.

17. Fungi Pensylvaniae mediae. 1 vol. In Latin and German. Fungi observed and described, 1793 and later.

18. Plantae cryptogamicae Lancastriensis, 1795. 1 vol. In Latin and German.

19. "Forsetzung meines journals von botanic und der natur-historie," 1799-1807. 1 vol. Much the same as No. 2 above.

20. Botanisches tagebuch, 1807-15. 1 vol. Much the same as No. 2 above.

21. Catalogue of the hitherto known plants in the United States, 1808. 1 vol. Bound with this is Folio plantarum Lancastriensium, 1808. 1 vol., with 222 figures.

22. Botany, a notebook. 1 vol. An early version of the author's *Catalogue of the*

Hitherto Known . . . Plants of North America. In this volume is a catalogue of plants found in Burlington and Gloucester Counties, N.J., by C. S. Rafinesque.

23. Gräser die bei Lancaster wild wachsen. 1 vol. In German. Lists of grasses seen in the vicinity of Lancaster or on his travels, such as meadow grasses, white timothy, miller's grass, sedges, etc.

24. Botanical notebook. 1 vol. In Latin. Descriptions of plants, with some sketches; extracts from published descriptions of oaks, pines, etc.

Presented by the author, 1785 (No. 3 only); the remainder by Rev. Frederick A. Muhlenberg, 1890.

479. ——

Letters, 1779-1815. Film. 1 reel.

From Lutheran Theological Seminary, Mount Airy, Philadelphia. Correspondents include C. D. Ebeling, Alexander von Humboldt, Henry Melchior Muhlenberg, and others.

480. ——

Observationes botanicae de plantis Americae septentrionalis, 1807-11. Film.

From Academy of Natural Sciences of Philadelphia.

481. MUHLENBERG, HENRY AUGUSTUS (1823-54), Politician, biographer
482. MUHLENBERG, HENRY AUGUSTUS PHILIP (1782-1844). Clergyman, politician.
    DAB

Papers. Film. 11 reels.

From Mrs. Jesse Wagner and Frederick W. Nicolls, Reading, Pa., 1949. Principally personal correspondence, business and legal papers of two prominent Pennsylvania-German citizens, each of whom represented his district in Congress. Correspondence with the elder Muhlenberg, mostly on Democratic politics and Lutheran church business, is from:

William Bigler	Charles B. Penrose
Earl of Buchan	John Meredith Read
Simon Cameron	Joseph Reed
DeWitt Clinton	Richard Rush
William J. Duane	Henry Simpson
Henry Helmuth	Daniel Webster
Henry Horn	Lloyd Wharton-Bickley
William J. Leiper	

Correspondents of the younger Muhlenberg include Benjamin H. Brewster, George M. Dallas, John K. Kane, Robert M. Patterson, and Seth Salisbury. There is also a group of letters to and from Muhlenberg relating to his biography of General Peter Muhlenberg. The collection includes a volume of commissions. Table of contents (41 pp.).

483. MUHLENBERG FAMILY

Papers, 1769-1866.

Miscellaneous letters, letter books, certificates, diplomas, etc., of various members of the family. Among them are: letters and papers to and from General John Peter Gabriel Muhlenberg (1746-1807) and officers of the Continental Army on military affairs in the Southern Department during the American Revolution, 1772-1804; letters to Albert Gallatin, Nathanael Greene, Edward Hand, Winthrop Sargent, Baron von Steuben, the Earl of Stirling, and George Washington; General Muhlenberg's journal of trips to the Ohio, 1784 and 1797; also letters and notes of Gotthilf H. E. Muhlenberg

(1753-1815), including a diary kept at Halle, 1771, and extracts of 30 letters to Stephen Elliott of Beaufort and Charleston, S.C., 1808-15; also letters of Henry A. Muhlenberg about his biography of General Muhlenberg, 1848-49; also letters of Henry Melchior Muhlenberg (1711-87); also a letter book of Peter Muhlenberg, paymaster of the U. S. Army, kept at Augusta and Savannah, Ga., 1836-42; also a group of certificates and diplomas, including G. H. E. Muhlenberg's diploma from Halle, 1769, General Muhlenberg's certificate of membership in the Order of the Cincinnati, civil and military commissions signed by Presidents Jefferson, Madison, Jackson, and Lincoln. Included are photostats of materials in the William L. Clements Library, Essex Institute, New-York Historical Society, Harvard University Library, Indiana Historical Society, New York Public Library, Henry E. Huntington Library, Yale University Library, and Wisconsin Historical Society.

Presented by Rev. Frederick A. Muhlenberg, 1891 (part), and Mrs. Jesse Wagner, 1952 (part).

484. MUIR, JAMES (d. *ca.* 1796). Philadelphia bookbinder

Ledger, 1782-89. Xerox copy.

From Historical Society of Pennsylvania. A record of his work for Robert Bell, Francis Bailey, Joseph Crukshank, Mathew Carey, Thomas Dobson, William Prichard, William Young, Charles Varlo, and other printers and accounts; with a few entries to 1795.

485. MULHERN, EDWARD (d. 1833?)

Dissertation on the doctrine & principles of magnetism &c., 1829. 1 vol.

The APS minutes of November 15, 1833, read: "An application from Alex Mulhern to have returned to him a paper on the 'doctrine of Magnetism' laid before the society by his deceased father, was received and the Librarian was directed to return the same."

Presented by the author, 1829.

486. MURCHISON, SIR RODERICK IMPEY (1792-1871). Geologist. APS 1860. *DNB*

American correspondence, 1830-67. 32 pieces. Copies.

Letters from American men of science, principally on geology; correspondents include:

Louis Agassiz	Richard Harlan
American Academy of Arts and Sciences	Isaac Lea
	Henry D. Rogers
James Dwight Dana	P. Campbell Ross
Edward Everett	Benjamin Silliman, Sr.
George W. Featherstonhaugh	Lardner Vanuxem
James Hall	

From the originals in the Geological Society of London.

487. MURPHY, ROBERT CUSHMAN (1887–   ). Zoologist, ornithologist. APS 1946

Journals, 1912-62. 34 vols.

The diaries, journals, and observations of a naturalist, generously illustrated with newspaper clippings, photographs, letters, sketches, maps, and charts. Original manuscript notes of some journals are also in the Library. The contents are as follows:

I-VIII. Long Island and elsewhere, 1949-59.
    IX. Baja California, 1915.

X. Florida fisheries, 1919. West coast of Florida and North Carolina capes.
XI. Tring, 1932. Visit to England to secure the Rothschild collection of birds.
XII. Peruvian Littoral Expedition, 1919-20.
XIII. Peru, 1953-54. Oceanography, fish, birds, fishing operations, guano.
XIV. Florida and the Gulf Stream, 1937.
XV. Askov Expedition, 1941. Voyage in the schooner *Askov* along the coasts of Darien, Colombia, and Ecuador to the Malpelo Islands, investigating shorelines and outlying pelagic waters, from the points of view of geographer, oceanographer, and marine biologist.
XVI-XVII. New Zealand, 1947-49. New Zealand flora, fauna, and sea-life; Seventh Pacific Science Congress.
XVIII. Low Country, 1928-47. South Carolina and southeastern United States.
XIX. Bermuda, 1951. Rediscovery of the cahow, or Bermuda petrel.
XX. Coast to Coast, and Mexico, 1955-56. A 12,000-mile motor trip to British Columbia, the west coast of the United States, and Mexico.
XXI. Around the World, 1957-58. Ninth Pacific Science Congress.
XXII. Operation Deep Freeze, 1960. Cruise of the U.S.S. *Glacier* in Antarctica, to the head of the Bellingshausen Sea.
XXIII. South Georgia Expedition, 1912-13. Microfilm. Printed as *Logbook for Grace*. See volume 30 below.
XXIV. Venezuela, 1952. Birds and fish of the coastal areas.
XXV. Philippines, 1953. Eighth Pacific Science Congress.
XXVI. Europe, 1950. Congressus Internationalis Ornithologicus, at Upsala.
XXVII. Stranger Pacific Cruise, 1956. Journal of the Scripps Cooperative Oceanic Productivity Expedition.
XXVIII. San José Island, 1945. Flora and fauna of an island "which has had almost no human inhabitants since the extermination of the native Indians early in the 16th century."
XXIX. Panama, 1924-25. Third Pan-American Scientific Congress, Lima.
XXX. "Logbook for Grace." Copy. See volume 23 above.
XXXI. Europe, 1926.
XXXII. Coast to Coast, 1951.
XXXIII. Inagua, 1956, 1958.
XXXIV. Long Island and elsewhere, 1960-62.
XXXV. Land Island and elsewhere, 1964-65.
Presented by Dr. and Mrs. Robert Cushman Murphy, 1961-66.

488. NEAGLE, JOHN (1796-1865). Portrait painter. *DAB*

Notebooks, 1825-50. 5 vols.

No. 1: "On Whist," 1850; No. 2: "Receipts for making Megellup, Varnish, & Drying Oil; also for cleaning pictures . . . ," 1825; No. 3: "Hints for a painter with regard to his Method of Study, etc.," n.d.; No. 4: [On artists and works of art], 1826; No. 5: "Lessons on Landscape painting . . . Illustrated with copies from Sully's copies, Varley and others," 1827.

489. NEVINS, PIM (fl. 1802-17)

Journal of a visit to America, 1802-03. 1 vol.

Account of travels, with descriptions, through New York, Philadelphia, Wilmington, Baltimore, Washington, Alexandria, Bethlehem, Pa., Easton, Pa., the Pocono Mountains, northern New Jersey, New Brunswick, N.J., and Trenton, N.J. Nevins was a member of Hardshaw West Monthly Meeting, Society of Friends, in Liverpool. See the journal of Joshua Gilpin, who accompanied Nevins on his journey to Bethlehem, in *Penna. Mag. Hist. Biog.* **46** (1922): p. 15.

490. NEW HAMPSHIRE. ADMIRALTY COURT

Proceedings relating to the armed brigantine *McClary* vs. the brigantine *Susanna*, 1777. 1 vol.

Endorsed by Charles Thomson as secretary of Congress: "Novr. 28, 1778. I have looked over the foregoing pages. I find on the first trial an appeal made to Congress from the judgment of the court, which being denied, the claimants appealed to a superior court where the cause is again heard & judgment given, but I do not find any appeal from this last judgment. I therefore do not know for what purpose the papers are lodged with me." Purchased at the sale of Benjamin Franklin's library, March 18, 1803.

491. NEW JERSEY. GENERAL ASSEMBLY

Acts, 1727, 1746, 1747. 3 pieces.

Acts for issuing bills of credit, 1727; for victualling the forces on an expedition to Canada, 1746; and for further victualling forces lately raised in New Jersey on an expedition to Canada, 1747.

492. NEW SWEDEN

Documents in the archives at Stockholm, 1640-55. 1 vol. In Swedish and French.

Copies of documents relative to New Sweden, made at the expense of Jonathan Russel, United States minister to Sweden, 1820. Printed in Hazard's *Register of Pennsylvania* 4 (1829): p. 177 through 5 (1830): p. 219. Bound with this is Per Lindeström, Description de la nouvelle Suède et des Indes Occidentales, 1691 (chapter 5 only).

Presented by Jonathan Russel, 1820 (documents), and William Jones, 1822 (Lindeström).

493. NEW-YORK HISTORICAL SOCIETY

Selected materials on Indian affairs, 1791. Film. 1 reel.

From New-York Historical Society. Letters and papers from the McKesson Collection on the Indians of New York State; correspondents include George Clinton, Joseph Brant, and Timothy Pickering.

494. NEWHOUSE, SETH (1842?-1921). Mohawk

Cosmogony of De-ka-na-wi-da's government, 1885. 1 vol. Photocopy.

From the original formerly in possession of Ray Fadden of St. Regis Mohawk Reservation, Hogansburg, N.Y. Described by William N. Fenton, "Seth Newhouse's Traditional History and Constitution of the Iroquois Confederacy," APS *Proc.* 93 (1949): p. 141.

495. NEWMAN, JOHN. Physician of Salisbury, N.C. APS 1797

A short account of the situation, soil, productions &c. of the State of Tennessee, 1797. 1 vol.

Dated January 19, 1797; read at a meeting of APS, February 17, 1797. Bound in is William Dunbar, Plan of a settlement near the Natches, noted as received from C. Ross, August, 1803.

496. NORTH AMERICAN INDIAN LANGUAGES

In addition to many manuscripts entered elsewhere in this Guide, the Library has dictionaries and vocabularies and other materials relating to North American Indian languages, as follows:

Choctaw: Vocabulaire Chacta, *ca.* 1820. 1 vol.

French words with Choctaw equivalents; numerals and sample phrases.
Presented by Peter S. Du Ponceau, 1827.

Delaware: Mingo vocabulary, taken from the mouth of William Sack, a Conestoga Indian, 1757. 1 vol.

The list was compiled at Fort Augusta; the volume contains accounts, 1757-71,
kept at Fort Augusta and elsewhere.
Presented by John Vaughan.

Micmac: Instruction sur la langue Mickmaque, *ca.* 1814. 1 vol.

Ottawa: Dictionarium Gallico-Outa-okum, 1771. 1 vol.

This volume includes Age-Epei only.

Miscellaneous vocabularies and papers, 1 vol.

This volume includes letters, vocabularies, committee reports, etc., drawn together
from several sources. Among the correspondents are:

Benjamin Smith Barton	William Vans Murray
Peter S. Du Ponceau	Constantine S. Rafinesque
John G. E. Heckewelder	William Thornton
George Izard	John Vaughan
Thomas Jefferson	David Zeisberger

497. NORTH AMERICAN LAND COMPANY

Miscellaneous documents, 1768-1843. 1 vol. and 56 pieces.

Ledger, 1795-1805, showing accounts with:

Tench Coxe	Frederick A. Muhlenberg
Thomas Fitzsimons	John Nicholson
William Temple Franklin	Thomas Ruston
Jared Ingersoll	Benjamin Shoemaker
Pierre L'Enfant	John Vaughan
Robert Morris	James Wilson

Also many deeds and other documents to which Robert Morris was a party. The volume
is indexed.

498. NUTTALL, THOMAS (1786-1859). Naturalist. APS 1817. *DAB;* APS *Proc.* **7**
    (1860)

Diary, 1810. Photostat.

Journal of a trip from Philadelphia by stage to Pittsburgh, then afoot through
Franklin, LeBœuf, and Erie to the Huron River; thence by boat to Detroit, where he
remained July 26–July 29, when he set out by canoe for Michilimackinac. Descriptions
of Detroit, plants, animals, springs, Indian mounds; notes on goitre. Edited by Jeanette
Graustein and published in *Chronica Botanica* **14**, 1-2 (1950-51).

499. OLBRECHTS, FRANS M. (1899-1959). Belgian linguist and anthropologist

Papers on the Iroquois Indians, *ca.* 1910-30. 46 folders and volumes. In Flem-
ish, French, and English.

Materials on the Onondaga, Tuscarora, Seneca, Cayuga, and Oneida Indians, collected under auspices of the American Council of Learned Societies' Committee on

Native American Languages; included are field notes, grammars, dictionaries, studies of Handsome Lake religion, medical prescriptions, comparative linguistics, and some correspondence with Franz Boas. Table of contents (2 pp.).

Presented by Mme Olbrechts, 1959.

500. OLITSKY, PETER KOSCIUSKO (1866-1964). Pathologist

Papers, 1917-64. *ca.* 2,500 pieces.

Consists chiefly of materials relating to his work in developing vaccines for various viruses and bacteria—encephalitides, typhus, rickettsioses, poliomyelitis, meningococcus, trachoma, etc. Also materials on intraperitoneal protection tests; records of experiments on production of intranuclear inclusions by means of chemicals; results of work by Dr. Harold R. Cox on viruses; medical research during World War II; and materials relating to the Rockefeller Institute. There are also corrected proofs of *Viral Encephalitides* (Springfield, Ill., 1958). Correspondents include:

Harold L. Amoss
A. Ascoli
Joseph W. Beard
Alex Blumstein
Detlev W. Bronk
Gina Castelnuovo
Harold R. Cox
Geoffrey Edsall
Simon Flexner
Herbert S. Gasser
H. C. Givens
Frank L. Horsfall, Jr.
Dorothy M. Horstmann
E. Elizabeth Jones
K. D. Leung
Perrin H. Long
Henry Makower
Isabel M. Morgan

Stuart Mudd
Hideyo Noguchi
F. F. Russell
Albert B. Sabin
Florence R. Sabin
A. A. Sadow
Walter Schlessinger
Henry E. Sigerist
Carl tenBroeck
Augustus B. Wadsworth
Kurt Wagener
L. T. Webster
Carl V. Weller
George H. Whipple
Ralph W. G. Wycoff
Robert H. Yager
Hans Zinsser

Presented by Mrs. Peter K. Olitsky and the Rockefeller Institute, 1965.

501. OPIE, EUGENE LINDSAY (1873–   ). Pathologist

Papers, *ca.* 1919-50. *ca.* 15,000 pieces.

Laboratory notes and files on dysentery, meningitis, viruses, poliomyelitis, rickettsiae, influenza, trachoma, and other diseases; a large body of papers on the study, vaccination, and cure of tuberculosis, including Opie's efforts to alleviate the disease in Jamaica, among Philadelphia school children, and in New York City. A large body of material pertaining to the United China Relief and the American Bureau for Medical Aid to China includes memoranda, budgets, committee reports, and correspondence with James L. McConaughy, Alfred Kohlberg, Donald D. Van Slyke, and others. Also material pertaining to the International Health Division of the Rockefeller Foundation, the University of Pennsylvania, the Milbank Memorial Fund, and other institutions. There are *ca.* 300 clinical autopsies performed at the Base Hospital, Camp Pike, Ark., of soldiers who died in the flu epidemic of 1918. Also notes of Opie's course in pathology at the University of Pennsylvania. Among the correspondents are:

George W. Bachman
Ward Brinton
Walter S. Cornell

Walter Ekhart
John A. Ferrell
Hubert W. Hetherington

H. H. Howard	David Seegal
Persis Putnam	Andrew J. Warren
F. F. Russell	C. W. Wells
Wilbur A. Sawyer	

Presented by Dr. Opie, 1965.

502. ORD, GEORGE (1781-1866). Naturalist and philologist. APS 1817. *DAB*
Letters to Charles Waterton, 1832-64. 71 pieces.

Correspondence of a lifetime friendship, with much incidental material on the life of a wealthy Philadelphia gentleman of the time. The following persons, institutions, and topics figure prominently: natural history, ornithology, John James Audubon (especially his deficiencies as a scholar and a gentleman and the defects of *Birds of America*), John Vaughan, the United States South Seas Exploring Expedition, Peale's Museum, APS, Bank of the United States, Charles L. J. L. Bonaparte, Titian R. Peale, Louis Agassiz, Sir Charles Lyell, Paul du Chaillu, and current events. Table of contents (4 pp.).

503. ——
Extracts from letters on John James Audubon. 1 vol.

Extracts, chiefly in an unknown hand, from Ord's letters, 1831-33, criticizing Audubon as a man and as a naturalist. Ord wrote the last part of the volume, and there are manuscript comments by Charles Waterton.
Presented by Mrs. Yvonne Waterton, 1962.

504. ——
Notes on the use of French verbs. 1 vol.

Ord presented this volume to his cousin Gregory B. Keen.

505. ——
Letters to Titian R. Peale, 1844-52. Film.

From Historical Society of Pennsylvania.

506. ORDWAY, JOHN (*ca.* 1775–*ca.* 1817). Explorer. *DAB*
Journal, 1804-06. 3 vols.

Kept on the Lewis and Clark expedition; edited by Milo M. Quaife and published in *The Journals of Captain Meriwether Lewis and Sergeant John Ordway, Kept on the Expedition of Western Exploration, 1803-1806* (State Historical Society of Wisconsin, *Collections* **22** [1916]).
Presented by Charles J. Biddle, 1949.

507. O'REILLY, HENRY, collector
Selections from papers relating to the Six Nations, 1789-1820. Film. 1 reel.

From New-York Historical Society. Letters, bills, accounts, receipts, memoranda, official communications and documents relating to the Iroquois in New York state, selected from vols. 6-15 of O'Reilly's collection, "Mementos of western settlement." Many manuscripts appear to be from the papers of General Israel Chapin, Indian agent; and correspondents include:

Joseph Brant	Joseph Ellicott
Théophile Cazenove	John Jay
Moses Cleaveland	Henry Knox

James McHenry	Oliver Philips
Robert Morris	Philip Schuyler
Thomas Morris	John Sergeant, missionary

508. OSTERHOUT, WINTHROP JOHN VANLEUVEN (1871-1964). Botanist and physiologist. APS 1917. *Year Book* 1964

Papers, 1894-1961. *ca.* 750 pieces, 80 photographs.

Principally letters on family matters, education, and scientific topics. Correspondents include:

Svante Arrhenius	Rudolf Höber
Detlev W. Bronk	John Nichols Loeb
Walter B. Cannon	Robert Loeb
Hugo de Vries	G. Howard Parker
Mrs. Helen Thomas Flexner	Silvestre Prât
Simon Flexner	

Table of contents (2 pp.).
Presented by Mrs. Marian Irwin Osterhout, 1962.

509. OWEN, SIR RICHARD (1804-92). English naturalist. APS 1845. *DNB*

Papers, 1837-89. *ca.* 125 pieces.

Correspondence on natural history, especially mollusks, fishes, and birds, and on medicine and social affairs with:

Charles L. J. L. Bonaparte	Sir John W. Lubbock
Charles Buxton	Sir Charles Lyell
Philip Pearsall Carpenter	Henri Milne-Edwards
Sir William Fothergill Cooke	Sir James Paget
Lady Mary Cooper	John Richardson
Sir William White Cooper	Adam Sedgwick
Thomas C. Eyton	

Also a synopsis of a course of lectures, 1857. Table of contents (3 pp.).

510. PAGET, SIR JAMES (1814-99). Surgeon. APS 1854. *DNB*

Letters, 1784-1932. 192 pieces.

Mostly addressed to Paget, these letters were assembled by Lady Paget as a collection of autographs; the subjects are medicine, science, and family. Correspondents include:

Sir Frederick August Abel	John Ericsson
John Couch Adams	Michael Faraday
Sir George B. Airy	Sir William Henry Flower
Louis Agassiz	Edward Forbes
Charles Babbage	Sir Douglas Strutt Galton
John Shaw Billings	Sir Francis Galton
Elizabeth Blackwell	Sir Archibald Geikie
Andrew Clark	Asa Gray
Georges L. C. F. D. Cuvier	Sir Joseph Dalton Hooker
Charles R. Darwin	Sir William Jackson Hooker
Sir Humphry Davy	Alexander von Humboldt
James Dewar	Thomas Henry Huxley
Thomas A. Edison	Joseph Lister
John L. Ellerton	Sir John William Lubbock

Sir Charles Lyell	Herbert Spencer
Sir Roderick Impey Murchison	Robert Stephenson
Sir William Osler	John Tyndall
Sir Joseph Prestwick	Rudolf Virchow
George Rolleston	Albert Russel Wallace
Sir William Siemens	Sir Thomas Watson
Sir James Young Simpson	Sir Charles Wheatstone

Table of contents (5 pp.).

511. PANELLA, SILVIA

Benjamin Franklin: writer and humanist. Typed, carbon.

Submitted for a degree at Universita Commerciale Luigi Bocconi, Milan, Italy, 1962

Presented by the author.

512. PARKE, THOMAS (1749-1835). Philadelphia Quaker physician. APS 1774

Journal, 1771-73. Film. 1 reel.

From Historical Society of Pennsylvania. Kept while a medical student in London and Edinburgh.

513. PARKER, ELY SAMUEL (1828-95). Seneca sachem, engineer, soldier, Commissioner of Indian Affairs. *DAB*

Papers, 1794-1946. *ca.* 600 pieces.

Printed and manuscript materials, principally on Seneca affairs and culture. Letters on these subjects, as well as politics, education, engineering, and war, are to and from: Henry Clay, Millard Fillmore, Henry M. Flagler, Lewis H. Morgan, Henry R. Schoolcraft, Daniel Webster, Asher Wright, and others. A number of letters relate to Parker's service as engineer of public buildings at Galena, Ill., and to his Masonic activities; others are written from Vicksburg and other centers of war. The collection includes essays on Seneca subjects; a fragment of Parker's diary, 1847; biographical data; and miscellaneous materials on Indian history and linguistics. Table of contents (56 pp.).

Presented by Arthur C. Parker, 1950.

514. PARKINSON, GEORGE H.

Charles Darwin's influence on religion and politics of the present day. Film.

Doctoral dissertation, University of Chicago, 1942.

515. PARRAS, PEDRO JOSEPH DE. Spanish priest

Diario y derrotero de los viages que ha hecho desde que salió de la Ciudad de Zaragosa en Aragón para La América, 1748-59. 1 vol.

Includes a narrative of a trip through the Paraguay missions, with descriptions of the life of the Indians there; also descriptions of Montevideo and Buenos Aires.

Presented by Joel R. Poinsett, 1820.

516. PARRISH, JASPER (1767-1836). Indian interpreter and agent

Letters and documents relating to his government service among the Indians of New York state, 1790-1831. Film. 1 reel.

Edited by Mrs. Dorothy May Fairbanks Newton.

Thesis, Vassar College, 1940.

517. PARSONS, MRS. ELSIE CLEWS (1875-1941). Anthropologist, folklorist

Papers, 1835-1944. *ca.* 11,000 pieces, 77 notebooks, 600 photographs, 265 negatives; also drawings, artifacts, newspaper clippings, etc.

Correspondence, 1921-41 (*ca.* 1,300 items), with Ruth Benedict, Franz Boas, Alfred V. Kidder, Alfred L. Kroeber, Oliver La Farge, Robert Redfield, Stith Thompson, Leslie A. White, and others; notes, papers, documents, etc., relating to the tales, proverbs, folklore, etc., of the West Indies; Jamaica Negro proverbs and sayings, collected by George R. Drinkwater, 1892; "Filipino Village Reminiscences" by Mrs. Parsons; riddles, folk tales, poems from York Village, Maine; materials on birth control; "Indian trait survey" by Edward W. Gifford; miscellaneous materials on Indians of the Southwest, Central America, and South America; unpublished manuscripts on sleep, a trip to Greece, and "The World Changes"; paintings of the Isleta pueblo of the Tewa Indians of New Mexico (published, with introduction and commentary by Mrs. Parsons, as *Isleta Paintings* [Smithsonian Institution, Bureau of American Ethnology *Bulletin* 181, 1962]). Table of contents (12 pp.).

Presented by the Parsons family, 1949.

518. PASTI, GEORGE (1923–)

Consul Sherard: amateur botanist and patron of learning, 1659-1728. Film.

Doctoral dissertation, University of Illinois, 1950.

519. PATTERSON, ROBERT (1743-1824). Mathematician. APS 1785. *DAB*

Letters and papers, 1791-1821. *ca.* 50 pieces.

Principally letters from Thomas Freeman and John Garnett; with some miscellaneous writings, such as "Hints towards a primer for my little boy," and a commencement address at the University of Pennsylvania, 1813.

520. PATTERSON, ROBERT MASKELL (1787-1854). Professor of natural philosophy, University of Pennsylvania; director of the United States Mint. APS 1809. APS *Proc.* 6 (1854)

Papers, 1775-1853.

Letters to and from Alexander D. Bache, John Gummere, Ferdinand R. Hassler, Samuel M. Leiper, Robert C. Reid, John Sergeant, John Vaughan, and others; 15 letters to President Franklin Pierce from various persons recommending Patterson's son for the directorship of the Mint, 1853; a large number of miscellaneous notes and papers on a great variety of topics, including astronomy, algebra, annuities, coal, canals, electricity, the deaths of Adams and Jefferson, music, and natural philosophy; notes of lectures and experiments made at Paris as a student at the Jardin des Plantes, 1810-11 (4 vols.). There are a number of lectures, a set of accounts at the University of Virginia, and letters to the trustees of the University of Virginia, University of Pennsylvania, and Girard College. Among unrelated items in the collection are Phineas Pemberton's meteorological observations, 1775-77; Ferdinand R. Hassler's list of books and instruments for the United States Coast and Geodetic Survey, 1817; and papers on Thomas Leiper's stone quarry and canal. Table of contents (9 pp.).

Presented by James O. Patterson, 1955 (in part).

521. PATTERSON, THOMAS LEIPER (1816-1905). Lawyer, engineer

Papers, 1834-1905. Film. 1 reel.

From manuscripts in possession of Mr. and Mrs. Leiper Patterson Read, Pottsville, Pa., 1965. Chiefly personal and family letters, with a few of earlier and later date. There is also a film of a transcript of the letters, made by Mrs. Eliza Leiper Woolford Jones, Vinings, Ga. Table of contents (7 pp.).

522. PEALE, MRS. BURD

Notes on the paintings of Charles Willson Peale. 1 vol.

Compiled in the latter part of the nineteenth century, this volume contains extracts from Charles Willson Peale's writings about his paintings and the subjects. Part of the volume is a list, with description, of Peale's portraits with the (then) location of each.

523. PEALE, CHARLES (1709-50). Schoolmaster, painter, father of Charles Willson Peale

Letter book, 1745-47. 1 vol.

Letters written from Maryland, principally on family affairs, financial conditions, health, and life in Maryland; with some references to Maryland politics. With typed copies.

524. PEALE, CHARLES WILLSON (1741-1827). Artist, naturalist, soldier. APS 1786. DAB

Note: For a brief description of the Peale Papers, see *Year Book* 1945: p. 74. The papers were fully and carefully used, with generous quotations from them, by Charles Coleman Sellers in *Charles Willson Peale*, APS *Memoirs* 23, 1, 2 (2 vols., Philadelphia, 1939-47). The principal groups of manuscripts are listed below:

Diaries, 1765-1826. 26 vols.

Daily entries relating to family and business, travels, sittings, museum work, etc. Three of the diaries are duplicated from originals elsewhere: No. 3 in the Henry E. Huntington Library, and Nos. 7 and 9 in Fordham University Library. Also the diary of June 9–July 4, 1824, which covers the period of Peale's last courtship.

525. ——

Letter books, 1767-1827. 18 vols.

Business and personal correspondence on a wide variety of topics with a great many persons. Subjects include events in Philadelphia; the Philadelphia Museum, its exhibits, and Peale's hopes for its acquisition by the city or state; the exhumation and exhibition of the mastodon; construction and promotion of the polygraph; agricultural concerns, including the operation of his farm Belfield; natural history; false teeth, etc. Correspondents include, among many others:

Sir Joseph Banks	Henry Laurens
Joel Barlow	Benjamin Henry Latrobe
John Beale Bordley	Thomas McKean
John Dickinson	Rembrandt Peale
James De Peyster	Titian R. Peale
William Duane	Franklin Peale
Peter S. Du Ponceau	Mrs. Angelica Robinson
Andrew Ellicott	Pennsylvania Academy of the
Benjamin Franklin	Fine Arts
Robert Fulton	Thomas Jefferson Randolph
John Hawkins	David Ramsay
Joseph Hopkinson	Isidore Geoffroy Saint-Hilaire
Michael Hillegas	William Smith
David Hosack	Thomas Sully
Thomas Jefferson	John Vaughan
Marquis de Lafayette	George Washington

Volumes 7 and 19 of the Letter books are missing. There is a 3-volume calendar and an index.

526. ——

Autobiography. 3 vols.

Autograph copy, manuscript copy, and typed copy by Horace W. Sellers, with notes and an index.

527. ——

Lectures, Nos. 1-39. 42 vols.

Lectures on natural history, describing the elements, physical phenomena, quadrupeds, fishes, and birds, systems of identification; delivered at the Philadelphia Museum and illustrated by specimens in that establishment.

528. ——

Lectures. 1 vol.

Lectures on natural history, the Philadelphia Museum, health, domestic happiness; one is entitled "a voice in behalf of the oppressed."

529. ——

Account book, 1785-95. 1 vol.

Accounts of Peale's museum, which was housed in Philosophical Hall. Only a few accounts are itemized, as "for Musick," "for Hand bills," etc. A few receipts for payment of taxes are included, with some sketches of animals and scenes.

530. ——

Belfield farm accounts, 1816-20. 1 vol.

For an account of Peale's country place, see Jessie J. Poesch, "Mr. Peale's Farm 'Persevere,'" APS *Proc.* **100** (1956): p. 545.

531. ——

Day books, 1805-23, 1810-24. 2 vols.

The day book of 1805-23 contains, among other things, an account with Robert Fulton for painting supplies; account with Thomas Jefferson Randolph for admission to lectures on chemistry, purchase of instruments, etc., with notes of payment by Thomas Jefferson; accounts with his children, etc. The day book of 1810-24 consists chiefly of farm accounts for Belfield, with notes on the construction of a mill, out-buildings, and farm work and purchases; with some notes of daily activities and a description of a plough made by Peale patterned after Jefferson's.

532. ——

Sketch book, 1801. 1 vol.

28 water-colors of scenes along the Hudson River, including Slaughter Landing, Verplank's Point, Stony Point, Dunderberg or Thunder Hill, Haverstraw Bay, Anthony's Nose, and several of West Point.

533. ——

Portrait list, *ca.* 1772. Fragment.

Names of 55 persons whom Peale painted, with notes on the sizes of paintings, and prices charged. This information appears in another form in Charles Coleman Sellers, "Portraits and Miniatures by Charles Willson Peale," APS *Trans.* **42**, 1 (1952).

534. ——

Memorandum book, 1794. 1 vol.

Entries for recipes for curing food, mixing oil paints, making black ink, cleaning teeth, making cements; also prescriptions for illness; notes on grafting, etc.

535. ——

Notes about his paintings. 8 notebooks.

Notes, newspaper clippings, photographs, etc., about the paintings of Peale and Rembrandt Peale, compiled by Charles Coleman Sellers for his biography of Charles Willson Peale.
Presented by Charles Coleman Sellers.

536. PEALE, FRANKLIN (1795-1870). Naturalist, paleontologist, traveler. APS 1833. APS *Proc.* 11 (1870)

Songs for guitar and piano, 1822-23. 2 vols.

One volume contains songs for guitar and piano, the other compositions and arrangements for guitar. Peale copied some, if not all, from the works of various composers; a few were copied by his wife.

537. PEALE, JAMES (1749-1831). Artist. *DAB*

Sketch book. 1 vol.

Sketches of scenes, animals, mills, machinery, persons, ships, furniture, etc.; also brief notes.

538. PEALE, MARY JANE PATTERSON (1827-1902)

Journal, 1844. 1 vol.

Commenced at Deer Park, April 26, 1844, and continuing to October 8, 1844, this is the record of a young lady's uneventful round of rising, dressing, sewing, making and serving meals, walking out, visits, outings, etc.

539. PEALE, REMBRANDT (1778-1860). Portrait and historical painter. *DAB*

Sketch books. 2 vols.

One book contains sketches of the Delaware Water Gap, Mount Vernon, and Washington's tomb; the other contains pencil sketches made on a trip on the Hudson River, October, 1850, including views of the Palisades, Castle Garden, the Catskill Mountains, etc.

540. ——

Palettes. 8 sheets.

The palettes show 153 colors, with notes by the author explaining the reasons for locating the colors. One note refers to Peale's painting of Washington, 1853.

541. ——

Miscellaneous manuscripts. Film.

From manuscripts in possession of Edward L. Davis, Philadelphia, 1962. Contains 7 letters to his wife, 1808-33; a fragment of autobiography on his painting and studies; a notebook containing copies of correspondence about his portrait of Washington; John Godman's Ode suggested by Rembrandt Peale's National Portrait of Washington (1824), a commonplace book containing kitchen and medicinal recipes.

542. PEALE, RUBENS (1784-1865). Artist

Letter books, 1802-14, 1824. 2 vols.

Chiefly letters to members of his family on the business of the museums in Philadelphia, New York, and London. The letters of 1824 are press copies, chiefly to Charles Willson Peale and Franklin Peale about the Baltimore museum.

Presented by Charles Coleman Sellers, 1945 (in part).

543. ——

Correspondence, 1822-49. 1 vol. and 23 pieces.

One volume of correspondence and miscellany relating to the New York museum, 1826-49, including the exchange of specimens; with some family correspondence. Also 23 letters to Franklin Peale about the Baltimore museum and its relations to the Philadelphia and New York museums. These letters mention Thomas Sully, Thomas Birch, Charles Willson Peale, and other Philadelphia artists; also the physiognotrace, galvanic experiments, gasometers, balloons, Indians, natural history, etc.

544. ——

List of pictures, 1855-65. 1 vol.

Subjects of 131 paintings, with dates and the names of the purchasers or those to whom the completed work was presented.

545. ——

Memorandum and events of his life. 1 vol.

An autobiographical work.

546. ——

Sketch book, 1864. 1 vol.

Pencil sketches of landscapes, designs for cards and figures, etc.

547. PEALE, ST. GEORGE (1745-78). Clerk of the Maryland Assembly, commissary of military stores

Accounts with the Board of War, 1777-78. 1 vol.

Entries for labor, barrels, wagon hire, freight, powder, muskets, bayonets, balls, cartridges and cartridge paper, powder horns, and other supplies; with some entries of the character of a commonplace book.

548. PEALE, TITIAN RAMSAY (1780-98). Student, painter

Miniature painting with the necessary instructions, ca. 1798. 1 vol.

Identifies miniatures as distinct from other paintings; instructions on fixing canvas, mixing paints, arranging subject, painting draperies, flowers, etc. Probably copied from a printed volume.

549. PEALE, TITIAN RAMSAY (1799-1885). Naturalist, explorer, artist. APS 1833.
DAB

Correspondence, 1820-68. 56 pieces.

Letters from Franklin Peale, chiefly on family affairs; but also on the United States Mint, agriculture, Civil War, photography, current events, and Franklin Peale's collection of artifacts of the Stone Age; with some letters from Titian Peale and his wife.

Presented by Charles Coleman Sellers, 1945.

550. ――――

Sketch books. 4 vols.

Principally sketches of subjects of natural history—flora, fauna, insects; also hunting scenes from the American West, sketches made on the Wilkes Expedition; portraits and sketches of Indians; with a group of Chinese scenes. A few sketches are by Charles Willson Peale and Thomas Say. For a short description of the sketch books, see Robert Cushman Murphy, "The Sketches of Titian Ramsay Peale (1799-1885)," APS *Proc.* **101** (1957): p. 523.

551. ――――

Charles Willson Peale, a biography. 1,039 pp.

Unpublished, and now superseded by Charles Coleman Sellers' biography of the artist.

552. ――――

Journal kept as assistant naturalist of Long's expedition west of the Rocky Mountains, 1819. Film.

From Library of Congress.

553. PEALE FAMILY

Papers, 1705-1898. *ca.* 400 pieces.

Principally correspondence among members of the family on family matters and genealogy. Most of the material is dated in the latter part of the nineteenth century. Principal correspondents include Charles Willson Peale, Rembrandt Peale, George Washington Parke Custis, Mrs. Eliza Burd Patterson Peale, Mrs. Harriet Peale, Rubens Peale, Mrs. Angelica Peale Robinson, Titian Ramsay Peale, Franklin Peale, and Albert Charles Peale, who appears to have assembled the collection. There is some material on the Philadelphia Museum, natural history, and Charles Willson Peale's portraits.

554. ――――

Genealogies. 3 vols.

One volume contains the line of descent from William Peale (fl. 1630) of Rutland-shire, through Charles Peale of Maryland, to 1950; a second volume is a Xerox copy of a family genealogy prepared by Joseph M. Peale, 1931, with emphasis on the line of James Peale (1749-1831), brother of Charles Willson Peale; the third volume, compiled by Horace Wells Sellers, contains notes, letters, photostats of documents relating to the family genealogy in England and the United States.

Presented by Charles Coleman Sellers, 1956, 1963.

555. PEALE-SELLERS FAMILY

Correspondence, 1686– . 12 boxes.

Wide-ranging, miscellaneous correspondence, with some other manuscripts, of members of the Peale and Sellers families, on natural history, the Philadelphia Museum, engineering, current events, and family matters. There is a group of letters and papers of Titian Ramsay Peale, including a sketch book and a large number of loose sketches; also a group of letters of Rubens Peale and one of letters of Raphaelle Peale; also photostats of letters of Rembrandt Peale concerning his portrait of George Washington, from the original manuscripts in Morristown, N.J., National Historical Park. Other correspondents include:

Jacques Boucher de Crèvecœur de Perthes	Samuel P. Langley
	Benjamin H. Latrobe
Park Benjamin	J. Peter Lesley
Alexander J. Cassatt	James Madison
Paul Philippe Cret	S. Weir Mitchell
John Philip de Peyster	Henry Morton
Thomas A. Edison	George Ord
Frederick Fraley	Robert M. Patterson
Benjamin Franklin	William Pepper
Robert Fulton	Charles Augustus Stetson
Isidore Geoffroy Saint-Hilaire	Elihu Thomson
Mrs. E. D. Gillespie	William Thornton
Oliver Wendell Holmes	John Vaughan
Thomas Jefferson	Benjamin West
Lord Kelvin	George Westinghouse

Presented by Charles Coleman Sellers, 1945 and 1962, Horace Sellers Colton, 1959, Dr. and Mrs. William J. Robbins, 1963 (parts).

556. PECKHAM, STEPHEN FARNUM (1839-1918). Chemist. APS 1897. *DAB*

The Lollard influence in colonial America: a history of the struggle for religious liberty in the Old and New World from the thirteenth to the eighteenth century. 1 vol. Typed.

557. PEMBERTON, ISRAEL (1715-79). Philadelphia Quaker merchant and philanthropist. APS 1768. *DAB*

Letter book D, 1744-47. 1 vol.

Mercantile letters relating to the purchase and shipment of goods in America, Europe, and the West Indies. Some are signed by Matthias Aspden, Israel Pemberton, Jr., John Reynell, and John Smith. There is an index of addressees (3 pp.).

558. PENN, THOMAS (1702-75), and RICHARD PENN (1706-71). Proprietors of Pennsylvania

Correspondence with James Hamilton, 1747-71. 1 vol.

About 175 letters on public business. A few are copies of letters by Hamilton and by or to Abraham Taylor, member of the Provincial Council.

Presented by J. Francis Fisher, 1834.

559. PENN, WILLIAM (1644-1718). Religious and political thinker, statesman. *DAB*

Miscellaneous letters and documents, 1665-1801. 4 vols.

Three vols. contain letters, laws, charters, reports, proclamations, petitions, and other official and semi-official documents relating principally to early Pennsylvania and New Jersey, signed by, or addressed to, Penn and, among others:

James Claypoole	William Markham
John Eckley	Isaac Norris
Benjamin Fletcher	Hugh Roberts
Andrew Hamilton	John Simcock
Thomas Lloyd	Robert Turner
James Logan	

Also included is Jonathan Williams' patent for molds for whitening refined sugar, 1793. Some documents are manuscripts, others copies. A fourth vol. is Penn's cash book, 1699-

1703, which records expenditures, payments of quit rents, etc.; tipped in is "Catalogue of Goods left at Pensbury," and of goods left at Philadelphia, 1701, of which the first was printed, with omissions and changes, in *Correspondence between William Penn and James Logan* 4: 62 (Historical Society of Pennsylvania, *Memoirs* 9). Table of contents, vols. 1-3 (7 pp.).

Presented by (among others) Thomas Biddle, Redmond Conyngham, Bernard Gratz, Dr. and Mrs. George Logan, Joseph Parker Norris, William Rawle, and Hugh Roberts, various dates.

560. PENN FAMILY. ESTATES

Quit rent rolls, 1688/9, 1788-93. 2 vols.

List of quit rents due in Philadelphia County, March 1, 1688/9, and in Philadelphia and Lancaster Counties, 1788-93.

Presented by Arthur Bloch, 1952 (Philadelphia and Lancaster list).

561. PENNSYLVANIA

Miscellaneous records.

These include a volume of records of early settlements on the Delaware in English and Dutch archives, copied from records in the office of the Secretary of State, Harrisburg; a volume of original manuscripts relating to Pennsylvania and the American Revolution (including messages and proclamations of governors of the province, petition to the King from the province of Georgia, draft of an address of the University of the State of Pennsylvania to George Washington, 1781, letter of Arthur Lee to Alexander Wedderburn, 1774, letter of Timothy Matlack to Abiel Holmes, 1819, George Wythe's draft of resolutions, 1775, etc.); a volume of extracts from provincial records, 1748-58 (printed in part in Hazard's *Register of Pennsylvania* 4 [1829]: p. 205 and subsequent pages through 6 [1830]: p. 369); and a volume of documents on the Wyoming Controversy, 1751-1814 (many of which are printed in *Pennsylvania Archives*), including correspondence of Lord Amherst, John Armstrong, Jr., Charles Biddle, John Boyd, Zebulon Butler, Thomas Cooper, Thomas Fitch, John Franklin, James Hamilton, Joseph Hamilton, William Montgomery, John Penn, Richard Rush, Jonathan Trumbull, and Roger Wolcott.

Presented by Redmond Conyngham, 1819, 1823 (part), Joseph Parker Norris, and John Bannister Gibson.

562. PENNSYLVANIA (Province)

Miscellaneous manuscripts on Indian affairs, 1737-75. 5 vols. Copies.

Reports on conferences and treaties with the Indians; extracts from the journals of Conrad Weiser and Christian Frederick Post; Charles Thomson's An Enquiry into the causes of the alienation of the Delaware and Shawanese Indians from the British interest, 1759; selected letters and documents in the Pennsylvania state records on Indian relations, French and Indian War, Braddock's campaign. Correspondents include:

John Armstrong	Robert Orme
Thomas Barton	Ferdinand J. Paris
Edward Braddock	Thomas Penn
Daniel Claus	Horatio Sharpe
George Croghan	Joseph Shippen
James Hamilton	William Shirley
James Logan	John Stanwix
Hugh Mercer	Robert Stobo
Andrew Montour	William Trent
Robert Hunter Morris	Conrad Weiser

Some manuscripts are in the hands of Deborah Norris Logan and Charles Thomson. Presented by Joseph Parker Norris, 1815, and Redmond Conyngham, 1816.

563. ———

Minutes of Indian treaties and conferences, 1721-60. 7 vols.

The following treaties and conferences are included:

1. Particulars of an Indian treaty at Conestogoe, July 5-8, 1721. Manuscript copy of a printed work, with a preface dated July 26. See *Colonial Records,* 3: p. 121.

2. Treaty of peace and friendship, made . . . at Albany, in . . . 1722. Nineteenth-century copy. Printed in part in *Colonial Records* 3: p. 196.

3. Treaty held with the Ohio Indians at Carlisle in October, 1753. Manuscript copy. Printed in facsimile in Carl Van Doren, ed., *Indian Treaties Printed by Benjamin Franklin* (Philadelphia, 1938), p. 123.

4. Minutes of conferences held with the Indians at Easton, July and November, 1756. 2 vols. Copies. Printed in facsimile in Van Doren, *Indian Treaties,* cited above, p. 135 and p. 150 respectively.

5. Minutes of the Indian treaty council held at Easton, July 21–August 7, 1757. With a letter from Charles Thomson to Isaac Norris, August 1757, enclosing this copy, which may have been prepared from Thomson's notes; also copies of five treaties with the Indians, 1686-1749, and three maps. Printed in facsimile in Van Doren, *Indian Treaties,* cited above, p. 189.

6. Minutes of conferences with Indians in the Council chamber, 1758-60. The records appear in *Colonial Records* 8: *passim.*

Presented by Dr. George Logan, 1820.

564. PENNSYLVANIA (Province). ASSEMBLY

Laws, 1682-1719. 2 vols.

One volume, prepared possibly for James Logan, contains copies of Charles II's grant to William Penn of the Lower Counties, 1683, an act of the Privy Council, 1705, the charter of Pennsylvania of 1701, acts of the Assembly, 1682-1719. The other volume contains the texts of laws enacted in the administrations of Governors Benjamin Fletcher and William Markham, 1693-1700. Much of the material in both volumes is printed in *Charter to William Penn, and Laws of the Province of Pennsylvania* . . . (Harrisburg, 1879).

Presented by Joshua Francis Fisher, 1835 (part).

565. ———

Laws enacted 1700. Film. 1 reel.

From Public Record Office, London. Manuscript copy of the laws, submitted to the King, 1702; also a copy of the laws enacted by the Duke of York, 1667; and other documents relating to early Pennsylvania history.

566. PENNSYLVANIA (Province). COMMISSIONERS FOR DETERMINING THE PENNSYL-
VANIA-MARYLAND BOUNDARY

Minutes, 1760-68. 2 vols. and 1 reel of film.

One volume was copied from the original minutes in possession of Ferdinand R. Hassler; the other is composed of original vouchers signed by Richard Peters and Joseph Shippen, Jr. The film is of the Minutes of the Commissioners, which are in Historical Society of Pennsylvania.

Presented by George M. Justice, 1844.

567. PENNSYLVANIA (Province). COUNCIL

Rough minutes, 1693-1717. 3 vols.

From this manuscript the minutes for 1700-12 were printed in Hazard's *Register of Pennsylvania* 6 (1830): p. 9 and following.

Presented by George and Deborah Norris Logan, 1817.

568. PENNSYLVANIA (Province). FRENCH AND INDIAN WAR

Military records and accounts, 1756-63. 7 vols.

1. Accompt book, Fort Granville, 1756. 1 vol. Record of purchases of stockings, shoes, hats, knives, shirts, and "sundries" by soldiers, February 19–May 21, 1756.

2. Receipt book, Camp at Shamokin, 1756. 1 vol. Soldiers' receipts for pay, July 21–October 22, 1756.

3. Orderly book, Fort Augusta, 1757. 1 vol.

4. Receipt book, Fort Augusta and Carlisle, 1757. 1 vol. Officers' and men's receipts for pay, April 4, 1757–June 4, 1758.

5. Muster roll, 1757-58. 1 vol. Muster roll of the Augusta regiment, May 10, 1757–November 23, 1758, with receipts of men for pay made at Carlisle, Rays Town, and Loyalhanna.

6. Diaries, Fort Augusta, 1760, 1763. 2 vols. Kept by James Burd, Samuel Hunter, and others. Printed in *Pennsylvania Archives*, ser. 2, 7: p. 415.

569. PENNSYLVANIA (Province). NON-IMPORTATION AGREEMENT

Manuscript and documents, 1765-75. 2 vols.

A small group of miscellaneous manuscripts and printed material relating to the Stamp Act, 1765, the Non-Importation Agreement, 1765-66, the Tea Tax, 1773, and the Non-Importation Agreement of 1774. There are letters of Governor John Penn and John Hughes, correspondence between the Sons of Liberty at Philadelphia and those of New York, 1766, an address of the committee of Boston merchants to a committee of Philadelphia merchants, August 11, 1768. In the back of one notebook are some accounts of expenditures by a private person unknown, Philadelphia, 1780.

570. PENNSYLVANIA (Commonwealth). CONSTITUTIONAL CONVENTION OF 1837-38

Autographs of the delegates. 1 vol.

Contains signatures only.

Presented by John Kintzing Kane, 1838.

571. PENNSYLVANIA (Commonwealth). STATE PENITENTIARY FOR THE EASTERN DISTRICT

Papers, 1819-35. 5 pieces.

Minutes, with several reports, 1835; statement of the amounts of bread and tea consumed; statement of expenses, 1819-33; resolution of March 24, 1823; letter of Thomas Bradford, Jr., November 6, 1826.

572. PENNSYLVANIA (Commonwealth). Taxation

Forms for the return of slaves for tax purposes, 1798. 1 vol.

The forms apply to York and Franklin Counties; they are printed, the blanks filled in by hand.

573. ——

Materials on revenue from the distilling and retailing of liquors, 1794-1803. 35 pieces.

Applications to possess and operate stills and to retail spirits and liquors; receipts for distilled liquors; accounts of monies collected by Lawrence Erb and James Brice, collectors. Counties covered are Berks, Fayette, Franklin, Philadelphia, and York.

574. Pennsylvania Hospital

Archives, 1751-1861. Film. 42 reels.

From the Pennsylvania Hospital. Minutes and rough minutes of the Managers; Attending Managers' accounts; treasurer's and other financial records; cash books, ledgers, monthly accounts, and receipt books of the steward and matron; materials relating to the medical staff and instruction; patients' records and accounts; materials on buildings and grounds and on the library, museum, and painting of "Christ healing the Sick" by Benjamin West; records of the Philadelphia Dispensary, Preston Retreat, Philadelphia Lying-In Charity, Humane Society, and other small hospitals absorbed by the Pennsylvania. Table of contents (14 pp.).

575. Penrose, Richard Alexander Fullerton, Jr. (1863-1931). Geologist. APS 1905. *DAB;* APS *Proc.* **72** (1933)

Letters and papers, 1885-1931. 2 boxes.

Correspondence with Charles Francis Adams, Jr., Edgar Fahs Smith, Thomas Sovereign Gates, and others, about undergraduate days at Harvard College, his interest in Harvard, University of Pennsylvania, and the Wistar Institute; list of publications; biographical data; papers on Robert G. Le Conte and Daniel Moreau Barringer; certificate of membership in the Governor Thomas Dudley Family Association; 25 drawings of crystals and 35 original colored sketches made to accompany his Harvard thesis, *The Nature and Origin of Deposits of Phosphate of Lime.*

Presented by members of the Penrose family, 1932, and by Edward L. Stokes, 1952.

576. Perez, Antonio (1539-1611). Spanish statesman, secretary of state under Philip II. Hoefer

El conocimiento de las naciones, 1599. 1 vol.

In a letter to the Librarian of APS, 1901, Henry Charles Lea noted that a manuscript of this work was known to the compiler of *Biblioteca nova scriptorium Hispaniae,* but no printed edition.

Presented by Joel R. Poinsett, 1820.

577. Pershouse, John (1769-1841). Philadelphia merchant

Papers, 1749-1899. 62 pieces and 5 vols.

Principally business correspondence between Pershouse and his brother James in England, with comments on conditions and events in the United States, such as anti-British feeling, Thomas Paine's return to America, Jefferson's administration, immigration, etc. Also Pershouse's journal, 1800-38, with accounts of travels in England and the United States; letter books, 1836-62, of Henry Pershouse, chiefly on business matters; and 2 vols. of Pershouse genealogical data, compiled by B. M. Pershouse Bayley, 1899. Table of contents (2 pp.).

578. Philadelphia. City Planning Commission

Preliminary report on historical sites in the Independence Mall. Typed.

Prepared by Harbeson, Hough, Livingston & Larson, architects, from research by Mrs. Hannah Benner Roach. The reports are on the Jones-Kinsey-Pennsylvania Hospital site; the Madison site; the site of the Presidential Mansion; the Galloway-Morris mansion site; the site of the office of the Department of Foreign Affairs; the Ridgway-Meredith site; and the site of the State House Inn.

Presented by Mrs. Hannah Benner Roach, 1951.

579. PHILADELPHIA. DR. FRANKLIN'S LEGACY

Ledgers and accounts, 1791-1870. 4 vols.

Account ledger, 1791-1870; bond account ledger, 1791-1861; bond books, 1791-1826, 2 vols., relating to the administration of Franklin's bequest to the city of Philadelphia of a fund to provide financial aid to young married artificers.

580. PHILADELPHIA. MAYOR

Record of indentures, 1771-73. 1 vol.

List of apprentices and servants, and of German and other redemptioners, bound in the mayor's office. Indexed. Printed in Pennsylvania-German Society, *Proceedings* **16** (1907): p. 4.

Presented by Thomas P. Roberts, 1835.

581. PHILADELPHIA. OVERSEERS OF THE POOR

Tax book for Chestnut and Walnut wards, April 1767. 1 vol.

Tax book of William Savery, one of the overseers of the poor, for collecting the poor tax in Philadelphia. Edited with an introduction by Mrs. Hannah B. Roach in *Pennsylvania Genealogical Magazine* **22** (1962): p. 159.

Presented by Samuel Moyerman, 1958.

582. PHILADELPHIA COUNTY. REGISTER OF WILLS

Wills of Signers of the Declaration of Independence and others. 11 pieces.

Testators are:

Benjamin Franklin Bache	Thomas McKean
Richard Bache	Thomas Mifflin
George Clymer	Robert Morris
Benjamin Franklin	George Ross
Francis Hopkinson	Benjamin Rush
Jared Ingersoll	

Deposited by the Register of Wills, 1953-54.

583. PHILADELPHIA ASSEMBLY

Book of expenses, 1748-49. 1 vol.

Kept by John Swift, treasurer of this dancing association; with a record of Swift's personal expenses, 1747-49. Described by Thomas W. Balch in APS *Proc.* **41** (1902): p. 260, and in his *The Philadelphia Assemblies* (Philadelphia, 1916).

Presented by Edwin Swift Balch and Thomas Willing Balch, 1902.

584. PHILADELPHIA MUSEUM COMPANY

Minutes and accounts, 1820-36, 1841. 5 vols.

Minutes, 1821-36 (2 vols.), recording actions of the trustees of Peale's Museum (John Bacon, Pierce Butler, Reuben Haines, Joseph Parker Norris, Robert Patterson, Robert M. Patterson, Coleman Sellers, George Escol Sellers, and others), including exhibits, purchase of specimens, appointment of personnel, financial statements, etc.; an account book, 1820-24 (1 vol.), being a record of daily income of the museum; and stock books, 1827-36, 1841 (2 vols.), consisting of stubs of certificates of stock sold to subscribers to the museum, with a quantity of unused certificates.

Presented by Charles Coleman Sellers, 1945.

585. PHYSICS

A system of physicks, 1670. 1 vol.

A compendium of natural philosophy.
Presented by Arthur W. Goodspeed.

586. PICKERING, TIMOTHY (1745-1829). Soldier, Indian agent, Secretary of War.
   APS 1744. *DAB*

Selected papers on Indian affairs, 1790-93. Film. 4 reels.

From Massachusetts Historical Society (3 reels) and Essex Institute, Salem, Mass.
(1 reel). Letters, reports, minutes, memoranda, and addresses to Indian chiefs, selected
from the Pickering papers. Correspondents include:

S. Bauman	Henry Knox
Israel Chapin	Benjamin Lincoln
Isaac Craig	George Morgan
Henry Drinker	John Parrish
Samuel Hodgdon	Arthur St. Clair
William Hull	Philip Schuyler

587. PIERCE, MRS. CATHARINE J., collector

Collection of family letters, 1787-1869. 83 pieces. Film. 1 reel.

From manuscripts owned by Mrs. Pierce, Charlotte, N.C. (1965). Family letters
of the Eccles, Jones and Lanneau families of North Carolina and Florida. Some letters
are written from Philadelphia (and speak of the Peale family), New York, and New
Haven.

588. PIKE, ZEBULON MONTGOMERY (1779-1813). Soldier and explorer. *DAB*

Journal of a voyage to the source of the Mississippi in the years 1805 and
1806. 1 vol.

Printed, with variations and omissions, in *Account of expeditions to the sources of
the Mississippi & through the western parts of Louisiana to the sources of the Arkansas,
Kans, La Platte & Pierre Jaun rivers performed during . . . 1805, 1806 & 1807 & a tour
through the interior parts of New Spain . . . in 1807* (Philadelphia, 1810). The journal
is edited in Donald Jackson, ed., *The Journals of Zebulon Montgomery Pike: with
Letters & Related Documents* (2 vols., Norman, Okla., 1966).
Presented by Daniel Parker, 1817.

589.——

Biographical materials. 51 pieces.

Transcripts, photostats, maps, and some original manuscripts collected by W. Eugene
Hollon for his biography of Pike, *The Lost Pathfinder* (Norman, Okla., 1949). Corre-
spondents include John C. Calhoun, William Clark, Richard Rush, John Sibley, and
James Wilkinson. Table of contents (2 pp.).
Presented by Eugene Hollon, 1950.

590. PLANCK, MAX (1858-1947). Physicist, author of the quantum theory

Letters, 1919-48. 18 pieces.

Letters from and concerning Planck.
Presented by Hans T. Clarke, 1964.

591. PLÉE, AUGUSTE (1787-1825). French botanist and traveler

Sketches, notes, and catalogues, *ca.* 1820-24. Film. 2 reels.

From Muséum d'Histoire Naturelle, Paris. Sketches made on a trip to the United
States, Canada, and the West Indies; catalogues of objects of natural history (fish,
animals, insects, fossils, etc.) sent by him to the Museum; also notes, etc.

592. POINSETT, JOEL ROBERTS (1779-1851), collector. Diplomat, statesman. APS 1827. *DAB*

Collection of Peruvian manuscripts. 1 vol. Copies. In Spanish.

Some 20 pieces relating principally to the revolt of Tupac Amaru II, last claimant to the throne of the Incas, 1780-83; also to medicine, manners, learned societies, and law of Spanish America, and the history of the Spanish conquest of Oran, 1505-09. Table of contents (5 pp.).

Presented by Joel R. Poinsett, 1820.

593. POST, CHRISTIAN FREDERICK (*ca.* 1710-85). Missionary, traveler. APS 1768. *DAB*

Journal to the great Council of the different Indian nations, 1760. Film.

From manuscript in possession of Mrs. Henry P. Gummere, Upper Darby, Pa., 1942.

594. POTIER, PIERRE (1708-81). Jesuit missionary

Miscellanea, 1743-44. Photocopy.

Huron vocabulary with French equivalents, names of Huron villagers, names of chiefs, etc., recorded by Father Potier, missionary at Sandwich on the Detroit River and written down at Lorette near Quebec. From the original manuscript in the archives of the Collège Sainte-Marie, Montreal.

Presented by Charles Marius Barbeau, 1952.

595. POTOCKI, Count JAN (1761-1815). Polish historian, archaeologist, and traveler. Larousse

Journal of travels in Russia, 1797-98. 1 vol. Copy. In French.

Part of Potocki's journey was made to search for the origins of the ancient Scythians. In 1828 the German Orientalist and traveler Heinrich Julius Klaproth asked the Society's permission to have a copy made of this manuscript. From this copy he prepared the work for publication, adding his own notes: *Voyage dans le steps d'Astrakhan et du Caucase . . . Histoire primitive des peuples qui ont habité anciennement ces contrées* (2 vols., Paris, 1829).

596. POTTER, GEORGE REUBEN

Idea of evolution in the English poets from 1744 to 1832. Film.

Doctoral dissertation, Harvard University, 1922.

597. POWELL, JOHN WESLEY (1834-1902). Geologist, ethnologist; director, United States Geological Survey. APS 1889. *DAB*

Materials relating to Powell and the Colorado River. Typescripts, photostats. 1 box.

Papers collected by Wallace E. Stegner for *Beyond the Hundredth Meridian: John Wesley Powell and the Second Opening of the West, 1868-1899* (Boston, 1954): they relate to explorations and geological surveys, the Hayden-Powell controversy, the Cope-Marsh-Powell controversy, the Colorado expedition of 1868, including extracts from Powell's scrapbook about the reported loss of the party, 1869.

Presented by Mr. Stegner, 1955.

598. ————

Correspondence of the Powell Survey, 1869-79. Film. 10 reels.

From National Archives, Washington. Letters received by the Geographical and

Geological Survey of the Rocky Mountain Region; also a selection of *ca.* 100 letters sent by the Survey, 1876-78. Correspondents include:

Alexander Agassiz	Henry W. Longfellow
E. W. Ayres	Othniel C. Marsh
Spencer F. Baird	Fielding B. Meek
Elliott Coues	Thomas Moran
James Dwight Dana	Thomas H. Morgan
Clarence Edward Dutton	John S. Newberry
Henry Gannett	James C. Pilling
James A. Garfield	John J. Stevenson
Albert S. Gatschet	Almon H. Thompson
George Gibbs	G. W. Vasey
Arnold Guyot	Lester F. Ward
Joseph Henry	A. G. Weatherby
Abram S. Hewitt	George M. Wheeler
Clarence King	Olin D. Wheeler
Joseph Leidy	Josiah D. Whitney
J. Peter Lesley	

599. ———

Diaries and letters, 1871-1907. Film. 1 reel.

From New York Public Library. Diary of Frederick S. Dellenbaugh of the Colorado River Expedition, 1871-73; correspondence of Robert B. Stanton and Jack Sumner about Powell, 1907; and J. F. Steward's "Through the Canyons of the Colorado," 1871.

600. POYNTELL, WILLIAM

Thermometrical journal, 1803. 1 vol.

The journal was kept on a voyage from the Downs to the Capes of Delaware on board the ship *Three Sisters,* June 26–August 20, 1803. The volume includes "Observations on the storm glass," made on the same voyage. The storm glass, with an explanation of its use and the journal of observations, and also the thermometrical journal were laid before the Society, November 4, 1803.

Presented by the author, 1803.

601. PRICE, ALAN

Humanities versus science in mid-nineteenth-century educational thought in England. Film.

Doctoral dissertation, Queens University, Belfast, 1957.

602. PRICE, ELI KIRK (1797-1884). Philadelphia lawyer. APS 1854. *DAB;* APS *Proc.* 23 (1886)

Papers, 1820-53. 35 pieces.

On business and legal affairs, including his writings on the law of real and personal property, private wrongs, etc.; also a letter to Daniel Webster.

603. PRICE, RICHARD (1723-91). English Nonconformist minister and writer on politics and economics. APS 1785. *DNB*

Papers, 1767-90. 90 pieces.

Letters from and to Price on British politics, the American Revolution, the peace of 1783, the future of the United States, prisons, slavery, etc. Correspondents include:

William Bingham	Arthur Lee
James Bowdoin, Sr.	Benjamin Rush
Charles Chauncy	Ezra Stiles
Benjamin Franklin	J. D. Van Der Capellen
William Gordon	John Wheelock
William Hazlitt	William White
John Howard	Edward Wigglesworth
Jan Ingenhousz	Joseph Willard
Thomas Jefferson	John Winthrop, IV

Many of these letters were printed in Massachusetts Historical Society, *Proceedings,* ser. 2, **17** (1903): p. 263.

604. PRIESTLEY, JOSEPH (1733-1804). Educator, scientist, theologian. APS 1784. *DAB, DNB*

Experiments relating to phlogiston and the conversion of water into air, 1783. 1 vol. Copy.

Presented by Samuel Vaughan, 1784.

605. ———

Letters and papers, 1771-1803. 2 boxes.

Manuscripts and photostats of manuscripts in the Municipal Library, Warrington, England, on theological questions, the internal development of the United States, the French Revolution, the Napoleonic wars, Unitarianism, science, chemistry, his publications, APS, and the like. The correspondence includes 41 letters to John Vaughan, 1791-1800; 68 letters between Priestley, Joseph Priestley, Jr., and John Wilkinson, 1787-1802; and 11 letters to various persons, 1774-1803. Table of contents (7 pp.).

606. PRIME, MRS. PHOEBE PHILLIPS, compiler

Alfred Coxe Prime directory of craftsmen, 1785-1800. Film. 1 reel.

Lists of Philadelphia craftsmen, compiled from the city directories, 1785-1800, and arranged alphabetically and by craft or trade. Included in the index are similar data gleaned from Philadelphia newspaper advertisements.

Photographed, by permission, from one of a limited number of copies issued by the compiler.

607. PURSH, FREDERICK (1774-1820). Botanist, horticulturist, explorer. *DAB*

Journal of a botanical excursion in the Northeastern parts of Pennsylvania & in the state of New York, 1807. 1 vol.

This manuscript was found among papers of Benjamin Smith Barton, who was Pursh's patron, 1817. It was published at Philadelphia, 1869, and for the Onondaga Historical Association, Syracuse, N.Y., with notes by William M. Beauchamp, 1923.

608. PYRLAEUS, JOHN CHRISTOPHER (1713-85). Moravian missionary

Lexicon der macquaischen [Mohawk] sprachen. 1 vol.

Deposited by the Society of United Brethren, 1819.

609. QUATTROCCHI, ANNA MARGARET

Thomas Hutchins, 1730-1789.

Biography of the military engineer, map-maker, and "Geographer of the United States."

Doctoral dissertation, University of Pittsburgh, 1944.

610. QUEBEC. UNIVERSITÉ LAVAL, SÉMINAIRE DE QUÉBEC

Selected materials on Indian linguistics. Film. 6 reels.

From Université Laval. Grammars, glossaries, books of prayers and hymns, in Iroquois, Huron, and Algonkin languages, almost all in the hands of Jesuit missionaries before 1760; also a register of baptisms and marriages of Indians; a brief history of the Hurons; etc. Table of contents (17 pp.).

611. QUESTEBRUNE, JOHN, M.A., Dublin

A short introduction to natural philosophy, 1720. 1 vol.

The author was chaplain to the 6th Earl of Galloway. The manuscript is embellished with colored drawings, illustrations, and decorations. It was owned by William Hamilton, 1785 (of The Woodlands, Philadelphia?).

Presented by J. Francis Fisher, 1834.

612. QUETELET, LAMBERT ADOLPHE JACQUES (1796-1874). Astronomer, meteorologist, statistician. APS 1839

Selected correspondence. Film. 2 reels.

From Bibliothèque royale de Belgique, Brussels. Correspondents include:

Charles Babbage	Edward C. Herrick
Alexander D. Bache	Sir John F. W. Herschel
Samuel Brown	George W. Hough
Thomas G. Clemson	Alexander von Humboldt
Robley Dunglison	Joseph C. G. Kennedy
James P. Espy	Auguste A. de la Rive
Michael Faraday	Urbain J. J. Le Verrier
William Farr	Humphrey Lloyd
James D. Forbes	Hubert A. Newton
James A. Garfield	Sir Edward Sabine
Charles Frederic Gauss	E. A. Sanford
J. Melville Gilliss	Lemuel Shattuck
Arnold Guyot	Charles Wheatstone
William R. Hamilton	William Whewell
Joseph Henry	Edward L. Youmans

613. QUIMBY, IAN M. G.

Apprenticeship in colonial Philadelphia, 1963. 1 vol. Typed. Copy.

Dissertation submitted for the degree of master of arts at the University of Delaware, 1963.

Presented by the author, 1963.

614. ——

Edward Duffield, artisan gentleman, 1963. 1 vol. Typed, carbon.

A biographical sketch of the eighteenth-century Philadelphia clockmaker, who was an executor of Benjamin Franklin's will.

Presented by the author, 1963.

615. RADIN, PAUL (1883-1959). American anthropologist

Writings. 21 boxes, 79 notebooks.

Notes, transcriptions, essays, etc., on the language and customs of several Indian tribes. There are a number of vocabularies, dictionaries, and grammatical notes on the Winnebago, Patwin, and Huave tribes; 79 notebooks, in English and Winnebago, on myths, legends, stories, customs, dances, religious observances, costume, etc., of the Winnebagos, with some on the Ottawa and Ojibwa; notes on Winnebago history; 2

boxes of Winnebago phonetic texts; etc. Some of the items are typed copies of Radin's published studies. Table of contents (*ca.* 50 pp.).

Presented by Mrs. Doris Radin, 1960.

616. RAFINESQUE-SCHMALTZ, CONSTANTINE SAMUEL (1783-1840). Naturalist. *DAB*

Letters and papers, 1808-40. 3 boxes. In English, French, and Italian.

Contains letters from Rafinesque, principally to Zaccheus Collins, 1810-40, with bills, receipts, and notes on Rafinesque vs. Parker; letters to Rafinesque from Collins, L. A. Tarascon, Lewis C. Beck, John Torrey, Charles W. Short, and others, 1817-35; miscellaneous correspondence and documents relating principally to Rafinesque vs. Parker, with an account of the Felician Society of Feliciana County, Ill., 1820. Also a large number of writings, chiefly on botanical topics, but including notes and essays on Indians, Negroes, grapes and wine-making, banking, and speculation. There is an account of his scientific travels in North America and southern Europe, 1800-32, and an American bibliography. The botanical notes include descriptions of specimens collected by Lewis and Clark, Patrick Gass, and Gotthilf H. E. Muhlenberg. For a description, see Charles Boewe, "The Manuscripts of C. S. Rafinesque (1783-1840)," APS *Proc.* 102 (1958): p. 590. Table of contents (14 pp.).

Deposited by the Academy of Natural Sciences of Philadelphia, 1943, 1952.

617. ——

Letters to John Torrey, 1819-40. Film. 1 reel.

From New York Botanical Garden.

618. ——

Correspondence with William Swainson. Film. 1 reel.

From Linnean Society of London.

619. ——

Ancient monuments of North and South America, 1822-25. Film.

From University Museum, University of Pennsylvania.

620. ——

Miscellaneous manuscripts. Film. 1 reel.

From University of Kansas Library. A few letters to John Torrey, Amos Eaton, and Reuben Haines; journals of travels to the Appalachian mountains, 1833, and to the source of the Schuylkill River, 1834.

621. RAUSCHARDT, FELIX HANNIBAL

Arithmetica decimalis; oder, Rechenkunst der Geometrischen Zehen theiligen Ruthen, 1648. 1 vol.

Problems in geometry and trigonometry; fortifications and their layout. A note on the fly-leaf says: "Found in the Bastile and Presented by Peter S. Du Ponceau Esqr to Wm Duer junr the 12 of Nov. 1796. W. Duer, Junior."

622. RELAND, ADRIAAN (1676-1718). Dutch Orientalist. Hoefer

Vocabularia variarum linguarum Americanarum, 1822. 1 vol. Copy.

A manuscript copy made in 1822 of 9 Indian vocabularies taken from Reland's *Dissertationum miscellanearum pars tertia* (Utrecht, 1708).

Presented by Peter S. Du Ponceau, 1844.

623. REYNELL, JOHN (1708-84). Philadelphia merchant. APS 1768

Daybook, 1731-32. 1 vol.

Purchases and payments for sugar, tobacco, clothing, nails, shipments of goods to the West Indies, etc., by, among others, John Bard, Benjamin Franklin, Andrew Hamilton, Israel Pemberton, William Rawle, Charles Read.

Presented by Seymour Adelman, 1947.

624. RHOADS, CHARLES JAMES (1872-1956). Banker, United States Commissioner of Indian Affairs. APS 1921. *Year Book* 1956

Papers, 1929. 1 box.

Principally letters and telegrams, mostly of congratulation, about Rhoads' appointment as Commissioner of Indian Affairs, 1929; with drafts of replies. Correspondents include Emily G. Balch, Felix Frankfurter, and Herbert C. Hoover. In the collection are several letters from James E. Rhoads to Capt. Richard H. Pratt, 1883-94, and copies of several letters from Pratt to the Commissioner of Indian Affairs, 1913-21, on Indian matters.

Presented by Brown Brothers, Harriman & Co., 1965.

625. RICHARDS, ALFRED NEWTON (1876-1966). Pharmacologist, medical administrator. APS 1935

Survey of medical affairs, University of Pennsylvania, 1931. Copy.

Confidential report on all aspects of the University of Pennsylvania medical school and hospital, research and teaching, prepared by Richards and T. Grier Miller for the president of the University, Thomas Sovereign Gates. This copy was made from the original in possession of Dr. Richards.

626. RITTENHOUSE, DAVID (1732-96). Instrument-maker, astronomer, treasurer of Pennsylvania. APS 1768. *DAB*

Meteorological observations, 1784-1805. 2 vols.

The first volume also contains notes of expenses and of observations while surveying the western boundary of Pennsylvania, 1785. The observations were continued in the second volume after Rittenhouse's death.

Presented (vol. 2) by Mrs. Henry S. Lowber, 1898.

627. ———

Observations made at Wilmington for determining the longitude, July 1–October 14, 1784. 1 vol.

Presented by Mrs. Henry S. Lowber, 1898.

628. ———

Receipt book, 1779-1785. 1 vol.

Record of payments principally by John Hart, treasurer of Bucks County, Pa., of taxes, such as militia fines, forfeited debts, supplies, monthly taxes, second-class tax, excise taxes, etc.

Presented by Mrs. Henry S. Lowber, 1898.

629. ROBBINS, WILLIAM JACOB (1890–   ). Botanist, plant physiologist. APS 1941

Papers, 1909-64. 10 boxes.

Correspondence on personal and scientific topics, including botany, APS, National Academy of Sciences, New York Botanical Garden, Lehigh University, University of Missouri, etc., with, among others:

C. O. Appleman	Alan Gregg
George W. Beadle	Ross G. Harrison
Lloyd V. Berkner	Mark H. Ingraham
Detlev W. Bronk	Frank B. Jewett
J. McKeen Cattell	John T. Lloyd
Ralph E. Cleland	Elmer D. Merrill
William D. Coolidge	John H. Northrop
Henry S. Drinker	Alfred N. Richards
B. M. Duggan	Jacob R. Schramm
Henry F. du Pont	Edmund W. Sinnott
John F. Enders	Rodney H. True
Frank D. Fackenthal	Alan T. Waterman
Lewis S. Greenleaf, Jr.	Raymund L. Zwemer.

Also *ca.* 100 letters to and from E. B. Wilson and others on the affairs of the National Academy of Sciences, 1941-62, and *ca.* 150 letters to and from Albert F. Blakeslee about the Smith College Genetics Experiment Station, 1938-54. Also letters and diaries of trips to Europe, Japan, and India; invitations; correspondence concerning the Tropical Plant Conference, 1959, the Animal Medical Center, Rockefeller Foundation; and some correspondence as president and executive officer of APS. Table of contents (32 pp.).

Presented by William J. Robbins, 1959-65.

630. ROBERTS, HELEN HEFFRON (1888–   )

Songs of the Nootka Indians of Western Vancouver Island, 1935-55.

Music for 97 songs. Printed in APS *Trans.* 45 (1955): p. 199.
Presented by the author, 1955.

631. ROBERTS, JOSEPH, JR. (1793-1835). Schoolmaster. APS 1829

Astronomical calculations, 1820-21. 1 vol.

Calculations of the distances of stars, eclipses, longitude, etc., made by William Maule, James Cresson, Joseph Jeanes, James James, and Robert Hutchinson, pupils in the Friends Academy, in which Roberts was a teacher.

Presented by John B. Roberts, 1913.

632. ——

Philosophical and mathematical papers. 3 vols.

One volume of mathematical and philosophical papers, 1814, which appear to be college exercises; an essay on the projection of the sphere and spherical trigonometry, to which is added an appendix on astronomy (1 vol.); and a lecture on natural philosophy, which appears to have been prepared for delivery.

Presented by John B. Roberts, 1913.

633. ROGERS, ROBERT (1731-95). Soldier, frontiersman. *DAB*

An estimate of the fur and peltry trade in the district of Michilimackinac, according to the bounds and limits, assign'd to it by the French, when under their government: together with an account of the situation and names of the several out-posts, 1767. 1 vol.

This communication was sent by Major Rogers, by the hand of Captain Jonathan Carver, to Thomas Barton, of Lancaster, Pa., who sent it to APS, where it was received and referred to the Committee on Trade and Commerce, December 20, 1768. Printed by William L. Clements, "Rogers' Michillimackinac Journal," American Antiquarian Society, *Proceedings,* n.s., 28 (1918): p. 224.

634. ROSSETER, JOHN (d. 1811?). Ship captain

Log of the China Packet, 1804-05. 1 vol.

The voyage was from Philadelphia to Canton and return. The concluding statement reads: "One hundred & thirty days from Maccoa out of which time we had 30
Calm days, the longest passage I Ever had from China. With this Journal I have done
and glad Am I."

635. ROTH, JOHANNES, translator. Moravian missionary

Ein Versuch! der Geschichte unsers Herrn u. Heylandes Jesu Christi in das
Delawarische übersetzt der Unami von der Marter Woche an bis zur Himmelfahrt
unsers Herrn, 1770-72. 1 vol.

A life of Jesus during Passion Week until his alleged ascent to Heaven, compiled
from Gospel sources and translated by Roth, missionary at Sheshequin on the Susquehanna River.

Presented by John Rhodes, 1832.

636. ROTHROCK, JOSEPH TRIMBLE (1839-1922). Physician, botanist, forester. APS
1877. *DAB*

Letters to Eli Kirk Price, 1878-84. 9 pieces.

Correspondence relating to botanizing expeditions in the Chesapeake Bay and
Virginia area, the University of Pennsylvania, APS, etc.

637. ROWLAND, HENRY A. (1848-1901). Physicist. APS 1896. *DAB*

Scrapbook. Film. 1 reel.

From Miss Harriette H. Rowland, Baltimore, 1966. Clippings about Rowland's
career at Johns Hopkins University, his inventions, lectures, public services, and family
events.

638. ROYAL SOCIETY OF ARTS, LONDON

Selected materials relating to America, 1754-1806. Film. 2 reels.

From Royal Society of Arts, London. Principal correspondents include:

William Alexander, Earl of Stirling	Thomas Gilpin
Edward Antill	Jared Ingersoll
Nathaniel Appleton	Benjamin Lincoln
Francis Bernard	Jonathan Mayhew
Charles Carter of Cleve	Samuel More
Thomas Clap	John Mervin Nooth
Thomas Cushing	Joseph Ottolenghe
Jared Eliot	Thomas Paine
Lewis Evans	William Shipley
Benjamin Franklin	William Tatham
Benjamin Gale	Benjamin West
Alexander Garden	Charles Woodmason

Also included are extracts from minutes and committee reports. Table of contents (12
pp.).

639. ROYAL SOCIETY OF LONDON

Minutes of the Council, 1747/8-1810. Film. 4 reels.

From the Royal Society.

640. ——

Letters and communications from Americans, 1662-1900. Film. 10 reels.

From the Royal Society. Letters from and to Americans (including South America and the West Indies) and about America, selected from the Society's manuscripts (Classified Papers, Letter Books, Letters and Papers, Royal Society Letters, Miscellaneous Correspondence, and other official groups) and from collections of private papers (Sir Charles Blagden, William Buckland, John Canton, Sir John F. W. Hershel, Sir Edward Sabine, and others), ranging in time and character from John Winthrop, Jr., "A Description of the Artifice & Making of Tarr & Pitch in New England," 1662, to letters from Sir Thomas Edward Thorne to his wife describing the American West, where he was on a surveying party in the 1880's. Unpublished papers by the following names are in some of the early collections:

Thomas Banister	Hugh Jones
Thomas Brattle	Richard Lewis
William Burnet	Cotton Mather
Mark Catesby	Alexander Moray
John Churchman	Joseph Morgan
John Clayton	Christopher Middleton
Peter Collinson	Francis Nicholson
Paul Dudley	Thomas Robie
Isaac Greenwood	Wait Winthrop
Nehemiah Grew	Christopher Witt

In the Blagden papers are letters from:

William Bingham	William Pepperell
Robert Fulton	Benjamin Thompson,
Rufus King	Count Rumford
Arthur Lee	Benjamin Vaughan
Andrew Merry	Robert Walsh

In the papers of Sir Edward Sabine are letters from Louis Agassiz, Alexander D. Bache, George P. Bond, Joseph Henry, J. Peter Lesley, Elias Loomis, Charles Smallwood, and Charles Wilkes. Table of contents and index (107 pp.).

641. ROYALE, JOSEPH (fl. 1766). Printer of Williamsburg, Va.

Journal, 1764-66. Xerox copy.

From University of Virginia Library. A daily record of sales of books, stationery, advertising, printing, binding, etc.; and of other income and expenses.

642. RUSH, BENJAMIN (1746-1813). Physician, patriot, humanitarian. APS 1768.
DAB

Commonplace book, 1792-1813. 1 vol.

Printed in George W. Corner, ed., *The Autobiography of Benjamin Rush: His "Travels through Life," Together with His Commonplace Book for 1789-1813*, APS *Memoirs* 25 (Philadelphia, 1948).

643. ——

Correspondence, 1759-1813. 5 boxes. Photostats.

Collected by Lyman H. Butterfield for his *Letters of Benjamin Rush*, APS *Memoirs* 30 (2 vols., Philadelphia, 1951). Table of contents (13 pp.).

644. ——

Memorable facts, events, opinions, thots, &c., 1789-1791. Photostat.

Selections from the original manuscript in Library Company of Philadelphia, where it is a portion of a volume entitled "Letters, facts, and observations upon a variety of subjects." Printed in George W. Corner, ed., *The Autobiography of Benjamin Rush*, cited above.

Presented by George W. Corner, 1948.

645. ——

Memorandum book, 1805-1813. 1 vol.

Notes on lands owned and sold and on leases of Philadelphia houses; accounts with Daphne Peterson, a free Negro, Mary Spence of Dunfermline, and Baynard Hall; list of books lent; list of those receiving copies of Rush's publications, 1805-06, among whom was Thomas Jefferson; and an "account of property belonging to the estate."

646. ——

Travels through life: or an account of sundry incidents and events in the life of Benjamin Rush . . . written for the use of his children, 1800. 8 vols.

The ninth surviving volume of this autobiography is in Library Company of Philadelphia. The complete Travels have been edited by George W. Corner, *The Autobiography of Benjamin Rush*, cited above.

647. ——

Lectures upon the mind. Film.

From the College of Physicians of Philadelphia.

648. Rush, James (1786-1869). Physician and psychologist. APS 1827. *DAB*

Cards of admission to medical lectures, 1807-16. 17 pieces. Photocopies.

Cards of admission to lectures at the University of Pennsylvania, St. George's Hospital, London, and Edinburgh University. On the back of several Rush has written sharp comments on the lecturers. The originals are in Library Company of Philadelphia; the notes have been edited and printed by Whitfield J. Bell, Jr., "Dr. James Rush on his . . . Teachers," *Journal of the History of Medicine* 19 (1964): p. 419.

649. Rush, Samuel (1795-1859). Lawyer, recorder of Philadelphia, son of Benjaman Rush

Notebook, 1859. 1 vol.

Contains short, generally splenetic essays on public singers ("the Mountebanks of the Voice"), the embarrassments of public men (Daniel E. Sickles and Philip Barton Key), songs, wit, wealth, suicide, Benjamin Rush, "that little sneak Kossuth," and modern authors ("the present wretches of the pen").

650. Rutty, John (1698-1775). Quaker physician. *DNB*

Letters to William Clark. Film.

From Friends' Reference Library, London. Letters to a physician in London and Bradford, Wilts.

651. Sabin, Florence Rena (1871-1953). Anatomist and physiologist

Papers, 1907-40. *ca.* 20,000 pieces.

Correspondence relating principally to medical research (tuberculosis, cancer,

lymphatic system, pernicious anemia), writings and publications, learned societies, Johns Hopkins School of Medicine, Rockefeller Institute, Peking Union Medical College, and Institute for Advanced Study; including letters, papers, and other materials on Emmy Noether Fund, Simon Flexner medal, Henry Strong Denison Medical Foundation; National Academy of Sciences, National Research Council, White House Conferences, Association of University Women, Medical Aid to China, Medical Aid to Spain, M. Carey Thomas Prize; also abstracts and notes of unpublished scientific papers; also materials for her biography of Franklin Paine Mall, 1934; etc. Table of contents (25 pp.).
Presented by Rockefeller Institute, 1964.

652. SAGARD, GABRIEL (fl. 1624-36). French missionary priest
Dictionnaire de la langue huronne, 1632. 1 vol. Copy.

Transcribed by James R. Malenfant for Peter S. Du Ponceau from Sagard's *Le Grand voyage du pays des Hurons . . . avec un Dictionnaire de la langue huronne* (Paris, 1632).
Presented by Peter S. Du Ponceau, 1816.

653. SAGER, A.
Chemie. 1 vol. In Swedish.
Brief outline, possibly of lectures, of the subject of chemistry.

654. ST. ANDREW'S SOCIETY OF PHILADELPHIA
Minutes and accounts, 1749-1843. Film.

From St. Andrew's Society of Philadelphia. Minutes, 1749-76, 1786-1833; and Treasurer's accounts, 1759-1843.

655. SAPIR, EDWARD (1884-1939). Anthropologist, linguist. *Year Book* 1939
Nootka ethnographic texts, *ca.* 1920. Film.
From National Museum of Canada, Ottawa.

656. SAY, THOMAS (1787-1834). Entomologist, conchologist. APS 1817. *DAB*
Papers, 1819-83. *ca.* 40 pieces, 62 drawings and impressions.

Chiefly on natural history, shells, and insects, including miscellaneous notes on conchology by Say; photostats of 6 letters from Say to Jacob Gilliams, 1819-29, from Morristown, N.J., National Historical Park; and a biographical note on Say. The drawings and impressions of shells are by Mrs. Lucy Way Sistaire Say, prepared for W. G. Binney's edition of Say's complete works on conchology, 1858; also Mrs. Say's refutation of what she considered an unfair attack in George Ord's memoir of Say. Correspondents include André Étienne Férussac, Arthur F. Gray, John Lawrence Le Conte, Charles W. Short, and others. Table of contents (3 pp.).

657. SCALIGER FAMILY
Papers, fifteenth-nineteenth centuries. *ca.* 700 pieces. In Latin, French, Italian, and Gascon dialect.

Correspondence between the Poizat and Vérone branches of the family about descent, titles, efforts to obtain recognition; Poizat family manuscripts, which include lists of slaves in Santo Domingo, baptismal certificates, etc.; Scaliger family manuscripts, genealogies, coats of arms, titles of fiefs, 1402-1546, military commissions, royal proclamations, wills of Julius Caesar Scaliger and his son Joseph Justus Scaliger; documents concerning the effort of Joseph de Lescale de Vérone to obtain official recognition of his claims; documents relating to other members of the Scaliger family and the question of descent from the Della Scalas of Verona. The collection is described and its history recounted by Vernon Hall, Jr., in APS *Proc.* **92** (1948): p. 120.

Presented by Cécile Poizat, 1888.

658. SCHMICK, JOHN JACOB (1714-78). Moravian missionary at Wyalusing, Pa.

Miscellanea linguae nationis Indicae Mahikan dicta, *ca.* 1760. 2 vols.

Presented by John G. E. Heckewelder, 1820.

659. SCHOOLBOOKS

Miscellaneous notebooks. 4 vols.

A book of algebra, kept by a student at West Nottingham Academy, 1772; an arithmetic; a volume of solutions of practical problems in John Gummere's *Astronomy,* 1821 (presented by Seymour Adelman, 1948); and notes from a text on conic sections.

660. SCHULZ, THEODOR. Moravian missionary in British Guiana

Arawak dictionary and grammar, 1803. 2 vols.

The dictionary has German equivalents and examples, with an Arawak index; the grammar is based on Latin models, with Latin nomenclature.

Presented by the author, 1819.

661. VON SCHWEINITZ, LEWIS DAVID (1780-1834). Mycologist, botanist. *DAB*

Letters to John Le Conte, 1816-29. Film.

From Kelly Mycological Library, University of Michigan.

662. SCIENTISTS' LETTERS

A growing collection of miscellaneous letters and small groups of letters of American and European men of science which are not part of any other collection and have not been included in the Miscellaneous Manuscripts (No. 462). This collection includes photocopies as well as original manuscripts. At present it includes copies of letters from American physicians and scientists or from European members of APS preserved in the Wellcome Historical Medical Library (70 pieces); copies of letters from American scientists, principally astronomers, in the Academy of Sciences, Moscow (46 pieces); a group of manuscript letters of French scientists, including a group from Alexandre Henri Nadault de Buffon to his publisher (68 pieces); letters and papers from the Muséum d'Histoire Naturelle, Paris, and also several boxes of letters of American, English, and German scientists. Correspondents include:

Cleveland Abbe	Charles Caldwell
Louis Paul Abeille	Jean François Champollion
John Couch Adams	John Churchman
Louis Agassiz	Alexander Ross Clarke
Sir George B. Airy	Peter Collinson
Alexander D. Bache	Karl T. Compton
Benjamin Smith Barton	Sir Astley Cooper
Elias R. Beadle	Thomas Cooper
Elie de Beaumont	Edward D. Cope
Lewis C. Beck	John Redman Coxe
John J. Berzelius	Henri Louis Duhamel du Monceau
Johann F. Blumenbach	Robley Dunglison
Charles Lucien Bonaparte	Albert Einstein
Ruggiero Giuseppe Boscovitch	John Reinhold Forster
Sir William H. Bragg	Sir Francis Galton
F. L. Button	Joseph Louis Gay-Lussac

Asa Gray	François André Michaux
Robert Hare	O. A. L. Mörch
Ferdinand R. Hassler	Samuel G. Morton
Joseph Henry	Thomas Nuttall
John Stevens Henslow	Max Planck
Sir John F. W. Herschel	C. M. Poulson
David Hosack	Joseph Priestley
Alexander von Humboldt	Benjamin Rush
Thomas Henry Huxley	Adam Sedgwick
Samuel D. Ingham	Arnold Sommerfeld
Abraham Valentine William Jackson	Herbert Spencer
	Alfred Stillé
Sir William Jenner	William Stimpson
Sir William Jones	André Thouin
Thomas S. Kirkbride	John Tyndal
Charles Marie de La Condamine	Benjamin Vaughan
John Coakley Lettsom	Benjamin Lewis Vuillamy
Sir Charles Lyell	Alfred Russel Wallace
Theodore Lyman	Wilhelm Wien
Matthew F. Maury	

Table of contents (16 pp.).

663. SELLERS, ANN (1785-?)

Diary, 1828, 1830. 1 vol.

Contains a journal of her trip from Philadelphia to the Catskill Mountains, August 16-30, 1828, and of another trip to the Pocono Mountains and Susquehanna River, July 9-25, 1830. The author has sketched a rural scene.

Presented by Charles Coleman Sellers, 1945.

664. SELLERS, ANNA (1824-1908)

Diary, 1902-03. 2 vols.

An account of her life in Chattanooga, Tenn., where she was visiting relatives—visitors, naps, walks, letters, friends, the routine of a boarding house.

Presented by Charles Coleman Sellers, 1964.

665. SELLERS, COLEMAN (1781-1834). Inventor

Letters and accounts, 1806-38. 8 vols.

Contains a letter book, 1828-34, of the correspondence of Coleman Sellers, Sellers, Brandt & Company, and Coleman Sellers & Sons, much of it about the shipment of wire paper molds, wool cards, steam engines, locomotives, etc.; with sketches of machinery. Also business accounts, including a record of payments to workmen (1 vol.), and receipt books, 1814-34 (2 vols.), for work done at the mill, rent, taxes, plumbing, furniture, stabling, etc.; also Coleman Sellers & Sons' account of deposits and withdrawals in the Schuylkill Bank, 1837-38 (1 vol.). Also household accounts, 1806-38 (2 vols.); and a volume of orders drawn on the treasurer of the First Church of the New Jerusalem of Delaware, 1830-31 (1 vol.).

Presented by Charles Coleman Sellers, 1945.

666. SELLERS, COLEMAN (1827-1907). Engineer, inventor. APS 1872. *DAB*

Letters and papers, 1863-99. 2 vols. and *ca.* 130 pieces.

Contains a letter book, 1863-78, containing correspondence relating principally to the Photographic Society of Philadelphia, including letters to William Howard Furness,

Henry Greenwood, Oliver W. Holmes, and Benjamin Silliman, Jr., and a few to Coleman Sellers; a letter book composed of letters written from Europe, principally to his children, arranged in the form of a journal and supplemented and illustrated with sketches, theater programs, invitations, letters of other persons, etc., 1884; and a group of letters from Sellers to his son Horace Wells Sellers, 1889-99, written while Coleman Sellers was serving as consulting engineer of the Cataract Construction Company, the Niagara Falls Power Company, and the international commission developing electric power at Niagara Falls; with some related minutes, memoranda, etc.

Presented by Charles Coleman Sellers, 1945 (part).

667. SELLERS, MRS. CORNELIA WELLS (1831-1909). Wife of Coleman Sellers (1827-1907)

Letters from relatives and friends, 1856-58. 1 vol.

Friendly letters, 51 in number, from relatives and friends in Cincinnati, addressed to Mrs. Sellers after her removal to Philadelphia.

Presented by Charles Coleman Sellers, 1945.

668. SELLERS, GEORGE ESCOL (1808-99). Engineer, inventor

Memoirs and other papers, 1829-98.

Various materials including the following: Memoirs, or reminiscences, an autobiography in the form of letters addressed to Coleman and Horace Wells Sellers, 1887-98, 2 vols., typed; sketch book, of mechanical equipment for locomotives, with some caricatures and verses, 1829; 86 letters to Coleman and Horace Wells Sellers, 1892-98, principally on family news, genealogy, and George Sellers' life in Chattanooga; diary, 1898; personal recollections of Nathan Sellers, 1849, with additional notes and materials relating to paper-making; and miscellaneous manuscripts on the United States Mint at Philadelphia, Pennsylvania Railroad, plan for a railroad to San Francisco, etc. The Memoirs were edited by Eugene S. Ferguson and published in Smithsonian Institution *Bulletin* **238** (1965).

Presented by Charles Coleman Sellers, 1945, 1948 (part).

669. SELLERS, HORACE WELLS (1857-1933). Architect

Collection on Independence Hall. Film. 3 reels.

From Independence National Historical Park. Letters, documents, notes, etc., relating to the history and construction of the Pennsylvania State House and its restoration in the early twentieth century.

670. SELLERS, JOHN (1762-1847). Surveyor, farmer, miller of Upper Darby, Pennsylvania

Records, 1783-1852. 13 vols.

These consist of a ledger, 1783-1819 (1 vol.), listing sales and purchases, with names; day book, 1785-1817 (2 vols.), which records by date purchases of leather and skins and the sale of shoes, boots, soles, leggings, etc.; diaries 1808-46 (7 vols.), beginning with Sellers' removal from his house in Philadelphia to his farm, with entries noting work done there, at the mill, as well as family and business events; receipt book 1821-56 (3 vols.), containing signed receipts for payments for wheat, rye, flax seed, oats, corn, casks, cattle, etc.

Presented by Charles Coleman Sellers, 1945.

671. SELLERS, NATHAN (1751-1830). Surveyor, scrivener, manufacturer

Records, 1771-1844. 14 vols.

Miscellaneous personal and business records as follows: Commonplace books, 1771-

73, 2 vols., containing legal forms with some private accounts. Diaries, 1773-74, 1776, 1817-29, 4 vols., containing household records, records of carpentry for the Library Company of Philadelphia and other accounts, notes on surveys, molds for paper-making, drawing and weaving wire, reports on Quaker meetings, reflections on work, morality, etc. Account book, including accounts of the firm of Nathan and David Sellers, 1774-1815, 1 vol., with records of sales to Continental Congress, Pennsylvania Committee of Safety, Thomas Fitzsimons, Thomas Leiper, John Penn, Stephen Sayre, Edward Shippen, Anthony Wayne, and others; also sketches of watermarks designed for special customers. Surveying notebooks, 1775-84, 4 vols., consisting of notes on surveys, 1777-79; survey of the West Chester road; survey of the State-House Yard after 1785, with drafts of letters to Zeba Pyle, 1820-21; and diary of a survey from Tulpehocken Springs to Quitapahilla Spring with David Rittenhouse and Thomas Hutchins, 1784, with notes of a trip to Baltimore, 1784, and receipts, 1806-17. Notes, kept as a member of the Philadelphia Common Council, 1805-12, 1 vol., including record of expenditures for cleaning, paving, and repaving streets, for the town watch, for the care of wells and pumps for water, etc. Receipt book, 1813, 1819-29, 1 vol. Notes of financial transactions, 1814-44, including investments in mortgages, stocks, loans, etc., with records of payments.
Presented by Charles Coleman Sellers, 1945.

672. SELLERS, NATHAN and COLEMAN. Manufacturers
Order book, 1834-36. 1 vol.

Orders for paper molds, with descriptions, and for machine work of different kinds. Customers include William Duane, Thomas Gilpin, Adam Ramage, and John Shryock.
Presented by Charles Coleman Sellers, 1945.

673. SELLERS, NATHAN and DAVID. Manufacturers
Letter book, 1821-31. 1 vol.

Business correspondence of the firm, relating to the sale and shipment of wire and wire products. Correspondents include John Haviland and George Shryock.

674. SELLERS, MRS. SOPHONISBA ANGUSCIOLA PEALE (1786-1859). Daughter of Charles Willson Peale
Account books, 1834-45. 3 vols.

Accounts with Charles and George Escol Sellers, her sons, of sums given her by them, 1834-36, 1 vol.; receipt book, 1834-45, 1 vol., containing receipts for payment of taxes, ground rents, groceries, interest, etc., as administratrix of the estate of Coleman Sellers; and a record of expenses while keeping house for her son-in-law Alfred Harrold, 1840-45, 1 vol., including wages, carriage fares, "childrens board," and groceries.
Presented by Charles Coleman Sellers, 1945.

675. SELLERS FAMILY
Papers, 1675-1928. ca. 1,500 pieces.

Correspondence among members of the Sellers and Peale families, with special emphasis on the Sellerses, ca. 1780-1860. Topics include such family matters as travel, household expenses, children, deaths and funerals, social and cultural life in Philadelphia, with some doggerel verses. Principal correspondents include: Coleman Sellers (1781-1834) and his wife Sophonisba Angusciola Peale (1786-1859), and their children Anna (1824-1908), Coleman (1827-1907), and George Escol (1808-99); also Ann Sellers (b. 1785), Hannah Sellers and her husband Peter Hill (d. 1857); Mrs. Cornelia Wells Sellers (1831-1909); Mrs. Elizabeth Coleman Sellers (1751-1832); and the following members of the Peale family: Charles Willson, Raphaelle, Rembrandt, Franklin,

Charles Linnaeus, Rubens, and Titian Ramsay Peale. Described in APS *Proc.* **95** (1951): p. 262.

Presented by Charles Coleman Sellers, 1956 (part).

676. ——

Genealogical data. 1 vol. Typed.

Data collected from family diaries and other records, by Horace Wells Sellers (?).

677. Sessé y Lacasta, Martino de (1755-1809). Spanish botanist; founder and director, Botanical Gardens, Mexico City

Catalogo de animales y plantas mexicanas, 1794. 1 vol.

For a work for which this was a part, see *Plantae Novae Hispaniae* (Mexico City, 1887) by Sessé y Lacasta and Joseph Marianno Mociño.

Presented by J. G. Williamson, 1835.

678. Sharswood, William (1836-1905). Pennsylvania naturalist

Papers, 1865-67. *ca.* 100 pieces.

Subjects include minerals and mining, publications, his play "The Betrothed," education, St. John's College in Maryland, Reconstruction in South Carolina. Correspondents include:

George Allen	Wolcott Gibbs
Samuel A. Allibone	Samuel S. Haldeman
Edward E. Barden	Jean Hosmer
George H. Boker	Charles T. Jackson
John Ross Browne	John Le Conte
James D. B. DeBow	John Lawrence Le Conte
William Everett	

Table of contents (3 pp.).

Presented by Frances Lichten, 1959.

679. Shippen, Edward "of Lancaster" (1703-81). Merchant. APS 1768

Letters and papers, 1727-89. 3 boxes.

Consists principally of letters and papers of Edward Shippen, including letter books, 1753-81, and correspondence with Joseph Shippen (1 box), 1750-78. Topics are business in Philadelphia and Lancaster, provincial politics, army supply in the French and Indian War, land purchases and speculation, housebuilding, and family affairs; correspondents include:

William Allen	Benjamin Franklin
Harmanus Alricks	Joseph Galloway
John Armstrong	Thomas Lawrence
Henry Bouquet	William Logan
Charles Brockden	Robert Hunter Morris
Edward Burd	John Penn
James Burd	Richard Peters
Benjamin Chew	Edward Shippen, Jr.
William Coleman	William Shippen, Sr.
George Croghan	Charles Willing

Also 1 box of miscellaneous correspondence, 1727-81, including many letters to members of the Shippen family and to William Allen, James Hamilton, John Harris, David

Jameson, and other officers in the Provincial forces, principally on military affairs, 1755-60; with a fragment of Joseph Shippen's orderly book, 1758; several letters from Joseph Shippen at Rome, 1760; records of payment of wagon hire on the Pennsylvania frontier; military returns.

Presented by The Philip and A. S. W. Rosenbach Foundation, 1952.

680. ——

Docket of cases, 1764-65. 1 vol.

Lists of cases tried and judgments rendered; some entries relate to apprenticeships.

681. SHIPPEN, EDWARD (1729-1806). Chief Justice of Pennsylvania. APS 1768. DAB

Receipts, 1754-89. 19 pieces.

Receipts from tradesmen, mechanics, and storekeepers for sewing, carriage work, the making and repair of shoes, madeira, fabrics, sugar, hair-dressing, clothing, etc.

682. SHIPPEN, JOSEPH (1706-1793). Merchant

Waste book, 1749-50. 1 vol.

Accounts with various persons in Pennsylvania, Maryland, and New Jersey for drygoods, notions, rum, cutlery, glassware, medicines, etc.

683. SHIPPEN, JOSEPH, JR. (1732-1810). Soldier, judge. APS 1768. Appleton

Letter book, 1763-73. 1 vol.

Principally on provincial business (Shippen was Secretary of the Province), the letters comment on such topics as: Indians of Pennsylvania, the French and Indian War, survey of the Maryland-Pennsylvania boundary, and the Stamp Act. Correspondents include: James Burd, Jeremiah Dixon, Joseph Galloway, Humphry Marshall, Charles Mason, Edward Shippen of Lancaster, Edward Shippen, Jr., and others.

Presented by The Philip and A. S. W. Rosenbach Foundation, 1952.

684. SHIPPEN, WILLIAM, JR. (1736-1808). Physician, anatomist, teacher. APS 1768. DAB

Journal, July 19, 1759–January 22, 1760. 1 vol.

Kept while a student of medicine in London under Dr. Colin McKenzie and Dr. William Hunter; mentions Dennys DeBerdt, Mark Akenside, George Whitefield, John Fothergill, David Garrick, and Thomas Penn. Printed, with notes, in Betsy C. Corner, *William Shippen, Jr., Pioneer in American Medical Education,* APS *Memoirs* 28 (Philadelphia, 1951).

Presented by J. Hall Pleasants, 1951.

685. ——

Prescription book, October 1, 1789–July 10, 1791. 1 vol.

A daily record of professional visits and prescriptions. Patients include:

Count Andreani	Tobias Lear
John Beckley	Marquis de Barbé-Marbois
Baron de Bretagne	Moreau de St.-Méry
Benjamin Chew, Jr.	Charles Thomson
Ralph Izard	George Washington
Thomas Jefferson	Thomas Willing
Henry Knox	

Presented by J. Hall Pleasants, 1952.

686. SHORT, CHARLES WILKINS (1794-1863). Physician, teacher, botanist. APS
     1835. *DAB;* APS *Proc.* **10** (1865)

 Correspondence, 1813–67. 80 pieces.

 Principally letters to his brother John Cleaves Short, on personal, family, and general topics; some relate to botany and science and are from Sir William J. Hooker, Thomas Nuttall, John Torrey, John Vaughan, and Caspar Wistar.

687. SHORT, WILLIAM (1759-1849). Diplomat. APS 1804. *DAB*

 Correspondence, 1787-1838. 230 pieces.

 Chiefly personal correspondence between Short and the Duchesse de La Rochefoucauld on his courtship and wish to marry her and bring her to America; her letters describe the life of a powerful, wealthy, and noble family under the *ancien régime,* events of the Revolution and the Reign of Terror, and life in France thereafter. The collection includes letters of Lafayette, Count Luigi Castiglioni, Pauline Castiglioni, the Duc de La Rochefoucauld-Liancourt, and others. Table of contents (6 pp.).

688. SHULL, GEORGE HARRISON (1874-1954). Botanist, professor of botany and
     genetics, Princeton University. APS 1918. *Year Book* 1954

 Papers, 4 file drawers.

 Consist principally of reports to the Carnegie Institution of Washington on the work of Luther Burbank, whose plant-breeding farm at Sonoma, Calif., Shull visited 8 times, 1904-15. The collection includes a report by Edwin C. MacDowell which is a guide to the collection, which is not otherwise indexed.

 Presented by Carnegie Institution of Washington, 1965.

689. SIMPSON, GEORGE GAYLORD (1902–   ). Paleontologist. APS 1936

 Letters to Mrs. Martha Lee Simpson Eastlake, 1918-62. 261 pieces.

 Addressed to his sister, these letters recount his travels and experiences on scientific expeditions to New Mexico, Arizona, Argentina, and Chile; much is personal.

 Presented by Mrs. Eastlake, 1964.

690. ——

 The meaning of evolution: a study of the history of life and of its significance for man. 298 pp.

 The manuscript of a book published by Yale University Press, 1949.

 Presented by the author, 1949.

691. SLOANE, SIR HANS (1660-1753). Physician, naturalist, founder of the British
     Museum. *DNB*

 Correspondence. Film. 16 reels.

 From British Museum. A copy of Sloane Mss. 4036-69, comprising principally letters to Sloane from scholars, physicians, naturalists, collectors, and others in Great Britain, Europe, and America. Not all of Sloane's correspondence is to be found in the volumes filmed here. Edward J. L. Scott, *An Index to the Sloane Manuscripts in the British Museum* (London, 1904) is a useful guide to the entire collection, including the portion filmed here.

692. SMITH, ERWIN FRINK (1854-1927). Plant pathologist. APS 1916. *DAB*

 Papers, 1865-1940. 17 boxes.

 Principally personal and professional correspondence; with some genealogical data. The collection contains many data on Smith's studies on plant pathology, with photographs of diseased plants. There are also a journal of a European tour, 1906 (4 vols.), miscellaneous memoranda, arranged alphabetically by subject (1 vol.), recipes for making ink, 1877 (1 vol.), notebooks of articles and mailing addresses, 1895-1903 (4 vols.), diary, 1870 (1 vol.), an interleaved copy of *Michigan Flora*, 1881, with notations throughout, botanical notes and memoranda on animals observed, 1873 (1 vol.), notes and memoranda on methods of experimentation, descriptions of experiments, and observations, 1898 (1 vol.), etc. The collection is not yet arranged.

Presented by Andrew Denny Rodgers, III, 1952.

693. SMITH, LLOYD DEAN

The Five Nations of Indians in their relation to the colony of New York from 1700 to 1781. Film.

Master's thesis, University of Wisconsin, 1900.

694. SMITH, THOMAS PETERS (1777-1802). Chemist and mineralogist. APS 1799
Journal in Europe, 1800-02. 5 vols.

Record of a tour of Germany, Denmark, Sweden, France, and England, to inspect technological improvements in manufacturing and mining. There are accounts of visits to C. D. Ebeling, Friederich Klopstock, J. A. J. Reimarus, Anders Sparmann, Karl P. Thunberg, and others. The journal is copied, legibly but with many excisions, into the fifth volume.

Bequeathed by the author, 1802, with the request that the journal be published if found to contain information "useful to the manufactories of my country."

695. ——

List of minerals, 1801. 43 leaves.

Kept on the author's travels in France and Switzerland; with notes by John Vaughan, from whose scrapbook these sheets were removed, 1959.

Bequeathed (?) by the author, 1802.

696. SMITHSONIAN INSTITUTION

Letters pertaining to the bequest of James Smithson, 1838. 1 vol.

Copied from House of Representatives Executive Documents, 25th Congress, 3rd session, No. 11.

697. SMYTH, FREDERICK (1732-1815). Chief Justice of New Jersey
Papers, 1756-1816. 56 pieces.

Relating principally to Smyth's career in New Jersey before the American Revolution, the collection includes addresses to grand juries and their reports, a copy of a petition to the Earl of Carlisle and its response, 1778; with some documents on Smyth's appointments, and material on the collection of customs in Rhode Island. Signatories include:

Benjamin Chew	Jared Ingersoll
Sir Henry Clinton	William Livingston
George Clymer	Hugh Mercer
John Dickinson	Robert Morris
Joseph Hopkinson	John Penn
Richard, Earl Howe	

Table of contents (2 pp.).

698. SNYDER, JOHN KELLERMAN

Franklin and Canada. Film.

Doctoral dissertation, McGill University, 1932.

699. SOCIETY FOR PROPAGATING CHRISTIAN KNOWLEDGE AMONG THE GERMANS SETTLED IN PENNSYLVANIA

Minutes, 1754-56. Film.

From Historical Society of Pennsylvania. Kept in the hand of Provost William Smith, these minutes include letters and reports in full or abstract. Table of contents (1 p.).

700. SOCIETY OF ANTIQUARIES OF SCOTLAND

Minute Book, 1780-82. 1 vol. Duplicate.

Bound with this is William Smellie, *Account of the Institution and Progress of the Society of Antiquaries of Scotland* (Edinburgh, 1782).

Presented by the Earl of Buchan, 1795.

701. SOCIETY OF FREE QUAKERS, PHILADELPHIA

Papers, 1781-1947. *ca.* 400 pieces and 6 vols.

Minutes of the Society, 1781-1947, and of the directors of the Corporation, 1929-47; membership book, with signatures of early members, 1785, and names of later members; deeds to meeting house and burying ground; treasurers' accounts; reports of officers and committees; bills and receipts for constructing, maintaining, and repairing the meeting house; canceled checks; letters to the Society and its officers, especially Samuel Wetherill, 1883-84; register of births and burials, 1786-93; book of printed orders for opening graves; album of photographs of gravestones in the burying ground, 1899; copy of inscriptions on stones in the burying ground, with a plan of the reinterments in the Wetherill graveyard, Audubon, Pa., 1905; lists of books purchased for the Apprentices' Library, tenant of the meeting house after 1841. Among the first members of the Society were: Moses Bartram, Clement Biddle, Elizabeth Claypoole (Betsy Ross), Lydia Darragh, Christopher Marshall, Timothy Matlack, Benjamin Say, and Samuel Wetherill, Jr.

Presented by the Religious Society of Free Quakers, 1957.

702. SOCIETY OF FRIENDS. "INDIAN COMMITTEE"

Records, 1791-1892. Film. 10 reels.

Minutes, letters, reports, speeches, accounts, and other archival material of the Committee for promoting the improvement and gradual civilization of the Indian natives. See George S. Snyderman, "A Preliminary Survey of American Indian Manuscripts in Repositories in the Philadelphia Area," APS *Proc.* 97 (1953): p. 598. Table of contents (13 pp.).

703. SOCIETY OF FRIENDS. PHILADELPHIA YEARLY MEETING

Book of discipline of the Society of Friends in Pennsylvania and New Jersey, 1719. 1 vol. Copy.

Copied for APS "from an antient Copy in the possession of Timothy Matlack, Esqre."

Presented by Peter S. Du Ponceau, 1820.

704. SORBY, HENRY CLIFTON (1826-1908). English geologist, mineralogist
Diaries, 1859-1908. Film. 2 reels.
From Sheffield University Library.

705. SOUTH CAROLINA GAZETTE
Name index, 1732-38. Film. 1 reel.
From South Carolina Historical Society. Compiled by Hennig Cohen.

706. SOUZA PALHER, JOAO DE
Descripçao e uso do dynamometro, 1807. 1 vol.
The instrument was for measuring and comparing the relative strength of men,
horses, and other beasts of burden. Includes descriptions of other instruments. Illustrated by engraved plates.

707. SPARKS, JARED (1789-1866). Clergyman, editor, historian, president of Har-
vard College. APS 1837. *DAB*
Papers relating to Benjamin Franklin, *ca.* 1826-63. 7 binders. Photoprints.
Correspondence with Henry Stevens, Sr., Henry Stevens, Jr., Franklin Bache,
J. Francis Fisher, James Mease, Henry D. Gilpin, Benjamin Vaughan, Petty Vaughan,
and others on Franklin, Franklin's descendants, and Franklin's papers; extracts from
Philadelphia newspapers on Franklin; papers used in his biography; miscellaneous
entries in his diary, 1830-54, relating to his search for Franklin manuscripts and his
preparation of his edition of Franklin's writings. The originals, from which these copies
were made, are in the Harvard University Library.

708. ——
Selected papers, 1819-63. Film. 2 reels.
From Harvard University Library. Letters and papers relating to Sparks' research
on Benjamin Franklin and the publication of an edition of the latter's writings. Principal
correspondents include:

Franklin Bache	James Mease
S. D. Bradford	William B. Reed
William Duane	Henry Stevens, Sr.
Peter S. Du Ponceau	Henry Stevens, Jr.
J. Francis Fisher	Benjamin Vaughan
George Gibbs	Petty Vaughan
Henry D. Gilpin	William Vaughan
Edward D. Ingraham	

There are also extracts from Sparks' journal, 1831-41, relating to his Franklin researches.
Table of contents (11 pp.).

709. SPECK, FRANK GOULDSMITH (1881-1950). Anthropologist
Collection of American Indian anthropology, 1903-50. 31 boxes, 148 folders,
2 packages, 4 reels of movie film, 5 drawers of lantern slides, maps, and drawings.
Relating primarily to the Indians of the Eastern Woodlands, the materials are
arranged by area and tribe. There are notes and formal studies of social structures,
hunting territories, economic behavior, religion, language, myths, dances, genealogies,
medicine, wampum, natural history, physical measurements. Some material is published,
much unpublished. The collection includes some materials on African anthropology and

photographs of anthropological interest taken in Europe, Africa, Asia, Australasia, and Oceania. Correspondents include:

Charles Marius Barbeau	Edward Sapir
Franz Boas	Carl Voegelin
Fay-Cooper Cole	Erminie Voegelin
Loren Eiseley	Clark Wissler
Alfred V. Kidder	Paul A. W. Wallace
Alfred L. Kroeber	Leslie A. White
Eli Lilly	Conway Zirkle

The collection was arranged by Anthony F. C. Wallace, who described it in "The Frank G. Speck Collection," APS *Proc.* **95** (1951): p. 286. Table of contents (43 pp.).

Presented by Mrs. Frank G. Speck, 1950, 1952; with additions by William N. Fenton, 1951, and John Witthoft, 1952.

710. ——

Collection of notes and diaries in the Cherokee syllabary, 1840-1932. 22 pieces.

Contains diary of Will West Long, ledger of birth and death records, medical texts and prescriptions, charms, Cherokee-English vocabulary, etc., made principally by Long and Morgan Calhoun.

Presented by the University of Pennsylvania Museum, 1958.

711. SPENCER, NATHAN. Pennsylvania farmer

An account of Thomas Godfrey, 1809. 1 vol.

Prepared "with a view of having it inserted in Rees Cyclopedia," this account is preceded by the account of Godfrey and his quadrant taken from the *American Magazine*, 1758, and includes a copy of James Logan's communication to the Royal Society. A letter from Spencer to Alexander Wilson, editor of the *Cyclopedia*, 1809, discusses Godfrey and the sources for this essay. Spencer is identified as "a farmer who owns the place that was once Godfrey's."

712. STAUFFER, JACOB (1808-80). Pennsylvania naturalist

Correspondence, *ca.* 1850-79. 2 boxes.

Letters on various scientific subjects, e.g., fishes, insects, snakes, mice, fossils, mosses; on learned institutions, notably the Smithsonian Institution and the Academy of Natural Sciences of Philadelphia; and about some men of science, from various correspondents, including:

Spencer F. Baird	J. S. Houghton
Edward D. Cope	John Lawrence Le Conte
Ezra Townsend Cresson	Leo Lesquereux
William Darlington	John Gottlieb Morris
Elie M. Durand	Thomas Conrad Porter
William Gibson Farlow	S. S. Rathvon
Samuel S. Haldeman	Charles Valentine Riley
Hugh C. Hanson	John Jay Smith
Joseph Henry	

713. ——

Classification of orders, families and genera of fish, *ca.* 1866-79. 1 vol.

The classification is made on the plan presented in the *Encyclopedia Britannica*,

and includes genera and species not included, especially of North America; with many illustrations of specimens.
Presented by Frank Stick, 1957.

714. STEWART, WALTER (d. 1796). Soldier. Appleton
Orderly book, Second Pennsylvania Regiment, 1778-79.

715. STOCKTON, WILLIAM T. Proprietor, New York and Baltimore stages
Notebook, 1813-17. 1 vol.

Account with Farmers & Mechanics Bank; names of debtors and creditors; and "Feed Book," naming owners of animals and amount of oats consumed by the beasts.

716. STRAHAN, WILLIAM (1715-85). London printer and publisher, Member of Parliament, friend of Benjamin Franklin. *DNB*
Journals and account book, 1751-77. 4 vols.

The first three volumes contain accounts of journeys to Scotland, with records of expenses on the way, as follows: 1: 1751; 2: 1759, 1760, 1766; 3: 1768, 1773, 1777. Strahan and Franklin were in Edinburgh at the same time in 1759. The fourth volume contains "The Particulars of the estate of Wm Strahan as it stood on the first of January 1755: 1759: 1761," with some miscellaneous accounts.

717. STRONG, WILLIAM WALKER (1883-1955). Physicist
Phoenician and Punic inscriptions made and found in the Chesapeake watershed of America, 1945. Film. 2 reels.

Photographed from one of a limited number of copies in possession of Joseph C. Ayoob, Aliquippa, Pa., 1960.

718. SULLIVAN, THOMAS (1755- ?). Irish soldier, 49th Regiment of Foot
Journal of the operations of the American war, 1778. 1 vol.

Sullivan, who was later steward in the family of General Nathanael Greene, gives an account of Boston and its evacuation, 1776, a description of Halifax, an account of the Jersey campaign, 1776-77, and of the occupation of Philadelphia, 1777-78. Extracts of the journal, relating to Philadelphia in 1777, were printed in *Pennsylvania Magazine of History and Biography* 31 (1907): p. 406, and subsequent volumes to 34 (1910): p. 241.
Presented by Charles Smith, 1804.

719. SWANN, WILLIAM FRANCIS GRAY (1884-1962). Physicist. APS 1926. *Year Book* 1962
Papers, *ca.* 1900-62. *ca.* 50,000 pieces; also photographs, slides, recordings, films.

Correspondence on research, business, and professional matters, particularly as director of the Bartol Research Foundation of the Franklin Institute; personal correspondence relating to his studies, teaching, travels, lectures, and music (as cellist and conductor of the Swarthmore, Pa., Symphony Orchestra); 56 notebooks, work books, books of lectures, etc.; 5 scrapbooks; diplomas and certificates; manuscripts of a book *Electrodynamics* and of *The Architecture of the Universe* (1934); about 600 articles on atmospheric electricity, acceleration of particles, atomic bomb defense, atomic energy, cosmic rays and energy, electrets, electrodynamics, magnetism, music, physics, quantum theory, radiation, relativity and Einstein, science and civilization, stratospheric flights (by balloon and airplane), thermodynamics, wave mechanics, etc. Also Kodachrome film "Hunting cosmic rays in a B-29," 1947 (1 reel), and film of the stratospheric balloon flight of Jean Picard (1 reel). Table of contents for articles only (26 pp.). Presented by Estate of Dr. Swann, 1962.

720. TAMIL LANGUAGE

Grammar and vocabulary. Nineteenth century. 1 vol. In Tamil and English.

721. TAYLOR, JOHN. Pennsylvania clergyman

Hebrew Lexicon. 1 vol.

Transcribed and abridged from the author's Concordance. Taylor was rector of Trinity Church, Pittsburgh; later a minister in Philadelphia. A note by his widow says the transcription may be inaccurate, since it had not been compared with the original. Presented by Mrs. Mary Taylor, 1844.

722. THOMAS, ALEX, and FRANK WILLIAMS

Nootka Indian manuscript texts. Film.

From National Museum of Canada, Ottawa.

723. THOMSON, ELIHU (1853-1937). Scientist, inventor, manufacturer. APS 1876.
     DAB; Year Book 1937

Papers, 1870-1944. *ca.* 35,000 pieces.

A great collection of letters, papers, notebooks, drawings, telegrams, essays, photographs, etc., about his family, electrical experiments, inventions, patents, astronomy, geology, general scientific topics, medicine, APS, General Electric Company, Thomson-Houston Electric Company, Central High School, Philadelphia, etc. There are 30 boxes of letters to Thomson, 12 boxes of letters from him; 8 boxes of correspondence of Thomson and George W. Hewitt; 7 boxes of letters and papers concerning Thomson; 84 boxes of letters and papers from the files of the General Electric Company, 1891-1923, 43 letter books of the Thomson-Houston Electric Company. There are 8 boxes of Thomson's manuscript comments on his patents; 304 original papers on science and inventions, with drawings; notebooks kept in courses in Central High School; diaries of trips to Europe; 28 papers of personal reminiscence; notebooks on genealogy; diplomas, certificates, resolutions, programs; scrapbooks of cards, photographs, clippings, and other souvenirs; 2 vols. of tributes on his eightieth birthday, etc. Correspondents include:

William E. Ayrton	Dugald C. Jackson
George F. Barker	Sir James H. Jeans
Daniel Moreau Barringer	H. H. Jeffcott
Sir William H. Bragg	Alba B. Johnson
Vannevar Bush	William W. Keen
John A. Brashear	Arthur E. Kennelly
Charles A. Coffin, Jr.	Irving Langmuir
William D. Coolidge	J. Robert Lovejoy
Robert E. Crompton	Edward Mallinckrodt
George W. Cutter	T. Commerford Martin
Lee DeForest	William H. Meadowcroft
Francis X. Dercum	Thomas C. Mendenhall
Gano Dunn	Dayton C. Miller
Thomas A. Edison	P. F. Mottelay
John A. Fleming	Sir Charles Morgan
William H. Greene	William H. Pickering
George E. Hale	Joseph H. Pratt
George W. Hewitt	Henry S. Pritchett

E. Wilbur Rice, Jr.
George W. Riché
Harlow Shapley
Monroe B. Snyder
Henry J. Spooner
Charles P. Steinmetz

George Stockley
Samuel W. Stratton
George Stuart
Silvanus P. Thomson
David Todd
Willis R. Whitney

The collection is described by John L. Haney, "The Elihu Thomson Collection," *Year Book*, 1944.

Presented by the General Electric Company and Mrs. Elihu Thomson (parts), 1937-44.

724. THORNTON, WILLIAM (1759-1828). Physician, architect, official. APS 1787. *DAB*

Papers. Film. 6 reels.

From Library of Congress. Diaries, 1777-82; expense books, 1794-1804; notebooks; commonplace book, drafts of essays; excerpts from minutes of Friends' Monthly Meeting, Tortola, 1741-61; newspaper clippings; sketches; correspondence from, among others:

Robert Aitken
Sir Joseph Banks
J. P. Brissot de Warville
Robert Fulton
Thomas Jefferson
John Coakley Lettsom
Robert Patterson

David Rittenhouse
Granville Sharp
John Trumbull
Comte de Volney
George Washington
Caspar Wistar

There are also letters and papers of Mrs. Thornton. Table of contents.

725. TILGHMAN, WILLIAM (1756-1827). Jurist. APS 1805. *DAB*

Papers, 1771-1845. 61 pieces.

Letters on business and legal affairs, sales of land, payment of taxes, court sittings, affair of Dr. S. Bouchell; also 1 vol. check stubs for expenditures from his estate, 1827-38. Correspondents include: Henry Drinker, Robert Goldsborough, William Goldsborough, Richard Lloyd, George Meade, and Richard Tilghman. Table of contents (3 pp.).

726. TORREY, JOHN (1796-1873). Botanist. APS 1835. *DAB*

Papers, 1819-64. 15 pieces.

Miscellaneous letters and papers on natural history, metals and mineralogy, botany, insects, the geological survey of New York, and analyses of distilled liquors in the cause of temperance. Correspondents include: Samuel B. Buckley, Parker Cleaveland, Edward C. Delavan, Elie M. Durand, Amos Eaton, and Charles Wilkes.

727. TORREY. JOHN, collector

Autograph letters of naturalists, 1744-1894. Film. 1 reel.

From Academy of Natural Sciences of Philadelphia. A collection of 283 letters; correspondents include:

Louis Agassiz
Benjamin Smith Barton
Zaccheus Collins
Chester Dewey

Peter S. Du Ponceau
John C. Frémont
Asa Gray
Robert Hare

William Hembel	Charles W. Short
Joseph Henry	Benjamin Silliman, Sr.
George Ord	John Torrey
Charles Pickering	Alexander Wilson
Constantine S. Rafinesque	

Table of contents (6 pp.).

728. TOWNSEND, JOHN KIRK (1809-51). Naturalist. Appleton

Vocabularies of the Okonagan, Attnaha, and Walla Walla languages, 1834-36. 2 vols.

The vocabularies were obtained from Indians, half-breeds, and traders; most of the informants are identified. One volume appears to contain the notes from which the other was prepared.

Presented by the author, 1838, and by Peter S. Du Ponceau, 1844.

729. TREAT, JOHN BRECK

Meteorological observations made at Arkansas, 1805-08. 1 vol.

Writing from "Arkansa in Louisiana" to Thomas Jefferson, March 31, 1809, Treat sent these observations, adding, "If from their perusal you can derive, either information or amusement, respecting the Climate of this part of our Country, your acceptance will be highly gratifying."

Presented by Thomas Jefferson, 1809.

730. TREVELYAN, SIR CHARLES EDWARD (1807-86). Governor of Madras. *DNB*

The natural process by which a conquered people in an inferior grade of civilization adopt the language and system of learning of their more civilized conquerors, 1832. Copy.

This essay is accompanied by another, written two years earlier, entitled, "Consideration of the means by which the present highly advanced state of learning and civilisation in Europe can be most effectually communicated to the rest of the world and to our Indian empire in particular."

Presented by James P. Engles, 1839.

731. TRUDEAU, JEAN BAPTISTE (1748-1827). Schoolmaster, trader, traveler

Description abrégée du haut Missouri, 1794-96. Film. 1 reel.

From Université Laval, Séminaire de Québec. Account of a journey up the Missouri River, with descriptions of the life and manners of the Indian tribes, prepared for Don Zenon Trudeau, governor of the territory. Another copy of Trudeau's journal for 1795 was translated by Mrs. H. T. Beauregard and published as "Journal of Jean Baptiste Trudeau among the Arekara Indians in 1795," Missouri Historical Society, *Collections* 4 (1922-23): p. 9.

732. TRUE, RODNEY HOWARD (1866-1940). Botanist. APS 1923

Papers, 1861-1939. 10 boxes.

Correspondence relating to True's professional activities in the University of Pennsylvania, the Bureau of Plant Industry of the Department of Agriculture, the American Association for the Advancement of Science, the Philadelphia Society for Promoting Agriculture, and to his publications. Also much personal correspondence and some travel diaries.

733. TURKEY, DEPARTMENT OF STATE

Secretary's handbooks. 2 vols. In Turkish.

One volume is entitled "Inscha or Turkish Letter Writer" and contains forms of business letters; the other is docketed as "Turjiman Nameh Mss Turkish Interpreter's Assistant. Forms of letters."
Presented by John P. Brown, 1836.

734. TURNER, LUCIAN McSHAN
Notes on the caribou, *ca.* 1885. Photocopy and film.

Notes on Cabot's caribou (*Rangifer caboti*) from a longer manuscript on the mammals of Labrador; with notes by Francis Harper on the range of the Eastern Woodland and Barren Ground caribous (presented by Francis Harper, 1958). Also (film from United States Museum), notes on the woodland caribou or reindeer (*Rangifer tarandus caribou* [Kerr]).

735. TYSON, GEORGE, collector
Japanese flora, drawn by native artists, 1865. 300 leaves.

Made at Nagasaki for one Tyson, of Boston, then of Hong Kong. The pictures are indexed by native name and month of blooming.
Presented by William Morris Davis, 1883.

736. UNITED CHURCH BOARD FOR WORLD MINISTRIES
Papers relating to North American Indian missions, 1817-83. Film. 64 reels.

From manuscripts on deposit in Houghton Library, Harvard University. Letters, reports, accounts, memoranda, etc., relating to the work of the American Board of Home Missions among the Abnakis, Cherokees, Chickasaws, Choctaws, Creeks, Dakotas, Mackinaws, Maumees, Mayhaws, Ojibwas, Osage, Pawnees, Penobscots, Sioux, and Stockbridge Indians in Arkansas, New York, Oregon, and elsewhere.

737. UNITED STATES ARMY. DEPARTMENT OF NORTH CAROLINA
General orders pertaining to the defences of New Bern, North Carolina, 1863. 1 vol.

Some leaves of the volume contain printed orders. The commanding generals during the period were Brigadier General C. A. Heckman and Brigadier General Innis N. Palmer. The volume was received by the Society in 1867.

738. UNITED STATES EXPLORING EXPEDITION
Records, 1838-42. Film. 27 reels.

From National Archives, Washington (Film microcopy No. 75).

739. VATER, JOHANN SEVERIN (1771-1826). German theologian and philologist. APS 1817. Hoefer
An enquiry into the origin of the population of America from the old Continent, *ca.* 1820. 1 vol.

Translated by Peter S. Du Ponceau from the author's *Untersuchungen über Amerikas Bevölkerung aus dem alten Kontinente* (Leipzig, 1810). It was Du Ponceau's opinion that Vater was moved to write this book by Benjamin Smith Barton's *New Views of the Origin of the Tribes and Nations of America,* which Vater often quoted.
Presented by Peter S. Du Ponceau, 1840.

740. VAUGHAN, BENJAMIN (1751-1835). Diplomat, political economist, agriculturist. APS 1786. *DAB*
Papers, 1746-1900. 43 boxes.

Letters (including some transcripts and photostats) from and to Vaughan from many American and British correspondents, including:

John Quincy Adams	William Manning
William Allen	Samuel L. Mitchill
Jesse Appleton	Benjamin Rush
Sir Joseph Banks	Earl of Shelburne (later
Parker Cleaveland	Marquess of Lansdowne)
Aaron Dexter	Gideon Snow
Benjamin Franklin	Jared Sparks
James Freeman	John C. Warren
Robert Hallowell Gardiner	

Also personal correspondence and business papers of Benjamin, Charles, Petty, Samuel Sr., Samuel Jr., William, William Oliver, and Sarah Vaughan (2 boxes); lectures, mostly in shorthand (3 vols.); a large number of notes and memoranda on a wide variety of topics, such as agriculture, architecture, astronomy, diplomacy, diseases, dueling, electricity, hieroglyphs, internal improvements, medicine, meteorology, land, manufactures, politics, punctuation, religion, silk-manufacturing, stock-breeding, taxation, Unitarianism, Benjamin Franklin, John Locke, Napoleon I, Joseph Priestley, Bowdoin College, town of Hallowell, Me.; notes on the peace negotiations, 1782-83; miscellaneous legal papers; genealogy of the Abbott-Vaughan families. For a personal account of the collection, see Mrs. Mary Vaughan Marvin, "The Benjamin Vaughan Papers," APS *Proc.* **95** (1951): p. 246.

Presented by Mrs. Mary Vaughan Marvin, 1950 (in part).

741. VAUGHAN, JOHN (1755-1841). Merchant; librarian and secretary, APS. APS 1784

Papers, 1768-1841. 5 boxes.

Correspondence with, among others:

John Adams	Thomas Jefferson
George Bancroft	Dolley P. Madison
Nathaniel Bowditch	James Monroe
Aaron Burr	Joseph Priestley
Parker Cleaveland	Jared Sparks
Thomas Cooper	Marquis de Talleyrand
Edward Everett	Benjamin Vaughan
Benjamin Franklin	Samuel Vaughan, Sr.
William Temple Franklin	William Vaughan
Richard Harrison	George Washington
John Jay	Benjamin Waterhouse

Also correspondence with Pierre, E. I., and Victor Marie du Pont, 1801-16 (photostats from Eleutherian Mills Historical Library), and with George W. Featherstonhaugh (photostats from Mrs. Duane Featherstonhaugh); also Vaughan's commonplace book, 1783; inventory and other documents relating to his estate, 1841. The collection includes verses written for Vaughan by William H. Furness, 1826, and verses and a song prepared for the Vaughan Club by Benjamin M. Hollinshead and William Norris, 1839, 1841. There are also 2 boxes of papers relating to Vaughan's administration of the estate of Samuel Merrick, Philadelphia importer, 1796-1822. The collection also contains (Madeira-Vaughan Collection) a number of miscellaneous letters of members of the Madeira family to or from, among others: Edward Everett Hale, Washington Irving, Harriet Martineau, Richard Peters, Jr., Agnes Repplier, Roger B. Taney, and Daniel Webster; the journal of a voyage of the ship *Sampson*, 1819, a letter of Jan Ingenhousz to Jonathan Williams, many letters to Jacob Snider, etc. Table of contents (25 pp.).

742. ——

Papers, 1808-22. Film.

From First Unitarian Church, Philadelphia. Miscellaneous accounts, bills, memoranda, and 20 letters to Vaughan, mostly on church affairs.

743. ——

Letters from the Office of Indian Trade, 1812-19. Film.

From National Archives, Washington. On the subject of Indian Peace Medals.

744. VAUGHAN, SAMUEL (1720-1802). Merchant, philanthropist, horticulturist.
     APS 1784

Journal of a tour through Pennsylvania, Maryland, and Virginia, June 18–September 4, 1787. 1 vol. Photostat.

The Pennsylvania portion of the journal, through July 13, has been printed, with full annotation, by Edward G. Williams in *Western Pennsylvania Historical Magazine* 44 (1961): p. 51. The original manuscript, owned by Mrs. Mary Vaughan Marvin, was deposited in Yale University Library, 1951.

745. VIERECK, HENRY LORENZ (1881-1926). Entomologist

Papers, 1894-1926. Film. 7 reels.

From Academy of Natural Sciences of Philadelphia. An extensive correspondence, including copies of outgoing letters. Correspondents include Henry Bird, J. Chester Bradley, Wilton E. Britton, Charles T. Brues, Melbourn A. Carriker, Arthur Classen, Frederic E. Clements, Leland O. Howard, and Henry Skinner. All correspondents, with the number of letters from each, are listed in Venia T. Phillips, *Guide to the Manuscript Collections in the Academy of Natural Sciences of Philadelphia* (1963).

746. VOLTAIRE, FRANÇOIS MARIE AROUET DE (1694-1778). *Philosophe.* Larousse

Letters. Photocopies, film. 8 boxes.

Principally letters by Voltaire, collected from various places. They are described and listed in Ira O. Wade, "The Search for a New Voltaire," APS *Trans.* 48, 4 (1958).

747. WALLACE, ANTHONY F. C. (1923–   ). Anthropologist

William Parsons, surveyor and Proprietary agent, 1701-57. 5 notebooks, 2 bundles.

A biography, accompanied by transcripts from sources, photostats, microfilms, and notes.

748. WARNER, JOHN (d. 1873). Amateur mathematician, Pottsville, Pa.

Letters and papers, 1850-64. 255 pieces.

The major portion of the correspondence deals with the controversy which arose when Benjamin Peirce, after having seen the manuscript of Warner's *Studies in Organic Morphology* (Philadelphia, 1857), read a paper on the subject before the A.A.A.S., 1855. Other topics frequently discussed are: the alleged "Harvard clique" and its influence on the A.A.A.S., the administration of the Dudley Observatory in Albany, N.Y., and the United States Coast and Geodetic Survey. Correspondents include: Louis Agassiz, William P. Foulke, Frederick Fraley, Horace Greeley, Joseph Henry, J. Peter Lesley, William F. Miskey, C. F. Winslow. Table of contents (16 pp.).

Deposited by the Academy of Natural Sciences of Philadelphia, 1944.

749. WATSON, JOHN (d. 1826). Physician and antiquary of Bucks County, Pa.

A narrative of the Indian Walk, 1815. 1 vol. Copy.

This copy was made by Watson's son in 1822; it includes the younger Watson's report of the recollections of Moses Bartram as well as his own commentary on the Walking Purchase, and a letter from John Watson, Jr., 1822, about this manuscript. Printed in Hazard's *Register of Pennsylvania* 16 (1830): p. 209.

750. WAUGH, FREDERICK WILKERSON (1872-1924). Canadian ethnologist

Collection of Iroquois folklore, 1912-18. *ca.* 900 pp. Typed, carbon.

Copies of originals in the National Museum of Canada, collected by Waugh at Six Nations Reservation, mostly from Cayuga and Onondaga informants. Indexed. Presented by William N. Fenton, 1951.

751. WAVRAN, ABBÉ C. L. B. "Chapelain de St. Louis à Hesdin"

Essai de phisique. 1 vol.

Presented to Benjamin Franklin; contains chapters on electricity, fire, air, water, earth, earthquakes, etc. Purchased at the sale of Franklin's library, 1803.

752. WAYNE, ANTHONY (1745-96). Soldier. APS 1780. *DAB*

Receipt book, 1785-92. 1 vol.

Signed receipts for Wayne's payment, in money or kind, of debts, taxes, land, commodities, etc.

753. WEEDON, GEORGE (1730?-90). Brigadier general, Continental Army. Appleton

Military correspondence, 1777-86. 1 vol.

Correspondence with officers of the American army and others, principally with Horatio Gates, Nathanael Greene, Thomas Jefferson, Marquis de Lafayette, Richard Henry Lee, J. P. G. Muhlenberg, Thomas Nelson, Baron von Steuben, George Washington, in 1780. Calendared in: *Calendar of the Correspondence Relating to the American Revolution of Brigadier-General George Weedon . . .* (Philadelphia, 1900). Presented by Hugh Mercer, 1835.

754. ——

Valley Forge orderly book, 1777-78. 1 vol.

Published: *Valley Forge Orderly Book of General George Weedon . . .* (New York, 1902).

Presented by Hugh Mercer, 1839.

755. WEER, PAUL, compiler

Bibliography of the *Walam Olum*. Film.

From manuscript in possession of Paul A. W. Wallace, New Cumberland, Pa., 1952. Writings about a chronicle of the Lenape Indians, first studied by Constantine S. Rafinesque and subsequently by Ephraim G. Squier and Daniel G. Brinton. See Weer's letter on the subject in *Pennsylvania History* 18 (1951): p. 266.

756. WELCH, GEORGE (fl. 1671). London trader

Journal of a voyage to the West Indies. 1 vol.

Describes his journey from his home in England to the coast, the long wait for the wind, the voyage, preparations against possible attack by pirates, visits to Barbados, Nevis, and other islands, his arrival at Port Royal in Hispaniola. The manuscript was purchased at the sale of Franklin's library, 1803.

757. WERKMEISTER, WILLIAM HENRY

Driesch's philosophy: an exposition and a critical analysis. Film.

Doctoral dissertation, University of Nebraska, 1927.

758. WEST JERSEY AND SEASHORE RAILROAD

Record of train movements, 1883. 1 vol.

In general, this is a record of movements of trains into and from Camden, with the number of full and empty cars, the times of arrival and departure, reasons for lateness, etc. The donor has inscribed this assurance: "This Ms. vol. of records concerning the West Jersey Railroads for the entire year 1883 will be of value to Railroad men and other students in the future. It was purchased by me in Camden and is official."

Presented by William J. Potts, 1889.

759. WESTERN MISSIONARY SOCIETY OF PENNSYLVANIA

Records, 1804-26. 1 vol. Typed, carbon.

Minutes of a Presbyterian philanthropy (originally Western Missionary Society, for the purpose of promoting and spreading the knowledge of agriculture, literature, and Christianity among the Indian tribes of America) which supported missionaries and schools among the Indians on Lake Erie and in Ohio. Transcribed by Edward I. George under the direction of Rev. Gaius Jackson Slosser, from the original in the library of the Pittsburgh Theological Seminary, 1936.

Presented by Merle H. Deardorff, 1952.

760. WHIPPLE, MRS. GEORGE HOYT, compiler

Scrapbook of Dr. Whipple's Nobel Prize, 1934. 1 vol.

Pictures, newspaper clippings, letters, telegrams, programs, etc., which tell the story of Dr. Whipple's Nobel award—of the news reaching Rochester, N.Y., local comments, the trip to Sweden, the presentation ceremony, etc.

Presented by Mrs. Whipple, 1962.

761. WILBUR, WALTER K.

Comparative study of Aztec hieroglyphs, 1943. 1 vol. Typed.

A study of pre-Conquest hieroglyphs in the Codex Borgia group.

Presented by the author, 1943.

762. WILKS, SAMUEL STANLEY (1906-64). Mathematician, statistician, professor at Princeton University. APS 1948. *Year Book* 1964

Papers, 1940-63. *ca.* 25,000 items.

Chiefly working papers on subjects requiring statistical analysis, and letters, reports, and papers relating to professional organizations, among them: U.S. Air Force Systems Command; American Association for the Advancement of Science projects; study of the life span of the APS members; American Association for Public Opinion Research; American Council on Education; American Educational Research Association; American Institute for Biological Research; American Mathematical Society; American Ordinance Association; American Society for Human Genetics; American Society for Testing Materials; American Statistical Association; ballistic research; College Entrance Examination Board; Institute of Mathematical Statistics; International Statistical Institute; Mathematical Association of America; National Academy of Sciences; National Research Council; National Science Foundation; Office of Ordinance Research; Rand Project; Russell Sage Foundation; Social Science Research Council; Systems Development Corporation; John Wiley and Sons, Inc.; United States government bureaus; various universities. There is little personal material. Table of contents (12 pp.).

Presented by Mrs. Samuel S. Wilks, 1964, and Princeton University, 1965.

763. WILLIAMS, ELEAZAR (1789-1858). Missionary to the Indians. *DAB*

A grammar of the Mohawk dialect of the Iroquois language. Film.

From Missouri Historical Society. Read by title at APS meeting, October 5, 1838, and referred to the Historical and Literary Committee.

764. WILLIAMS, HENRY JONATHAN (1791-1879). Philadelphia lawyer. APS 1833

A brief account of the family of General Jonathan Williams (1751-1815). 1 vol.

Williams, a nephew of Benjamin Franklin, was subsequently chief of the Corps of Engineers, United States Army, and first superintendent of the United States Military Academy at West Point. The genealogical material was "compiled from family records and his own personal knowledge by his son," H. J. Williams, 1873.

765. WILLIAMS, JOHN. Storekeeper, Middletown, Pa.

Day book and ledger, 1773-74. 2 vols.

The day book is a chronological record of sales, with names of purchasers; the ledger arranges the same data by customer. Typical of the articles sold are: sugar, augers, knives, jewelry, thread, tea, linen, coffee, tobacco, combs, fabrics of various sorts, glass panes, wine, rum, ribbon, salt, and frying pans.

766. WILLIAMS, JONATHAN (1750-1815). Merchant, army officer. APS 1787. *DAB*

Selected papers, 1771-1813. Film. 1 reel.

From Indiana University Library. The papers selected are those relating to Benjamin Franklin and APS; they include correspondence among Franklin, William Franklin, Jonathan Williams, Sr., and Jonathan Williams, Jr. (the present figure); also Williams' journal of a trip through England with Benjamin Franklin, Jan Ingenhousz, and John Canton, 1771; also some memoranda and essays by Williams on trade, meteorology, sugar refining; also notes and drawings. Table of contents (5 pp.).

767. WILLIAMSON, Miss ———, and E. A. BOWLES

Crocus: drawings in water color, 1903-05.

768. WILSON, ALEXANDER (1766-1813). Ornithologist. APS 1813. *DAB*

Letters, 1800-09. Film.

From Museum of Comparative Zoology, Harvard University. Chiefly to William Bartram.

769. [WILSON, JAMES?] (1743-98). Lawyer, associate justice of the United States Supreme Court. *DAB*

Account book and diary. 1 vol.

The entries are made in a copy of *Aitken's General American Register* for 1773. Some entries are dated 1774, others 1782-86. The notes are in two hands. The book is a record of receipts and expenses and of some astoundingly intimate actions, the latter almost certainly not Wilson's.

770. WILSON, JAMES PATRIOT (1769-1830). Clergyman. APS 1814. Appleton

Observations while passing thro' the Choctaw, Chickasaw & Cherokee nations, 1803.

Two pages, with additions, addressed to John Vaughan.

771. WISTAR, CASPAR (1761-1818). Philadelphia physician and paleontologist. APS 1787. *DAB*

Letters, 1794-1817. 44 pieces.

Letters to Wistar on botany and paleontology, APS, and instructions to André Michaux for exploring the Missouri, from various persons, including:

Samuel Brown	François André Michaux
Adriaan Gilles Camper	Samuel L. Mitchill
J. F. Corrêa da Serra	Ambroise M. F. J., Baron de
Georges L. C. F. D. Cuvier	Palisot de Beauvois
John G. E. Heckewelder	David Bailie Warden
Thomas Jefferson	

Table of contents (3 pp.).

Presented by Mrs. Esther F. Wistar in memory of her husband, Dr. Mifflin Wistar, 1893.

772. ——

Medical commonplace book, 1796-1813. 1 vol.

Contains observations respecting the yellow fever, with arguments to prove its foreign origin; facts relative to the progress of the fever in 1797; infection of the ship *Deborah;* infection and death of Colonel Van Emburgh; infection of the crew of the Durham boat, 1802; account of the diseases which afflicted the family of James Hammar in Montgomery County; facts relating to the typhus fever of 1812-13; case histories, 1796-1803; temperature chart, 1758-59, 1760; thermometrical journal kept by Charles Norris, 1760-65, copied from his notes in possession of Joseph Parker Norris.

Presented by Mr. and Mrs. Henry G. Leach, 1951.

773. ——

Notes of anatomical lectures, *ca.* 1781-1809. 3 vols.

Presented by Mr. and Mrs. Henry G. Leach, 1952.

774. ——

Note necrologique sur le Docteur Wistar, 1818. By José Francesco Corrêa da Serra. 1 vol. In French.

Included are letters about Wistar written to John Vaughan by Catherine Bache Wistar, Elizabeth Wistar, and others; also the printed eulogiums on Wistar by William Tilghman and Charles Caldwell, and newspaper clippings about his death.

775. WISTER, CHARLES JONES, JR. (d. 1910)

Memoir of Charles J. Wister, 1782-1865. 3 vols.

The elder Wister was a member of APS 1811, and an amateur scientist who erected an astronomical observatory at his Germantown, Pa., home "Grumblethorpe." Printed in Charles J. Wister, Jr., *The Labour of a Long Life: A Memoir of Charles J. Wister* (2 vols., Germantown, 1866-86).

Presented by Charles Grossman, 1962.

776. WOOD, GEORGE BACON (1797-1879). Philadelphia physician. APS 1829. *DAB;* APS *Proc.* **19** (1880)

Papers, 1815-1913. 30 pieces.

Some correspondence relating to the publication and republication of his *Dispensatory of the United States* and *Treatise on Therapeutics and Pharmacology, or Materia Medica* by J. B. Lippincott & Co.; also 12 diplomas and certificates of membership in American and European professional societies.

777. ——

Journal, 1836-49. Film. 1 reel.

From College of Physicians of Philadelphia. A record of travels to Niagara Falls and Quebec, and of professional activities in Philadelphia. A similar journal, 1817-29, was reproduced by mimeograph by a collateral descendant of George B. Wood at Wynnewood, Pa., 1939.

778. WOOD, JOHN (1775-1822). Professor of mathematics, College of William and Mary

Vocabulary of the language of the Nottoway tribe of Indians, 1820. 1 vol.

Obtained from Edie Turner, "an old Indian Woman." This volume contains also John Heckewelder's English-Algonkian and Delaware comparative vocabulary and his Names of various trees, shrubs, and plants in the language of the Lenape.

Presented by Thomas Jefferson, 1820 (Wood manuscripti).

779. WOODORF, ——. Clerk to John Anstey, commissioner for American Loyalists' claims

Journal of a trip through the American states, 1785-88. 1 vol.

The author traveled in all the American seaboard states from Massachusetts and Rhode Island to Georgia. His journal relates their respective histories, describes the towns he visited, comments on episodes of the American Revolution and on the Federal Convention and state ratifying conventions. He and Anstey spent a night at Mount Vernon, 1786.

780. WORMLEY, THEODORE GEORGE (1826-97). Physician, toxicologist. APS 1878. DAB

Correspondence, 1853-96. ca. 75 pieces.

Letters, chiefly on professional appointments and honors, from Samuel D. Gross, Charles F. Himes, S. Weir Mitchell, Benjamin Silliman, Jr., and others; with drafts of replies. Table of contents (2 pp.).

Presented by Mrs. Hiram B. Eliason, 1965.

781. YOUNG, HUGH (d. 1822). Army officer

A topographic memoir on East and West Florida, with itineraries, 1818. Film.

From manuscript in possession of Francis W. Rawle, Albany, N.Y.

782. ZEISBERGER, DAVID (1721-1808). Moravian missionary. DAB

Grammar of the language of the Lenni Lennape, 1816. 1 vol.

Translated from the original German manuscript in the archives of the Society of United Brethren, Bethlehem, Pa., by Peter S. Du Ponceau, 1820; printed, with an introduction by Du Ponceau, in APS Trans., n.s., 3 (1830): p. 65.

Presented by Peter S. Du Ponceau, 1820.

783. ——

On the prepositions of the Onondago language. 1 vol. In German.

784. ——

Onondago-German vocabulary. 1 vol.

Presented by the author.

INDEX

References are to item number. **Boldface** indicates the principal collection.

Abbe, Cleveland, 14, 662
Abbot, Charles G., 82*a*
Abbott, Charles C., 28
Abbott, John, 415
Abbott-Vaughan family, 740
Abeille, Louis Paul, 662
Abel, Sir Frederick August, 510
Abernethy, John, 467
Abert, John James, 18, 114
Abnaki Indians, mission, 736
Abolitionism, 406
Abraham, Max, 104
Académie des Sciences, Paris. See: Institut de France, Académie des Sciences
Académie Royale des Sciences, Paris. See: Institut de France, Académie des Sciences
Academy of Natural Sciences, Philadelphia, 94, 712; letters, 93; minutes, 92
Academy of Philadelphia. See: University of Pennsylvania
Academy of Sciences, Moscow, letters from, 662
Accademia delle Scienze, Turin, corres., 94
Acland, Sir Henry Wentworth, 293, 467
Acoma Keresan Indians, dance music, 102
Adair, William, meteorological observations, 450
Adams, Charles Francis, 95
Adams, Charles Francis, Jr., 575
Adams, Henry, 189
Adams, John, **95**, 401, 520, 741
Adams, John Couch, 467, 510, 662
Adams, John Quincy, 9, 13, 52, **95**, 158, 205, 232, 740
Adams, Samuel, 401
Adams family, papers, 95
Adelung, Frederick, 9, 52
Affleck, Thomas, 306
Africa, anthropology, 709; North, travel and description, 282
Agassiz, Alexander, 28, 398, 598
Agassiz, Elizabeth C., 14
Agassiz, Louis Jean Rodolph, 93, 119, 272, 293, 301, 422, 462, 486, 502, 510, 640, 662, 727, 748
Agriculture, Europe, 234, 254; U.S.: Commissioner of Agriculture, 398; general, 478, 549, 740; Pennsylvania, 392, 525, (farm accounts) 530, 531, (farm diary) 670; Virginia, 430
Ainu language, 424

Air pressure, 234
Airplane, stratospheric flights, 719
Airy, Sir George Biddell, 293, 463, 464, 510, 662
Aitken, Jane, 96
Aitken, Robert, 29, 724; estate, 96
Akenside, Mark, 684
Alaska, Gwenhoot Indians, 102
Albers, J. A., 9
Aldini, Giovanni, 254
Alexander, Caleb, author, 97
Alexander, Jerome, 372
Alexander, John Henry, 117, 272, 333
Alexander, Robert, 121
Alexander, William, Earl of Stirling, 483, 638; author, 98
Algae, 196
Algebra, 520
Algeria, history, 282
Algic Indians. See: Chippewa Indians
Algonkian (Algonkin) Indians, 593; linguistics, 610; religion, 102; vocabularies, 330, 778
Alison, Francis, Sr., 176
Allen, Alexander Viets Griswold, 233
Allen, George, 272, 678
Allen, Harrison, 99
Allen, William, Chief Justice, 164, 679
Allen, William, Jr., 740
Allen family, genealogy, 99
Allibone, Samuel Austin, 678
Allman, George James, 293
Alricks, Harmanus, 679
Alston, Charles, 263
Amaldi, Edoardo, 104
American Academy of Arts and Sciences, 486
American Association for Public Opinion Research, 762
American Association for the Advancement of Science, 149, 732, 748, 762; 1884 meeting, 273
American Bureau for Medical Aid to China, 501
American Council of Learned Societies. Committee on research in American native languages, 499; collection, 101; corres., 100
American Council on Education, 762
American Educational Research Association, 762
American Indian ethnology and linguistics, 102. See also: Indians
American Indians. See: Indians

American Institute for Biological Research, 762

American Institute of Architects. Philadelphia Chapter, records, 103

American Mathematical Society, 762

American Medical Association, 171

American Ordinance Association, 762

American Ornithologists' Union, 426

American Philosophical Society, 1-91; advisory committee, 50a; "Archives," 9; bicentenary of the society, 71-72; building and endowment fund, 77-79; building fund, trustees, 76; centennial celebration, visitors, 84; committee on education and participation in science, 63a; committee on general meeting, 69a; committee on grants, 54a; committee on hall, 54b; committee on nomination of officers, 69b; committee on papers, 69; committees record, 50; committee on revision of laws, 50b; correspondence on the 150th anniversary of the Society, 83; corresponding secretary, 26; curators, 34-37; finance committee, 53-54; Franklin bicentenary, 67-68; "Franklin House," 80; historical and literary committee, 32, 51-52, 322, 367, 437; historical manuscripts, 66; history, 89-91; joint committee with the American Physical Society on theoretical physics, 104; laws and regulations, 7, 50b; letters acknowledging election, 14; librarian, 40-41; library, 42-49, 65, 81; Magellanic premium, 7, 73-74, 81; manuscript communications, 10, 98; mechanical and physical science committee, 64; members: autographs, 19, certificates, 16, deceased list, 17, memoirs, 18, 158, photographs, 20; membership and attendance lists, 12; minutes, 4-6; miscellaneous legal papers, 81; nominations, 13; officers, 21; officers and council, 33; Phillips prize essay, 75; Philosophical Hall, 81, 529; philosophical questions, 82; presidents, 21; printing accounts, 96; publications committee, 55-63; register of visitors, 85; reports of general meetings, 82b; rolls of members, 15; secretary, 26-28; South Polar Exploration, 70; standing orders, 8; treasurer, 29-32; verbal communications, 11; weekly broadcasts, 82a; 94, 132, 149, 171, 231, 240, 248, 255, 272, 408, 413, 455, 457, 502, 605, 629, 723, 762, 766, 771, 775

American Physical Society, joint committee with the APS on theoretical physics, 104

American Red Cross, 105

American Revolution. See: U.S., American Revolution

American Society for Promoting Useful Knowledge, 2, 3

American Society for Human Genetics, 762

American Society for Testing Materials, 762

American Statistical Association, 762

Amherst, Jeffrey, Baron, 170, 561

Amidei, Adolfo, 257

Amoretti, Carlo, 254

Amoss, Harold Lindsay, 500; papers, 105

Ampère, André Marie, 113

Amphlett, William, 428

Anatomy, lectures, U. of Penna., 773

Ancona, Mirella Levi d', author, 106

Anderson, Melford O., 358

Andrade, Edward Neville da Costa, 104

Andrade, Manuel José, 101, 178

Andreani, Count Paolo, 107, 685

Andrews, Emma B., author, 108

Andrews, Miss H. A., 151

Andrews, William, 293

Anemia, medical research, 651

Angiviller, Charles Claude Labillarderie d', count, 454

Anglo-American relations, Society of Friends, 279

Anguiano, Ramón de, author, 109

Angulo, Jaime de, 101

Animal Medical Center, 629

Anisson-Duperon, Jacques Laurent, 254

Annemours, Charles François Adrien Le Paulnier, chevalier d', 355; author, 110

Anstey, John, 779

Anthropology. See specific persons and places

Antill, Edward, 638

Anti-Semitism, 387

Anti-vivisection, 171

Apiculture, 388

Appalachian Mountains, travel and description, 620

Appleman, Charles Orval, 629

Appleton, Jesse, 740

Appleton, Nathaniel, 638

Apprentices Library, Philadelphia, 701

Apprenticeship, 580, 613

Arapaho Indians, Northern, linguistics, 102

Araujo, Antonio de, 112

Arawak Indians, dictionary, 660; grammar, 660

Archaeology, Central America, 474; Egypt, 108; Mexico, 239; South America, 619; U.S., 619, Pennsylvania, 174, Southeastern, 102, Southwest, 380

Architecture, 103, 234

Argentina, travel and description, 689

Arizona, travel and description, 689

Arkansas, Indians, missions, 736; meteorological observations, 729

Armstrong, Edward Cooke, 100

Armstrong, John, 562, 679

Armstrong, John, Jr., 561

Arrhenius, Svante, 508

Art, Rome, 310; U.S.: see under members of Peale family

Arusmont, Francis Wright d', 428

Ascoli, A., 500

Ascoli, Max, 182

Asia, anthropology, 709

Aspden, Matthias, Sr., 557
Astrology, Roman, 208
Astronomy, 98, 155, 272, 463, 464, 520, 723, 740; instruments, 250; observations and calculations: transit of Venus, 250, 275, Mason and Dixon survey, 298, 439, 440, Pennsylvania boundary, 463, 464, 626, miscellaneous, 627, 631; observatories: Lick, 271, Grumblethorpe, 775
Athabaskan Indians, dance, 225, 226; music, 225, 226
Athenaeum of Philadelphia, 29, 81
Athénée de Paris, corres., 113
Atomic bomb, defense, 719
Atomic energy, 826b, 719
Attnaha Indians, vocabulary, 728
Audubon, John James, 13, 114, 154, 415, 475, 502-503
Audubon, Lucy Bakewell, 114
Audubon, Victor Gifford, 114, 398
Auk, The (journal), 426
Aurora borealis, 141
Australasia, anthropology, 709
Ayen, duke of, 234
Ayer, Edward Everett, author, 115
Ayres, E. W., 598
Ayrton, William Eduard, 723
Azambuja, Jacob Frederico Torlade Pereira de, author, 116
Azara, Felix de, 229
Aztec Indians, calendar stone, 405; hieroglyphs, 761

Babbage, Charles, 117, 119, 349, 422, 510, 612
Babington, Charles Cardale, 293
Bache, Albert Dabadie, 118
Bache, Alexander Dallas, 13, 44, 117, 119, 233, 272, 310, 398, 406, 463, 464, 520, 612, 640, 662
Bache, Benjamin Franklin, 123, 338, 355; diary, 120; papers, 121; will, 582
Bache, Catherine (Wistar), 123
Bache, Franklin (1792-1864), 21, 86, 310, 366, 707, 708
Bache, Franklin (1869-ca.1947), 81
Bache, Richard, 121, 123, 321; will, 582
Bache, Sarah (Franklin), 121, 123, 268, 269
Bache, Theophylact, 123
Bache, Thomas Hewson, 122
Bache, William, 123
Bache family, papers, 123
Bachman, George W., 501
Bachman, John, 114, 475
Back, Ernst, 104
Bacon, John, 584
Bailey, Francis, 484
Bainbridge, William, 211
Baird, Spencer Fullerton, 213, 293, 398, 406, 598, 712
Balard, Antoine Jerome, 293

Balbo, Prospero, 94
Balch, Emily G., 624
Baldwin, William, 197
Ball, John, 422
Ball, Mary, 264
Ball, Robert, 253
Ball game, Cherokee, 102
Ballard, Edward, 333
Ballistics, 311, 762
Balloons, 543; stratospheric flights, 719
Bancker, Charles Nicoll, papers, 124
Bancker, James A., letters, 125
Bancker, John, 295
Bancroft, George, 14, 349, 741
Banister, John, Jr., 445
Banister, Thomas, 640
Bank of North America, 191
Bank of Stephen Girard, records, 286
Bank of the United States, 502
Banking, 616
Banks, Sir Joseph, 11, 141, 220, 254, 346, 355, 462, 525, 724, 740; papers, 126
Baptists, 159
Barbeau, Charles Marius, author, 102, 127, 128, 224, 296, 709
Barbé-Marbois, François, marquis de, 685
Barbeu-Dubourg, Jacques, 337
Barclay, Robert, 265
Bard, John, 176, 623
Barden, Edward E., 678
Barker, Anna E., 129
Barker, George Frederick, 723
Barlow, Joel, 158, 525
Barnard, Frederick Augustus Porter, 272, 398
Barns, plan of, 476
Barrett, Helen Jennings, 370
Barringer, Daniel Moreau, 575, 723
Barron, Samuel, 211
Bartlett, Harley Harris, collection, 130
Bartol Research Foundation, Franklin Institute, 719
Barton, Benjamin Smith, 10, 11, 42, 44, 176, 195, 496, 607, 662, 727; journals, 131; papers, 132; vocabularies, 133
Barton, Richard P., 11
Barton, Thomas, 307, 562
Barton, William Paul Crillon, 195, 197
Bartram, Isaac, 355
Bartram, John, corres., 134-136, 198, 415; John Bartram Association, papers, 137
Bartram, Moses, 10, 701, 749
Bartram, William, 132, 198, 768; diary, 138
Barus, Carl, autobiog., 139
Bass, Lawrence Wade, 144
Bassi, Laura, 141
Bate, Charles Spence, 293
Bates, W. H., 216
Batik language, 130
Bauer, Edmond, 104
Bauman, S., 586

Bayne-Jones, Stanhope, 105
Beaches, 314
Beadle, Elias R., 662
Beadle, George Wells, 144, 629
Beard, Joseph Willis, 500
Beasley, Frederick, 18
Beauchamp, W. M., author, 140
Beaumont, Elie de, 662
Beccari, Odoardo, 422
Beccaria, Giovanni Battista, 155; papers, 141
Beche, Sir Henry Thomas de la, 422
Beck, Lewis Caleb, 616, 662
Beckley, John, 685
Beckwith, H. K., 105
Beckwith, Martha Warren, 151
Becquerel, Jean, 104
Begue de Presle, Achille Guillaume le, 359
Belden, Louis C., author, 142
Belknap, Jeremy, 173, 210
Bell, Robert, 484
Bell, Thomas, 253
Belmar, Francisco, author, 143
Benedicks, Carl, 104
Benedict, Ruth Fulton, 517; biog., 446
Benezet, Anthony, 303
Benezet, Daniel, 306
Benezet, James, 164
Benjamin, Park, 555
Bentham, George, 422, 467
Berenson, Bernard, 108
Berger, John Eric, 220
Bergmann, Max, papers, 144
Berkeley, Miles Joseph, 293
Berkhofer, Robert Frederick, Jr., author, 145
Berkner, Lloyd Viel, 629
Berliner, Arnold, 104
Bernard, Sir Francis, 638
Berny, Pierre Jean Paul, author, 146
Bertin, Exupère Joseph, 465a
Berzelius, Johan Jakob, 220, 662
Bessey, Charles Edwin, 292
Biddle, Charles, 211, 561
Biddle, Clement, 355, 701
Biddle, Clement Cornell, 18, 117, 221
Biddle, Francis, 82a
Biddle, James, 211, 307
Biddle, Nicholas, 232, 409, 410; queries to William Clark, 147
Biddle, Owen, 303
Biddle, William, 164
Bienville, Jean Baptiste Le Moyne, Sieur de, 386
Bigelow, Jacob, 197, 415
Bigelow, Poultney, 231
Bigler, William, 482
Billings, John Shaw, 398, 510
Billings, William, journals, 148
Bingham, William, 158, 603, 640
Biological Abstracts, 149
Biological Society of Washington, 426

Bioluminescence, 311
Biot, Jean Baptiste, 220
Birch, Thomas, 543
Bird, Henry, 745
Bird, John, 250
Bird, Junius, 174
Bird, Robert Montgomery, 475
Birds. See: Ornithology
Birge, Raymond Thayer, 104
Birth control, 517
Bissell, Friedrich Wilhelm, 349
Bissing, Friederich Wilhelm von, 108
Black, Robert A., 102
Blackett, Patrick Maynard Stuart, 104
Blackwell, Elizabeth, 467, 510
Blagden, Sir Charles, 349, 640
Blainville, Henri Marie Ducrotay de, 293
Blair, John, 445
Blakeslee, Albert Francis, 149, 218, 629
Blanchard, Jean Pierre, 13
Bland, Thomas, 293
Blodget, Lorin, 150, 398
Blood, 387; groups, 149
Bloomfield, Leonard, 100
Bloss & Johnson, London, 305
Blumenbach, Johann Friedrich, 662
Blumer, Herbert, 372
Blumstein, Alex, 500
Blyth, Edward, 253
Boardman, Henry A., 18
Boas, Franz, 28, 100, 144, 231, 446, 499, 517, 709; family corres., 151; materials for American linguistics, 101; Nootka vocabularies, 152
Boerhaave, Hermann, 280
Bogoras, Waldemar, 151
Bohr, Niels Henrik David, 104
Bohrn, A., 216
Boilers, explosions, 272
Bok, Edward W., 171
Boker, George Henry, 678
Bonaparte, Charles Lucien Jules Laurent, **153**, **154**, 293, 502, 509, 662
Bond, George P., 640
Bond, Thomas, Sr., 176, 190, 303
Bonnet, Charles, 383
Bonomi, Joseph, 293
Book illumination, Italy, 106
Booth, James Curtis, 272
Bordley, John Beale, 525
Born, Max, 104
Boruet, E., 196
Boscovich, Roger Joseph (Boscovitch, Ruggiero Giuseppe), 254, 662; papers, 155
Bosse, Mme A. Weber von, 196
Bostock, John, 220
Botany, 138, 197, 199, 234, 263, 292, **379**, 422, 432, 616, 629, 636, 686, 726, 771; Europe, 254; United States, 196, **379**, 425, **452**, 453, **454**, 477, **478**, 480, Michigan, 692,

New Jersey, 375, New York, 607, Pennsylvania, 375, **478**, 607; Mexico, 677; Cherokee economic botany, 102; drawings, 735, 767; Lenni Lenape terms, 331, 778; John Bartram Association, 137; biog. of William Sherard, 518. See names of individual botanists
Botta, Carlo, 254
Bouchard-Chantereaux, Nicolas Robert, 293
Bouchell, S., 725
Boudinot, Elias, 52
Bouger, Pierre, 465*a*
Bouquet, Henry, 163, 170, 679
Bowden, Witt, 182
Bowditch, Charles P., 151
Bowditch, Henry Ingersoll, 117
Bowditch, Nathaniel, 117, 741
Bowdoin, James, Sr., 603
Bowdoin College, 740
Bowen, Thomas Bartholomew, 156
Bowerbank, James Scott, 215
Bowles, E. A., 767
Bowles, William Lisle, 293
Boyd, John, 561
Boyd, Paul Prentice, 372
Braddock, Edward, 562
Bradford, S. D., 708
Bradford, Thomas, Jr., 571
Bradley, James Chester, 745
Bragg, Sir William Henry, 662, 723
Brant, Joseph, 170, 493, 507
Brashear, John Alfred, 723
Brattle, Thomas, 640
Brazil, Christianity, 112
Breakwaters, 314
Breck, Samuel, 457, 475; Continental currency, 157; recollections, 158
Bree, Charles Robert, 253
Breintnall, Esther (Parker), 164
Breintnall, Joseph, 199
Breit, Gregory, 104
Bretagne, baron de, 685
Brewer, Joseph, author, 159
Brewing, Philadelphia, 303
Brewster, Benjamin Harris, 481
Brice, James, 573
Bridges, Calvin Blackman, 473
Brigham Young University, Archaeological Society, 285
Brillon de Jouy, Anne Louise Boyvin d'Hardancourt, 266; musical compositions, 160; plays, 161
Brinton, Daniel Garrison, 755
Brinton, Ward, 501
Brisson, Mathurin Jacques, 234
Brissot de Warville, Jean Pierre, 158, 724
British West Indies, 294
Britton, Nathaniel Lord, 151
Britton, Wilton Everett, 745
Brockden, Charles, 679

Broderip, William John, 293
Brodie-Innes, J., 216
Broglie, Louis de, 104
Brongniart, Alexandre, 475
Brongniart, Alexandre Théodore, 186
Bronk, Detlev Wulf, 500, 508, 629
Brooke, Charles Frederick Tucker, editor, 277
Brookes, Joshua, 293
Brooks, Phillips, 233
Brown, Robert, 349
Brown, Samuel, 10, 612, 771
Browne, John Ross, 678
Brown-Séquard, Charles Edouard, 467
Brues, Charles Thomas, 745
Brugnatelli, Luigi Gaspard, 254
Bryan, R. W., 100
Bryce, James, author, 162
Bryn Mawr College, 260
Buchan, Earl of. See: David Steuart Erskine
Buchanan, James, 221
Bucholz, John Theodore, 149
Buckland, Francis Trevelyan, 253
Buckland, William, 215, 293, 348, 349, 475, 640
Buckley, Samuel Botsford, 726
Buffon, Alexandre Henri Nadault de, 662
Bull, William, Jr., 199
Bumpus, Herman Carey, 151
Bunbury, Sir Charles James, 422
Burbank, Luther, 372, 688
Burd, Edward, 679
Burd, Edward Shippen, 240, 264
Burd, James, 170, 261, 568, 679, 683; accounts, 164; papers, 163
Burd, Joseph, 164
Burd family, 164
Burnet, John, 465
Burnet, John, Jr., 465
Burnet, Philip, 372
Burnet, William, 040
Burr, Aaron, 268, 741
Burr, Charles H., author, 165
Burroughs, Marmaduke, 428
Busby, C. A., 9
Bush, Vannevar, 149, 723
Bushnell, Horace, 406
Busk, George, 215, 293, 422
Buthe, J. M., 18
Butler, Benjamin F., 14
Butler, Elmer Grimshaw, 372
Butler, Nicholas Murray, 151
Butler, Pierce, 584
Butler, Richard, 170
Butler, Zebulon, 561
Button, F. L., 662
Buxton, Charles, 509
Buxtorf, Johann, author, 166
Byrd, William, author, 167

Cadwalader, Lambert, 9

Cadzow, Donald A., 174

Caille, Abbé de la, 465*a*

Cairns, Hugh, 260

Cakchiquel Indians, grammars and vocabularies, 168

Caldwell, Charles, 44, 355, 475, 662, 774

Calhoun, John Caldwell, 221, 589

Calhoun, Morgan, 710

California, travel and description, 370

Calkins, Gary Nathan, 372

Cameron, Simon, 482

Campbell, John, Earl of Loudoun, 228

Campbell, William M., 358

Camper, Adriaan Gilles, 771

Canada, travel and description, 193, 312, 591; Indians: materials in Public Archives, Ottawa, 170, catalogue of songs in National Museum, 169

Canals, 520

Candolle, Augustin Pyramus de, 248

Canisius, Sister Mary. See: Mary Canisius, Sister

Cannon, Walter Bradford, **171**, 182, 260, 508

Canton, John, 640, 766

Capital punishment, 310

Carey, Mathew, 18, 484; accounts, 172; letter books, 173

Caribou, Labrador, 734

Carlisle, Pa., 568

Carnegie Institution of Washington, 149, 688; Department of Genetics, 218

Carpenter, Edmund Snow, author, 174

Carpenter, Philip Pearsall, 509

Carpenter, William Benjamin, 422

Carpenters Company, Philadelphia, papers, 175

Carr, Malcolm, 178

Carr, Robert, 213

Carriker, Melbourn Armstrong, 745

Carroll, John, 173

Carter, Charles, of Cleve, 638

Carter, Howard, 108

Carson, Joseph, author, 176

Cass, Lewis, 427

Cassatt, Alexander J., 555

Cassini, Jacques, 465*a*

Cassini de Thury, César François, 465*a*

Castelnuovo, Gina, 500

Castiglioni, Count Luigi, 687

Castiglioni, Pauline, 687

Castle, William Ernest, 218; papers, 177

Caswell, Alexis, 272

Cataract Construction Company, 666

Catesby, Mark, 640

Cattell, James McKeen, 100, 144, 151, 372, 629

Cattell, Jaques, 144, 372

Cayuga Indians, 102

Cazenove, Théophile, 507

Central America, archaeology, 474; dictionaries, 178, 660; grammars, 178, 660; Indians, 517; Middle America cultural anthropology materials, 178; travel and description, 109, 474

Central High School, Philadelphia, 309, 723

Cercle des Philadelphes, Cap-François, 179

Ceuta, Africa, 282

Chalmers, George, papers, 180

Chambers, Robert, biog., 460

Champollion, Jean François, 662

Channing, William Ellery, 117, 310

Chapin, Israel, 507, 586

Chapman, Henry Cadwalader, 398

Charles II, king of England, 564

Charles, Jacques Alexandre César, 254

Chastellux, François Jean, marquis de, 158

Chattanooga, Tenn., social life, 664

Chauncy, Charles, 603

Chavez, Edward A., 151

Chemistry, 113, 220, 234, 310, 311; lectures, 531, 653; phlogiston theory, 604. See individual chemists

Cherokee Indians, ball game, 102; description, 285, 770; economic botany, 102; grammars and vocabularies, 710; medicine, 418, 710; missions among, 736; record book, 181

Chesney, Alan Mason, 105

Chew, Benjamin, 303, 679, 697

Chew, Benjamin, Jr., 685

Chew, Joseph, 170

Cheyenne Indians, texts, 102

Cheyney, Edward Potts, editor, 182

Chicago, University of, 231

Chickasaw Indians, description, 770; missions to, 736

Child, Lydia Maria, 406

Chile, travel and description, 689

China, Language and lexicons, 288, 424, 448; sketches and drawings, 550; trade, 125, 634; travel and description, Canton, 211; writing, 372

China Packet (ship), logbook, 634

China trade, 125, 634

Chippewa Indians, customs, 427; language, 364, 427

Choctaw Indians, description, 770; missions to, 736; vocabulary, 496

Cholti Indians, grammar and vocabulary, 469

Churchman, John, 10, 640, 662

Cigna, Gian Francesco, 141

Civil War. See U.S., Civil War

Clairaut, Alexis Claude, 465*a*

Clap, Thomas, 638

Clark, Alvin, 463, 464

Clark, Andrew, 510

Clark, Raymond P., Jr., author, 183

Clark, William (1732-1774), letters, 650

Clark, William (1770-1813), 147, 409, 410, 589, 616; biog., 419; diary, 184; journal, 185

Clarke, Alexander Ross, 662
Clarke, Cora Huidekoper, 196
Clarke, George, 416
Clarke, James Freeman, 406
Clarke, Thomas, 274
Classen, Arthur, 745
Claus, Daniel, 170, 562
Clay, Henry, 232, 513
Claypole, James, 559
Claypoole, Elizabeth (Betsy Ross), 701
Clayton, John (1657-1725), 640
Clayton, John (1694-1773), 176, 415
Cleaveland, Moses, 507
Cleaveland, Parker, 475, 726, 740, 741; papers, 186
Cleaver, Isaac, 197
Cleland, Ralph Erskine, 149, 629
Clements, Frederick E., 745
Clemson, Thomas Green, 612
Clifford, John, 11
Clinton, DeWitt, 415, 482
Clinton, George, 321, 493
Clinton, Sir Henry, 697
Clymer, George, 264, 697; papers, 187; will, 582
Clymer, L., 188
Coal, Japan, 424; U.S., 132, 424, 520
Coard, Robert L., author, 189
Coates, Beulah, 190
Coates, Margaret, 190
Coates, Mary, 190
Coates, Samuel, 190, 240; accounts, 191
Coates, Thomas, 192
Cobbett, William, 158
Cockcroft, Sir John Douglas, 104
Coffin, Charles Albert, Jr., 723
Coffin, Charles P., 388
Coffyn, Francis, 359
Cohen, Hennig, author, 705
Cohn, Alfred Einstein, 144
Coinage, Europe, 254
Colbert Maulevrier, Edouard Charles Victurnien, count de, journal, 193
Colchicine, 149
Colden, Cadwalader, 176, 198, 415
Coldspring longhouse (Seneca), 102
Cole, Fay-Cooper, 709
Cole, Sir Henry, 340, 356
Cole, Rufus, 105
Coleman, William, 679
Coleridge, Samuel Taylor, marginalia, 194
College Entrance Examination Board, 762
College of Philadelphia. See: University of Pennsylvania
College of Physicians, Philadelphia, 29, **195**
Collin, Nicholas, 9, 42, 45
Collins, Frank Shipley, papers, 196
Collins, Zaccheus, 44, 93, 191, **197**, 616, 727
Collinson, Peter, 176, **198**, **199**, 415, 416, 640, 662

Colorado River, travel and exploration, 597, 599
Columbia University, 151
Combe, George, 320, 475
Comets, 450
Commerce and navigation, Anglo-American relations (1794-1807), 252
Compass, variation of, 98
Compton, Arthur Holly, 104
Compton, Karl Taylor, 662
Comstock, William, 231
Conchology, 253, 656; Pacific area, 301
Condorcet, Marie Jean Antoine Nicolas de Caritat, marquis de, author, 200
Conestoga Indians, 496
Conference on Science Manuscripts, 201
Congo Free State, description, 111
Conklin, Edwin Grant, 22, 23, 28, 82a, 182, 260
Connecticut, University of, 149
Conrad, T. A., 475
Constable, William, 264, 265
Contrecœur, Claude Pierre Pécaudy, sieur de, 170
Conway, Moncure Daniel, 292, 406
Conybeare, William Daniel, 422
Conyngham, Redmond, 18, 52
Cooke, Charles, author, 102, 202
Cooke, Sir William Fothergill, 509
Coolidge, William David, 629, 723
Coombe, Thomas, Jr., 307
Cooper, Sir Astley, 662
Cooper, Lady Mary, 509
Cooper, Thomas, 11, 176, 186, 205, 220, 462, 561, 662, 741
Cooper, William (1754-1809), 265
Cooper, William (1798-1864), 114, **153**, 154, 475
Cooper, Sir William White, 509
Cope, Edward Drinker, 406, 597, 662, 712; diaries, 203
Cope, Thomas P., 232
Coqueral, Athanase Laurent Charles, 348
Coral islands, 215
Corbyn, Thomas, 355
Cornell, Walter S., 501
Corner, George Washington, 105
Corning, Howard, 114
Cornplanter, Edward, 204
Cornplanter, Jesse, author, 204
Corrêa da Serra, Edward J., 205
Corrêa da Serra, José Francesco, 18, 248, 348, 415, 771, 774; papers, 205; biog. materials, 206
Corwin, Edward S., 82a
Cosmic rays, 719
Costa Rica, Indian languages, 276
Coster, Dirk, 104
Coto, Thomas, author, 168
Coues, Elliott, 398, 462, 598

Councilman, William Thomas, 260
Court de Gébelin, Antoine, 254
Courtivron, marquis de, 465*a*
Cowan, Thomas William, 388
Cowdry, Edmund Vincent, 372
Cowles, Rheinhart Parker, 372
Cox, Harold R., 500
Coxe, Daniel T., 207
Coxe, John Redman, 186, 207, 662
Coxe, Julian Halliday, 207
Coxe, Tench, 173, 497
Craftsmen, Philadelphia, 606
Craig, Isaac, 586
Cramer, Frederick Henry, author, 208
Crane, M. E., 151
Craniology, 475
Crawford, Earl of. See: John Lindsay
Creek Indians, description, 315; missions to,
    736
Crell, Lorenz, 254
Crelle, August Leopold, 253
Cresap, Thomas, 180
Cresson, Ezra Townsend, 712
Cresson, Frank C., 174
Cresson, James, 631
Cresson, John C., 86
Cret, Paul Philippe, 555
Crèvecœur, J. Hector St. John, 158
Crèvecœur de Perthes, Jacques Boucher de,
    555
Crocus, drawings, 767
Croghan, George, 163, 344, 562, 679
Crompton, Robert E., 723
Cross, Wilbur Lucius, 372
Crozier, William J., 196
Crukshank, Joseph, 484
Cuming, Hugh, 253, 293
Cummings, Hubertis Maurice, author, 209
Currency, 310; Continental, 157; New Jersey,
    491; Portuguese, 116
Currie, William (1754-1828), 176
Curson, Samuel, meteorological observations,
    450
Curtis, George W., 233
Curtis, John, 422
Curtis, Peter, 11
Cushing, Thomas, 638
Custis, George Washington Parke, 553
Cutler, Manasseh, letters, 210
Cutter, George Washington, 723
Cuvier, Georges Léopold Chrétien Frédéric
    Dagobert, baron de, 254, 462, 510, 771

Da Costa, Jacob M., 86
Dadant, Charles, 388
Dakin, Henry Drysdale, 144
Dakota Indians, missions to, 736
Dale, Richard, papers, 211
Dallas, Alexander J., 42
Dallas, George Mifflin, 232, 481

Dana, James Dwight, 14, 293, 398, 406, 463,
    464, 486, 598
Dance. See: Indians
Dancing, Philadelphia, 583
Dandolo, Vicenzo, 254
Darcet, Jean, 254
Darlington, Benjamin Smith Barton, 212
Darlington, William, 176, 195, 415, 462, 712;
    letters, 212, 213
Darrach, Charles Gobrecht, author, 214
Darragh, Lydia, 701
Darrow, Karl K., 82*a*
Darwin, Sir Charles Galton, 104
Darwin, Charles Robert, corres., 14, 214, **215-
    216**, 217, 253, 293, 301, 356, 422, 510; in-
    fluence on religion and politics, 514;
    reminiscences of, by James Bryce, 162. See
    also: Evolution
Darwin, Sir Francis Galton, 467; letters, 217
Dashkova, Ekaterina Romanovna, princess, 13
Datura, 149
Daubenton, Louis Jean Marie, 234
Davenport, Charles Benedict, 149; papers, 218
Davezac, M., 18
David, Theodore M., 108
David Library of the American Revolution,
    Washington Crossing, Pa., collection, 219
Davidson, George, 272
Davis, Bradley Moore, 149, 196
Davy, Sir Humphry, corres., 220, 254, 510
Dawes, Elizabeth F., collector, 221
Day, Gordon M., 222
Dean, James, 223
Deane, Sidney Norton, author, 223
DeBerdt, Dennys, 684
DeBow, James Dunwoody Brownson, 678
Debye, Peter Joseph William, 104
Decompression sickness, 311
Deering, Frank C., collector, 224
DeForest, Lee, 723
De-ka-na-wi-da, 494
DeKay, James Ellsworth, 154, 475
de Laguna, Frederica, notes, 225, 226
DeLancey, William Heathcote, 18
Delavan, Edward Cornelius, 726
Delaware, grant to W. Penn, 564; Lewes,
    meteorological observations, 450; Wilming-
    ton, longitude, 627
Delaware Indians. See: Lenni Lenape Indians
Deleuze, Joseph Philippe François, 254
Dellenbaugh, Frederick Samuel, 599
Demerec, Milislav, 218
Dencke, Christian Frederick Heinrich, 324,
    477
Denny, William, 344
De Peyster, James, 525
De Peyster, John Philip, 555
Depping, George B., 18
Dercum, Francis Xavier, 23, 723
Desor, Edouard, 406
Detroit Indians, 170

de Vries, Hugo, 508
Dewar, James, 510
Dewey, Chester, 727
Dexter, Aaron, 210, 740
Dick, Sir Alexander, 471
Dickerson, Mahlon, 52, 211
Dickinson, John, 233, 307, 525, 697
Dictionaries. See under Indians, China, and Hebrew
Dieke, Gerhard Heinrich, 104
Dillingham, William H., 18
Diplomacy, 146, 740
Dirac, Paul Adrien Maurice, 104
Dix, Dorothea, 463, 464
Dixon, Jeremiah, 250, 441, 683. See also: Mason and Dixon survey
Dixon, Roland Burrage, 101, 151
Dobbs, Arthur, 199, **228**
Doblaz, Gonzalo de, author, 229
Dobson, Thomas, 484
Dodge, Bernard Ogilvie, papers, 230
Dohrin, Anton, 398
Doll, Eugene Edgar, 178
Domm, Lincoln Valentine, 372
Don, George, 422
Donaldson, Henry Herbert, papers, 231
Doornik, Jacob Elisa, 475
Dorsey, John Syng, 191
Dougherty, Denis, Cardinal, 23
Drake, Daniel, 13
Drew, Virginia, 178
Driesch, Hans Adolf Eduard, author, 757
Drinker, Henry, 187, 270, 586, 725
Drinker, Henry Sandwith, 629
Drinkwater, George R., 517
Duane, Charles William, 233
Duane, Deborah (Bache), 233
Duane, Mary (Morris), 233
Duane, Russell, 233
Duane, William (1760-1835), 233, 525, 672, 708
Duane, William (1807-1882), 233
Duane, William John, 233, 482; memoirs, 232
Duane family, papers, 233
Dubos, René Jules, 144
DuChaillu, Paul Belloni, 293, 502
Duché, Jacob, Jr., 307
Dudley, Paul, 640
Dudley Observatory, Albany, N.Y., 748
Duelling, 740
Duffield, Edward, biog., 614
Duggan, B. M., 629
Duhail, Louis Stephen, 18
Duhamel du Monceau, Henri Louis, 465a, 662; papers, 234
Duke of York's Laws, 565
Dumas, Jean Baptiste, biog., 235
Dumas, Jean Baptiste André, author, 235
Duméril, André Marie Constant, 293
Dunbar, William, 10, 352, 495; journal, 237

Dunglison, Robley, 86, 310, 612, 662; autobiog., 238
Dunn, Gano, 723
Dunn, Leslie Clarence, 177
Dunn, Nathan, Chinese museum, 81
Dunn, Thomas, 389
Dupaix, Guillermo, author, 239
Du Ponceau, Peter Stephen, 9, 32, 44, 93, 133, 191, 205, **240-247**, 255, 346, 348, 364, 366, 367, 475, 496, 525, 708, 727; Law Academy, 391; history of APS, 89; letters from J. G. E. Heckewelder, 323; translation, 284
du Pont (de Nemours), Eleuthère Irénée, 248, 741
du Pont (de Nemours), Henry Algernon, 248
du Pont (de Nemours), Henry Francis, 629
du Pont (de Nemours), Pierre Samuel, 10, 248, 741
du Pont (de Nemours), Victor Marie, 248, 741
du Pont de Nemours family, papers relating to the APS, 248
Dupré, Augustin, medals, 249
Duquesne de Menneville, Ange, marquis, 170
Durand, Elie Magloire, 93, 712, 726
Dutilh, Stephen, 244
Dutton, Clarence Edward, 598
Dwight, Timothy (1752-1817), 173
Dynamometer, 706

Eandi, Giuseppe Antonio Francesco Girolamo, 141
Earthquakes, 141
East India Company, transit of Venus, 250
Eastlake, Martha Lee (Simpson), 689
Eaton, Amos, 186, 346, 475, 620, 726
Eaton, William, 211
Ebeling, Christoph Daniel, 479, 694
Eccles family, 587
Eckley, John, 559
Eclipses, lunar, 275, 298; solar, 272, 275, 298
Eddington, Arthur Stanley, 104
Eddy, Caspar Wistar, 197
Eddy, Thomas, 264
Edinburgh, University of, 263; lecture tickets, 648
Edison, Thomas Alva, 462, 510, 555, 723
Edsall, Geoffrey, 500
Education, 272; of American Indians, 449, 513; in England, 356, 601; in France, 113; in Switzerland, 120; in United States, 119, 124, 233, 406, 475; in Philadelphia, 199; elementary, 468; legal, 391; medical, 260, 280, 332, 355, 387, 471, 512, 625, 648, 684, 773; schoolbooks, 97, 659
Edwards, Benjamin, 251
Egerton, Sir Philip de Malpas Grey, 253, 422
Egypt, hieroglyphs, 289; travel and description, 108
Ehrenfest, Paul, 104
Einstein, Albert, 104, 144, 462, 662, 719

Eiseley, Loren Corey, 709
Ekhart, Walter, 501
Electrets, 719
Electricity, 141, 234, 272, 520, 543, 723, 740; atmospheric, 719; Niagara Falls, N.Y., 666
Electrodynamics, 719
Eliot, Charles W., 14
Eliot, Jared, 638
Elkins, Wilson H., author, 252
Ellerton, John Lodge, 510
Ellicott, Andrew, 10, 355, 525
Ellicott, Joseph, 507
Elliott, Stephen, 197, 483; biog., 213
Ellis, John, 415
Elmsley, Peter, 359
Emerson, Ralph Waldo, 310, 406
Emory, William Hemsley, 272, 398
Enders, John Franklin, 629
Engerrand, G. C., 151
Engineering, 119, 314, 424, 468, 513, 555, **665, 666, 668,** 672
England, travel and description, eighteenth cent., 254, 434, 766; nineteenth cent., 577
Entomology, 138, 234, **398,** 478, 656, 726; drawings, 395, 656
Epidemics, 310
Eppes, John Wayles, 366
Erb, Lawrence, 573
Ericsson, John, 510
Erskine, David Steuart, Earl of Buchan, **482**
Erving, George William, 428
Espy, James Pollard, 612
Ethnography. See: Indians, ethnography
Ethnomedicine, Navaho, 102
Ettawageshik, Jane Esther (Willets), 102
Ettwein, John, 327
Eugene of Savoy, Prince, 412
Europe, travel and description, eighteenth cent., 107, 155, 412, 471; nineteenth cent., 115, 406, 428, 463, 616, 666, 692, 694, 695, 723; twentieth cent., 629, 692
Evans, Cadwalader, 392
Evans, Lewis, 638
Evans, Oliver, 10
Everett, Edward, 13, 117, 462, 486, 741
Everett, William, 678
Evolution, 171, 214, **215, 301,** 356, **372, 422;** and religion, 467; Robert Chambers and evolution, 460; in English poetry, 596; meaning of, 690; Darwin's influence on religion and politics, 514; reminiscences of Darwin, 162
Ewing, John, 355
Expedition to the Rocky Mountains (1819-1820). See: Stephen H. Long
Exploration. See under country or area, travel and description
Eyton, Thomas Campbell, 215, 356, 509; corres, 253

Fabroni, Giovanni Valentino Mattia, 220; papers, 254
Fackenthal, Frank Diehl, 151, 629
Fadden, Ray, 102
Falconer, Nathaniel, 306
Faraday, Michael, 14, 293, 310, 510, 612
Farlow, William Gibson, 230, 712
Farmer, Lewis, 303
Farmers & Mechanics Bank, Philadelphia, 715
Farr, William, 612
Farrand, Livingston, 231
Favi, Francesco, 254
Featherstonhaugh, George William, 117, **255,** 475, 486, 741
Febiger, Christian, 191
Feins, Claire K., author, 256
Felician Society, Feliciana County, Ill., 616
Fenger, ———, 332
Fenton, William N., 204
Fermi, Enrico, 104, 257
Fernandez de Medrano, Sebastian, poems, 282
Ferrell, John A., 501
Férussac, André Etienne, 656
Fessenden, William Pitt, 119
Fields, Harold B., author, 258
Fillmore, Millard, 513
Finley, John Huston, 218
Fire-fighting, 310
Fischer, Willie, 196
Fisher, G. S., 174
Fisher, Irving, 218
Fisher, John, 310
Fisher, Joshua Francis, 89, 333, 707, 708
Fisher, Richard, 310
Fitch, Asa, 293
Fitch, Thomas, 561
Fitton, William Henry, 422
Fitzpatrick, Franklin E., author, 259
Fitzsimons, Thomas, 497, 671
Five Nations. See: Iroquois Indians
Flagler, Henry Morrison, 513
Fleming, John, 422
Fleming, John Adam, 723
Fleming, William, 366
Fletcher, Sir Angus, 82a
Fletcher, Benjamin, 559, 564
Fletcher, Charles Robert Leslie, 467
Flexner, Abraham, 260
Flexner, Helen (Thomas), 508
Flexner, Simon, 105, 144, 500, 508; papers, 260
Flinn, John E., 149
Flint, Austin, 406
Florida, geography, 781; travel and description, 135, 281, 397
Flower, Sir William Henry, 215, 253, 293, 301, 422, 467, 510
Fogelson, Raymond D., 102
Fokker, Adriaan Daniel, 104
Folger, Walter, 464

Folklore, American Indian, 101, 750; Maine, 517; West Indian, 517
Fontana, Felice, 155, 254, 359
Fooks, Paul, 303, 307
Forbes, Alexander, of Balogie, 465
Forbes, David, 215
Forbes, Edward, 253, 293, 422, 510
Forbes, Elizabeth, 465
Forbes, Jacques C. B., 102
Forbes, James David, 612
Forel, Auguste H., 216
Forster, George, 254
Forster, Johann Reinhold, 254, 662
Forsyth, William, 379
Fort Augusta, Pa., 164, 351, 496, 568; accounts, orderly books, and records, 163; quartermaster, 261
Fort Bedford, Pa., 170
Fort Granville, Pa., accounts, 568
Fort Hunter, Pa., 163
Fort Pitt, Pa., 170; quartermaster, 262
Fort Wilkinson, Ga., 317
Fort William Henry, N.Y., 163
Fortnightly Club, 88. See also Wistar Association
Fortune, Reo Franklin, 446
Fosdick, Harry Emerson, 105
Foster, Sir Michael, 215
Fothergill, Anthony, 44, 338
Fothergill, John, 176, 199, 232, 263, 355, 684
Fougeroux de Bondaroy, Auguste Denis, 234
Foulke, William Parker, 748
Fowler, Alfred, 104
Fox, Charles Pemberton, family legal papers, 264
Fox, George (d. 1828), 264, 265, 270
Fox, Joseph, 264
Fox, Samuel M., 264
Foxcroft, John, 303
Frachtenberg, Leo Joachim, 151
Fraley, Frederick, 272, 555, 748
France, Revolution (1789), 445, 605; reign of terror, 687; travel and description, 203; treaty with Spain (1761), 282
Francis, Tench, 187
Franciscan Order, missionaries in Spanish America, 420
Franck, James, 104
Frankfurter, Felix, 624
Franklin, Benjamin, 120, 121, 141, 146, 173, 219, 233, 266, 303, 305, 307, 319, 321, 335, 338, 344, 359, 403, 416, 434, 525, 555, 603, 623, 638, 679, 716, 740, 741, 751, 764, 766; anecdotes, 470; autobiog., 189; biog., 511; bust, 443; and Canada, 698; estate, 123; houses, 81, 358; legacy to Philadelphia, 579; research on, by W. E. Lingelbach, 413, by Jared Sparks, 707, 708; will, 582
Franklin, Deborah (Read), 306
Franklin, James, Jr., 267

Franklin, John, 561
Franklin, Margaret (Markoe), 121
Franklin, William, 123, 268, 269, 766
Franklin, William Temple, 123, 264, 265, 268, 270, 497, 741
Franklin & Hall, 305
Franklin Institute, Philadelphia, 272; Bartol Research Foundation, 719; meteorological observations, 363
Franks, David, 303
Fraser, Thomas E., 271
Frazer, John Fries, 18, 233, 272, 398, 406
Frazer, Persifor, papers, 273
Frazer, Robert, 121, 274
Free Library of Philadelphia, 408
Freehauff, Daniel, 275
Freeman, James, 740
Freeman, Thomas, 519
Freemasonry, 513
French and Indian War, 170, 344, 679, 683; accounts, orderly books, etc., 163, 164, 261, 262, 351, 568; Indian affairs, 562
Frémont, John Charles, 232, 727
Fretageot, Marie Duclos, 428
Friedrich Wilhelm IV, 348
Friends Academy, Philadelphia, 199, 631
Friendship Carpenters Company, Philadelphia, 175
Frisi, Paolo, 155
Fulton, John Farquhar, 339
Fulton, Robert, 366, 525, 531, 555, 640, 724
Fur trade, 185; at Michilimackinac, 633
Furness, Horace Howard, 28, 398, 406
Furness, William Henry, 741
Furness, William Howard, 666
Fuss, Nicholas, 9

Gabb, William More, author, 276
Gage, Simon Henry, 231
Gager, William, Latin plays, 277
Gaggiotti-Richards, Emma, 348
Gale, Benjamin, 638
Gallatin, Albert, 52, 240, 246, 483
Gallerio, Giorgio, 254
Galli, Johann G., 349
Gallini, Stefano, 254
Galloway, Joseph, 268, 269, 679, 683
Galton, Sir Douglas Strutt, 510
Galton, Sir Francis, 293, 467, 510, 662
Galunsky, Louis Charles, 348
Gannett, Henry, 598
Garden, Alexander, 199, 415, 638
Gardiner, Emma (Hallowell), author, 278
Gardiner, Robert Hallowell, 740
Garfield, James Abram, 598, 612
Garnett, John, 519
Garnett, Thomas, 441
Garrick, David, 684
Garrigues, Samuel, 244
Garvin, Paul L., 102

Gary, Anne Thomas, author, 279
Gasometers, 543
Gass, Patrick, 616
Gasser, Herbert Spencer, 500
Gaston, William, 18
Gates, Horatio, 170, 262, 753
Gates, Thomas Sovereign, 575, 625
Gatschet, Albert Samuel, 336, 598
Gaubius, Hieronymus David, 280
Gauld, George, author, 281
Gauss, Charles Frederic, 612
Gauthier, Jean François, 234
Gaver, Antonio de, 282
Gay-Lussac, Joseph Louis, 662
Geikie, Sir Archibald, 510
General Electric Company, 723
Genetics (journal), 218
Genetics, **149**, 177, **218**, 372, 473, **688**
Genth, Frederick Augustus, 462; catalogue of minerals, 283
Geoffroy, Etienne Louis, 465*a*
Geoffroy Saint Hilaire, Isidore, 293, 348, 525, 555
Geology, 254, 356, **422**, 424, 475, **486**, 575, 723; Colorado River, 597, 598; Japan, 424; New York, 726; Pennsylvania, 406
George I, king of England, 227
Georgia, travel and description, 135
Gerard de Rayneval, Joseph Mathias, author, 284
Gerlach, Walther, 104
Germanistic Society, 151
Germany, travel and description, 149
Gibbs, George, 186, 598, 708
Gibbs, Wolcott, 14, 272, 406, 678
Gibson, John Bannister, 9
Giese, Arthur Charles, 372
Gifford, Edward Winslow, 517
Gillespie, Ellen (Duane), 555
Gillespie, John Douglas, 285
Gillette, Lucy F., 196
Gilliams, Jacob, 656
Gilliss, James Melville, 14, 612
Gilman, Daniel C., 28
Gilmor, Robert, 186
Gilmore, Raymond Maurice, 174
Gilpin, Henry D., 707, 708
Gilpin, Joshua, 489
Gilpin, Thomas (1728-1778), 638
Gilpin, Thomas (1776-1853), 11, 672
Girard, John, 244
Girard, Stephen, 232, **286**
Girard College, Philadelphia, 520
Girardin, Louis Hue, 366
Givens, H. C., 500
Gladstone, William Ewart, 356, 467
Glauert, Earl T., author, 287
Glemona, Basile de, author, 288
Glentworth, George, 307, 459
Gliddon, George Robins, 289

Gmelin, John George, 199
Goddard, David Rockwell, 230
Goddard, Pliny Earle, 100, 101
Goddard, William, 173
Godfrey, Thomas, biog., 711
Godman, John, 541
Goldsborough, Robert, 725
Goldsborough, William, 725
Gooch, Sir William, 416
Goodspeed, Arthur Willis, 290
Gordon, Eugene, 102
Gordon, George Angier, 233
Gordon, George Byron, 151
Gordon, Harry, 170
Gordon, William, 603
Gouband Carrera, Antonio, 178
Goudsmit, Samuel Abraham, 104
Gould, Benjamin Apthorp, 117, 272, 398, 463, 464
Gould, John, 253
Grace, Rebecca, 306
Graeme, Thomas, 307
Grammars. See: Tamil, Hebrew, and various Indian tribes
Granier de Cassagnac, Bernard Adolphe, author, 291
Grant, Ulysses S., 14
Gray, Arthur F., 656
Gray, Asa, 14, 93, 117, 215, **292**, **379**, 415, 462, 475, 510, 662, 727
Gray, John Edward, 215, 253, 293
Gray, George Robert, 253
Graydon, Alexander, 52, 164, 261
Graydon, Caleb, 163
Great Britain, Board of Trade, 294; commercial policy (1794-1807), 252; travel and description, eighteenth cent., 512, 716
Greece, travel and description, 517
Greenleaf, Lewis S., Jr., 629
Greeley, Horace, 748
Green, Jacob, 293
Green, John Henry, 194
Greene, Catharine (Ray), 266
Greene, Francis Vinton, 426
Greene, Nathanael, **295**, 355, 483, 718, 753
Greene, William Houston, 723
Greenwood, Arthur M., 296
Greenwood, Henry, 666
Greenwood, Isaac, 640
Gregg, Alan, 629
Gregg, Andrew, 297
Gregg, David M., author, 297
Grégoire, Henri, 254
Grew, Nehemiah, 640
Grew, Theophilus, 298
Griffith, Hiram H., 299
Grimaldi, Gabriel, 254
Gronovius, Johann Friedrich, 415
Gross, Samuel David, 780
Grote, Augustus Radcliffe, 398

Grote, George, 467
Grover, Frederick O., 196
Grund, Francis Joseph, 221
Guano, fish, 310
Guarani Indians, 229
Guatemala, history, 300; travel and description, 109
Guatimalteca Indians, vocabulary, 168
Günther, Albert Carl Ludwig Gotthilf, 215, 253
Guiteras Holmes, Calixta, 178
Guizot, F. P. G., 14
Gulf Stream, 148
Gulick, John Thomas, 215, **301, 302**
Gummere, John, 18, 520
Guthe, Carl, 380
Guyot, Arnold Henry, 14, 272, 406, 598, 612
Gwenhoot Indians, 102
Gyorgy, Paul, 144

Haber, Fritz, 104
Haeckel, Ernst, 422
Hagen, Herman August, 398
Haida Indians, carvings, 102
Haile, Berard, 101
Haines, Reuben, 154, 303, 584, 620; meteorological observations, 450
Haines & Twells, accounts, 303
Haldeman, Samuel Stehman, 272, 304, 398, 406, 475, 678, 712
Hale, Edward Everett, 14, 406, 463, 464, 741
Hale, George Ellery, 723
Hale, Kenneth, author, 102
Hale, Lucretia Peabody, 406
Hales, Stephen, 199
Hall, Baynard, 645
Hall, David, 163; biog., 376; papers, 305; receipt book, 306
Hall, James, 186, 398, 406, 486
Hall, Jonathan, 441
Hall, William, 306
Hall & Sellers, 307
Halle, Universität, 483
Hallowell, Maine, 740
Hambright, John, 163
Hamilton, Alexander, 158
Hamilton, Andrew (d. 1741), 559, 623
Hamilton, Andrew II (ca. 1707-1747), 308
Hamilton, Gavin, 264
Hamilton, James, 163, 303, 344, 558, 561, 562, 679
Hamilton, Joseph, 561
Hamilton, William Rowan, 612
Hamilton & Balfour, Edinburgh, 305
Hammar, James, 772
Hanbury, Josiah, 198
Hancock, Albany, 215, 216
Hancock, John, 321
Hand, Edward, 265, 483
Handsome Lake religion, 499

Haney, John Louis, papers, 309
Hanson, Hugh C., 712
Harden, Jane (Le Conte), 399
Harding, Warren Gamaliel, 462
Hare, Robert, 86, 154, 195, 662, 727; papers, 310
Hare family, 355
Hare Indians, Fort Good Hope, N.W.T., Canada, 102
Harlan, Richard, 10, 13, 44, 114, 475, 486
Harmand, Philippe Nicolas, 248
Harmand de Montgarny, J. B. T., 9
Harper, Francis, 734
Harper, Robert Almer, 230
Harrington, John Peabody, 101
Harris, John, 163, 679
Harris, Thaddeus William, 396, 398
Harris' Ferry, Pa., 261
Harrison, Richard, 741
Harrison, Ross Granville, 629
Harrold, Alfred, 674
Hart, John, 628
Hart, John Seely, 18
Hartley, Thomas, 265
Hartshorne, Edward Yarnell, 182
Harvard University, 474, 575, 748
Harvey, Edmund Newton, papers, 311
Harvey, Jacob, papers, 312
Harvey, William Henry, papers, 313
Haskins, Charles Homer, 100
Hassler, Ferdinand Rudolph, 9, 10, 520, 662
Hauch, Ferdinand, 196
Haupt, Lewis Muhlenberg, 314
Haven, Tracy E., 196
Haviland, John, 673
Hawkesworth, John, 338
Hawkins, Benjamin, 525; letters and journal, 315-317
Hawkins, John, 525
Hay, John, 28
Hayden, Ferdinand Vandiveer, 398, 406, 597
Hayes, Isaac Israel, 272
Hayes, Patrick, letters, 318
Hayes, Rutherford Birchard, 394, 398
Hayre, Charlotte Ruth Wright, author, 319
Hays, Isaac Minis, 81; author, 320
Hazard, Ebenezer, 173; papers, 321
Hazard, Samuel, 124; meteorological observations, 450
Hazlitt, William, 603
Hebrew language, grammar and dictionary, 166, 721
Heckewelder, John Gottlieb Ernestus, 52, 247, **322-331**, 375, 496, 771, 778
Heckman, Charles Adams, 737
Heiberg, Benjamin, 332
Heisenberg, Werner, 104
Heiser, Victor George, 105
Helmholtz, Hermann von, 14
Helmuth, Henry, 482

Helmuth, Justus Heinrich Christian, biog., 18
Hembel, William, 93, 727
Henry, Joseph, 117, 272, 293, 310, 394, 398, 406, 463, 464, 598, 612, 640, 662, 712, 727, 748
Henry, Matthew S., 333, 334
Henshaw, Henry Wetherbee, 426
Henslow, John Stevens, 215, 253, 422, 662
Hentz, Nicholas M., 9
Heraldry, 335
Herbert, John Maurice, 215
Herrick, Edward Claudius, 612
Herries, Sir Robert, & Co., 264, 265
Herschel, Sir John Frederick William, 349, 422, 463, 464, 612, 640, 662
Hervey, Frederick Augustus, Earl of Bristol and Bishop of Derry, 254
Hetherington, Hubert W., 501
Hewitt, Abram S., 598
Hewitt, George W., 723
Hewitt, John Napoleon Brinton, 336
Hewitt, Joseph W., 100
Hewson, Mary (Stevenson), 123, 266, 337, 338
Hewson, Thomas Tickell, 44, 337, 338
Hewson, William, 176, 337, 338
Heye, George Gustav, 151
Hicks, Henry, 423
Hieroglyphs, 740; Aztec, 761; Egypt, 289; Maya, 474
Hiester, Joseph, 355; biog., 297
Higgins, Jesse, 265
Higginson, Thomas Wentworth, 196, 406
Hilbert, David, 104
Hildreth, Samuel Prescott, 475
Hill, David, 449
Hill, Hannah (Sellers), 675
Hill, Henry, 264
Hill, Peter, 675
Hillegas, Michael, 525
Himes, Charles Francis, 780
Hindle, Brooke, author, 90
Historical and Literary Committee. See: American Philosophical Society
Historical Society of Pennsylvania, 29
History of Science Society, papers, 339
Hitchcock, Edward, 14, 186, 423
Hitchens, Arthur Parker, 105
Hodgdon, Samuel, 586
Hodge, Frederick Webb, 151
Hodgkin, Thomas, 475
Hodson, C. B. S., 218
Höber, Rudolf, 508
Hoeven, Jan van der, 293
Hoijer, Harry, 101
Holker, John, 244
Holland, Josiah Gilbert, 233
Hollinshead, Benjamin M., 741
Hollyday, Henry, 199
Holmes, Abiel, 13, 52, 561
Holmes, Oliver Wendell (1809-1894), 555, 666

Holmes, William Henry, 151
Holyoke, Edward Augustus, 158
Home, David Milne, 423
Hooker, Sir Joseph Dalton, 215, 340, **379**, 510
Hooker, Sir William Jackson, 216, 253, **379**, 422, 462, 467, 510, 686
Hoover, Herbert Clark, 624
Hopi Indians, language, 102; songs and words, 102
Hopkins, William, 423
Hopkinson, Francis, 303, **341**, 342, 343; will, 582
Hopkinson, Joseph, 18, 232, 525, 697
Hopper, Isaac, 191
Horn, George Henry, 398, 482
Hornaday, William Temple, 218
Horner, Leonard, 215, 348
Horner, William E., 18
Horsfall, Frank Lappin, Jr., 500
Horsfield, Thomas, 423
Horsfield, Timothy, papers, 344
Horsmanden, Daniel, 345
Horstmann, Dorothy Millicent, 500
Horticulture, 149, 374, 432. See also: Botany, and names of individuals
Hosack, David, 52, 256, 312, 347, 415, 525, 662; biog., 346
Hosack, Mary (Eddy), 123
Hosmer, Jean, 678
Houdon, Jean Antoine, 443
Hough, George Washington, 612
Houghton, J. S., 712
Howard, Charles, Duke of Norfolk, 198
Howard, Frederick, Earl of Carlisle, 697
Howard, H. H., 501
Howard, John, 603
Howard, Leland Ossian, 745
Howe, Julia Ward, 463, 464
Howe, Richard, Earl, 697
Howe, Sir William, 458
Howgate, Henry W., 117
Hoyt, William Deans, 196
Hrdlička, Aleš, 151
Hauve Indians, dictionary and vocabulary, 615
Hubbard, Henry Guernsey, 398
Huck-Saunders, Richard, 359
Hudson River, sketches, 532, 539
Hughes, George Wurtz, 117
Hughes, John, 268, 569
Hulings, William E., 405
Hull, Edward, 423
Hull, William, 586
Humane Society, Philadelphia, records, 574
Humboldt, Alexander von, papers, 52, 93, 205, 215, 254, **348**, 349, 422, 463, 464, 479, 510, 612, 662
Humboldt, Wilhelm von, 254
Hume, David, papers, 350
Hume, Edward H., 105

Humphrey, J. E., 196
Humphreys, David, 211
Hunt, George, 101
Hunt, Thomas Sterry, 423
Hunter, Alexander, 351
Hunter, George, journals, 352
Hunter, George H., 352
Hunter, Samuel, 163, 261, 568
Hunter, Thomas Marshall, author, 353
Hunter, William (d. 1761), journal, 354
Hunter, William (1718-1783), 337, 355, 684
Huntington, Samuel, 321
Huntington, William Reed, 233
Huron Indians, dictionary and grammar, 102, 594, 652; language, 610; narratives, 102; vocabulary, 594
Hutchins, Thomas, 170, 180, 281, 671; biog., 609
Hutchinson, Charles H., 355
Hutchinson, James, papers, 355
Hutchinson, Robert, 631
Huxley, Thomas Henry, 215, 253, 356, 422, 467, 510, 662; papers, 357
Hyatt, Alpheus, 301
Hyde, James H., 149
Hydrography, 155
Hydromechanics, 155

Iberville, Pierre Le Moyne d', 386
Ichthyology, 712, 713; North America, 132
Illinois-Miami Indians, dictionary, 393
Imperial Academy of Sciences, St. Petersburg, 9
Immunology, 105, 387
Incas, revolt (1780-1783), 592
Independence Hall, Philadelphia, 669; Square, 421, 671
Independence National Historical Park, Philadelphia, 358
India, acculturation, 730; travel and description, 629
Indians, 100, 285, 416, 543, 550, 616; affairs (1790-1793), 586; anthropology, 709; antiquities, 128; captivities: 127, narratives, 224, reports, 296; Central America: 517, dictionaries, 178, 660, grammars, 168, 178, 466, 469, 660, vocabularies, 168; dances, 102, 225, 226, 285, 615; dictionaries: 278, 334, 365, 378, 393, 435, 466, 496, 499, 608, 615, 652, Alaskan, 151, Southwestern, 615; ethnography: 101, 102, Alaska and Canada, 102, 151, 226, 655, Iroquois, 102, 336; ethnology, 101, 102; folklore, 101; grammars, 102, 435, 466, 499, 615, 740, 763, 782, 783; history, 322, 325, 328; languages, 100, 102, 143, 151, 222, 240, 242, 244, 247, 276, 322, 323, 364, 435, 496, 499, 658; linguistics, 100, 102, 242, 244, 285, 513, 610; Massachusetts (state), 442; Michigan (state), 170; missions and missionaries:

466, Methodist Episcopal Church, 415, North America, 736, Presbyterian, 759, Protestant, 145; mounds: 498, Pennsylvania, 174; music, 102, 169, 204, 225, 226, 630; mythology, 101, 336, 381, 615; names, 333; New York (state), 170, 362, 493, 516; Ohio River Valley, 180; origins, 739; peace medals, 743; Pennsylvania (state): 170, 344, 562, 683, 749, treaties, 563; Peru, 475; religion, 466; Society of Friends, 702; South America, 517; Southwest, 517; United States, 709, 731; vocabularies, 133, 152, 330, 368, 427, 469, 496, 594, 615, 622, 710, 728, 778, 784. See also under names of individual tribes. The Society has published *A Guide to the Manuscripts Relating to the American Indian in the Library . . .*, by John F. Freeman, which should be consulted for a complete survey of the Indian material which is but briefly touched upon in this *Guide.*
Influenza (1918 epidemic), 501
Ingenhousz, Jan, 254, 359, 366, 603, 741, 766
Ingersoll, Charles Jared, 233
Ingersoll, Jared, 497, 638, 697; will, 582
Ingham, Samuel Delucenna, 662
Ingraham, Edward Duffield, 213, 708
Ingraham, Mark Hoyt, 629
Institut de France, 149; Académie des Sciences, 200; reports on papers, 465a
Institute for Advanced Study, Princeton, N. J., 260, 651
Institute of Mathematical Statistics, 762
Instruments, scientific. See: Scientific instruments
Insurance (annuities), 520
International law, 576
International Statistical Institute, 762
Irish immigration, U.S., 259
Iron, U.S., 424
Iroquois Indians, 163; biogs., 140; confederacy, 494; description, 107; folklore, 750; grammars and dictionaries, 435, 499; languages, 102, 499, 610; in Massachusetts, 442; in New York, 102, 345, 507, 693; medicine, 499; personal names, 202. See individual tribes
Irving, Washington, 741
Isis (journal), 339
Isleta Indians, paintings, 517
Ives, Eli, 197
Izard, George, 496
Izard, Ralph, 685

Jackson, Abraham Valentine William, 662
Jackson, Andrew, 232
Jackson, Charles Thomas, 423, 678
Jackson, Dugald Caleb, 82b, 723
Jackson, Halliday, journals, 360-362
Jackson, Isaac Rand, 18

Jackson, Richard, 266
Jacobs, Melville, 100, 101
Jacobs, Michael, 363
Jacobs, William Stephen, 18
Jacquin, Nikolaas Joseph, 359
Jamaica, Negro folklore, 517; tuberculosis, 501
James, Edwin, 364, 365
James, Sir Henry, 423
James, James, 631
James, Thomas Chalkley, 44, 248
Jameson, David, 679
Jamieson, Thomas F., 423
Japan, ambassadorship of Roland S. Morris, 233; geological survey, 424; language, 372, 424; travel and description, 424, 629
Jardin des Plantes (also Jardin du Roi), Paris, 374, 520
Jardine, Sir William, 253, 293
Jay, John, 507, 741
Jeanes, Joseph, 631
Jeans, Sir James Hopwood, 723
Jeffcott, H. H., 723
Jefferson, Thomas, 36, 52, 173, 205, 237, 248, 321, 348, **366**, 367, **369**, 401, 403, 520, 525, 531, 555, 577, 603, 645, 685, 724, 729, 741, 753, 771; Declaration of Independence, 320; Indian vocabularies, 368, 496
Jenner, Sir William, 662
Jenness, Diamond, 101
Jennings, George Nelson, autobiog., 370
Jennings, Herbert Spencer, 370; diary, 371; papers, 372
Jessup, Philip C., 82a
Jesuits. See: Society of Jesus
Jewett, Frank Baldwin, 629
Jochelson, Waldemar, 151
Johns Hopkins University, 231, 260; School of Medicine, 651
Johnson, Alba Boardman, 723
Johnson, Caleb, 307
Johnson, Eldridge R., 81
Johnson, Joseph, 213
Johnson, Sir William, 180
Johnson & Unwin, London, 305
Joliot, Frédéric, 104
Jomard, Edmé François, 348
Jones, D. A., 388
Jones, E. Elizabeth, 500
Jones, Hugh, 640
Jones, John Paul, 211
Jones, N. Cantwell, 264, 265
Jones, Rebecca, 191
Jones, Robert Strettell, 373
Jones, Samuel, 175
Jones, William, 121
Jones, Sir William, 662
Jones family, North Carolina, 587
Jourdan, Pascual, 104
Judd, John Wesley, 422, 423

Judd, Neil Merton, 380
Jukes, Joseph Bette, 423
Junto, minutes, 1
Jussieu, Antoine Laurent de, 374, 465a

Kalm, Peter, 415
Kamerlingh-Onnes, Heike, 104
Kampmann, Christian Frederick, 331, 375
Kane, John Kintzing, 18, 86, 310, 481
Kany, Robert Hurd, author, 376
Kapitza, Peter, 104
Kappa Lambda fraternity, 29
Kauffmann, Angelica, 254
Kayser, Heinrich Gustav Johannes, 104; autobiog., 377
Kearsley, John, Sr., 199
Kearsley, John, Jr., 459
Keat, Roland G., 100
Keating, William Hypolitus, 36, 93, 154
Keen, William Williams, **24**, 28, 171, 231, 723
Keith, Sir William, 227
Kellogg, Vernon Lyman, 372
Kelly, John, 265
Kelso, Henry B., 378
Kelvin, Lord. See: Sir William Thomson
Kemble, Edwin Crawford, 104
Kendall, Amos, 232
Kennedy, Joseph Camp Griffith, 612
Kennelly, Arthur Edwin, 723
Kentucky, travel and description, 352, 452
Keppel, Frederick P., 151
Keppele, Henry, 303
Keppele, John, 306
Kern, Edward M., 289
Kew. See: Royal Botanic Gardens
Key, Harold H., 178
Key, Philip Barton, 649
Kidder, Alfred Vincent, 101, **380**, 517, 709
Kidder, Homer Huntington, recorder, 381
King, Clarence, 406, 598
King, Rufus, 211, 640
King George's War, 491
Kinloch, Francis, letters, 382, 383
Kinnersley, Ebenezer, 303
Kirkbride, Thomas Story, 310, 662
Kirwan, Richard, 254
Klaproth, Heinrich Julius, 595
Klein, Oskar, 104
Klett, Joseph F., author, 384
Kline, Howard F., 178
Klopstock, Friederich, 694
Knox, Henry, 158, 507, 586, 685
Kobawgam, Charles, 381
Kobawgam, Charlotte, 381
Kohlberg, Alfred, 501
Kossuth, Louis, 649
Kramers, Hendrik Anthony, 104
Kroeber, Alfred Louis, 100, 101, 151, 517, 709
Krumel, Donald W., author, 385
Kuhn, Adam, 415

Kunz, George Frederick, 105
Kurath, Gertrude Prokosch, 102
Kurjack, Dennis Charles, 358
Kwakiutl Indians, dictionary and grammar, 151

Lacépède, Bernard Germain Etienne de la Ville sur Illon, comte de, 254
Lacey, John, 212
La Condamine, Charles Marie de, 155, 465a, 662
Lacordaire, Jean Théodore, 398
Ladenburg, Rudolf, 104
La Farge, Oliver, 517
Lafayette, Marie Jean Paul Joseph Roch Yves Gilbert de Motier, marquis de, 158, 188, 219, 221, 254, 401, 525, 687, 753
La Fort, Thomas, 449
La Galissonière, Augustin Félix Elisabeth Barrin, comte de, 234
La Harpe, Bénard de, author, 386
Lalande, Joseph Jerome Le Français de, 155, 254
Lancaster County, Pa., law docket, 680; quit rents, 560
Land speculation, 740; Pennsylvania, 679
Landsteiner, Karl, 144; biog. data, 387
Lane, Sir Arbuthnot, 105
Langdale, Alice, 190
Langevin, Paul, 104
Langley, Samuel Pierpont, 555
Langmuir, Irving, 144, 723
Langstroth, Lorenzo Lorraine, papers, 388
Languages, Ainu, 424; Batik, 130; Chinese, 424; French, 424; Japanese, 372, 424; Tamil, 720. For American Indian languages, see under Indians, and under individual tribes.
Lankester, Sir Edwin Ray, 215
Lanneau family, 587
Lapique, Jacques, 381
Lardner, Lynford, 163, 303
La Rive, Auguste Arthur de, 612
La Roche, René, 389, 475
La Rochefoucauld, Duchesse de, 687
La Rochefoucauld-Liancourt, François Alexandre Frédéric, duc de, 158, 254, 687
Larrey, Baron Dominique Jean, letters, 390
Larrey, Baron Félix Hippolyte, 390
Latrobe, Benjamin Henry, 10, 11, 525, 555
Laue, Max von, 104
Laufer, Berthold, 151
Laurens, Henry, 525
Lavoisier, Marie Anne Pierrette Paulze, 254
Law, Samuel A., 187
Law, education, 391; profession in Philadelphia, 602; Roman, 208; Spanish-American, 592
Law Academy, Philadelphia, 391
Lawrence, Cornelius Van Wyck, 119

Lawrence, George Newbold, 301
Lawrence, Thomas, 679
Lea, Isaac, 18, 154, 415, 486
Leacock, John, 392
League of Nations, 171
Lear, Tobias, 685
Learned societies. See under particular society and members
Le Boulanger, Jean Baptiste, 393
Lecky, William E. H., 467
Le Conte, John, 661, 678
Le Conte, John Eatton, 396-399, 415; papers, 394; drawings, 395
Le Conte, John Lawrence, 14, 272, 394, 395, 399, 656, 678, 712; papers, 398
Le Conte, Joseph, 14, 398, 399
Le Conte, Louis, 399
Le Conte, Robert G., 575
Le Conte family, 399
Lederle Laboratory, 105
Lee, Arthur, 400, 401, 561, 603, 640
Lee, Frederick S., 260
Lee, Richard Henry, 366, 753; papers, 401
Lee, Richard Henry, Jr., 320
Leet, Isaac, 320
Lefevre, Jean-Jacques, 293
Legaux, Peter, 10, 402-404
Lehigh University, 629
Leidy, Joseph, 14, 195, 215, 598
Leighton, William Allport, 253
Leiper, Samuel M., 520
Leiper, Thomas, 520, 671
Leiper, William J., 482
Leishman, Sir William Boog, 260
Leland, P. W., 333
Leland, Waldo Gifford, 100
Le Monnier, Pierre, 465a
Lenard, Philipp, 104
L'Enfant, Pierre Charles, 497
Lenni Lenape Indians, 322, 496, 562, 635, 755; botanical names, 331, 778; dictionaries and grammars, 330, 334, 778, 782; place names, 326
Lennox, Charles, Duke of Richmond, 198
León y Gama, Antonio de, 405
Leonard, Levi W., 396
Lepine, Jeanne, 178
Le Roy, Jean Baptiste, 270
Lescale de Vérone, Joseph de, 657
Lesley, J. Peter, 248, 468, 555, 598, 640, 748; papers, 406
Lesley, Susan (Inches), 406
Lesquereux, Leo, 398, 406, 712
Lester, Robert MacDonald, 100
Lesueur, Charles Alexandre, 13, 428; sketches, 407
Letombe, Joseph Philippe, 158, 248
Lettsom, John Coakley, 355, 662, 724
Leung, K. D., 500
Le Verrier, Urbain Jean Joseph, 612

Lewis, G. Albert, 67
Lewis, John Frederick, Sr., papers, 408
Lewis, Meriwether, 147, 616; journals, 409, 410
Lewis, Richard, 640
Lewis, William Draper, 82a
Lewis and Clark expedition, 147, **185**, 409, 410, 506; botanical specimens, 616
Li, Fang-Kuei, 100
Library Company of Philadelphia, **411**, 671
Lick Observatory, University of California, 271
Lieber, Oscar, 349
Liesganig, Joseph, 155
Lightning, 141
Lilly, Eli, 709
Lincoln, Benjamin, 586, 638
Lincoln, Jackson Steward, 178
Lindeström, Per, author, 492
Lindsay, John, Earl of Crawford, journals, 412
Lingelbach, William Ezra, papers, 413
Linguistics. See under Indians and particular tribes
Linnaean Society, Lancaster County, Pa., 414
Linnaeus, Carl, 199, 205, 415, 478
Linnean Society, London, 217, 301, **415**
Lister, Sir Joseph, 171, 510
Livingston, William, 123, 697
Lloyd, Humphrey, 612
Lloyd, John T., 629
Lloyd, Richard, 725
Lloyd, Thomas, 559
Locke, John, 740
Locomotives, 668
Lodge, Sir Oliver, 467
Loeb, Jacques, 260
Loeb, John Nichols, 508
Loeb, Robert, 508
Loewi, Otto, 144
Logan, George, 10, 52
Logan, James, 241, 392, 415, 559, 562, 564, 711; corres., 416, 417
Logan, William (d. 1776), 679
Logbooks, *Apollo,* 148; *China Packet,* 634; *Harriet,* 299; *Sampson,* 741
Lollards, 556
London, Fritz, 104
London. Linnean Society. See: Linnean Society, London
London. Royal Society. See: Royal Society, London
London. Royal Society of Arts. See: Royal Society of Arts, London
Long, Perrin Hamilton, 500
Long, Stephen Harriman, 10, 251, 552
Long, Will West, **418, 710**
Longchamps, Charles J. de, 244
Longfellow, Henry Wadsworth, 598
Loomis, Elias, 117, 640

Loos, John Louis, author, 419
Lorich, Severin, biog., 18
Lorimer, John, 281
Loskiel, George Henry, 327
Loudoun, Earl of. See: John Campbell
Louis Philippe, king of the French, 13, 158
Louisiana Territory, boundaries, 367; French settlement, 386; travel and description, 110, 237, 352, 409, 410, 506, 588, 589
Lovejoy, Jesse Robert, 723
Lovett, Robert Williamson, 105
Loxley, Benjamin, 306
Loyalhanna, Pa., 568
Loyalists' Claims Commission, 779
Lozano, Pedro, 420
Lozières, Louis Narcisse Baudry de, 179
Lubbock, Sir John William, 215, 216, 467, 509, 510
Lukens, John 264, **421,** 441
Luminescence, 311
Lutheran Church, United States, 476, 482
Lyell, Sir Charles, 14, 215, 348, 356, 406, 502, 509, 510, 662; papers, 422, 423
Lyman, Benjamin Smith, 406; papers, 424
Lyman, Theodore, 415, 423, 662
Lyon, John, 425

McAtee, Waldo Lee, papers, 426
McCall, Archibald, 303
McClary, brigantine, 490
McClellan, Catharine, author, 226
Macclesfield, John, Earl of, 250
McClurg, James, 176
McConaughy, James L., 501
McCormick, Dennis, 163
McCrae, Thomas, 105
McCulloch, Thomas, Jr., 114
MacDowell, Edwin Carleton, 688
McDuffie, George, 221
McGee, William John, 151
McHenry, James, 507
McIlvaine, H. M., 124
McIlvaine, William, 18
MacInnes, Duncan Arthur, 144
McKean, Thomas, 232, 525; will, 582
McKean and Elk Land and Improvement Company, 355
McKee, Alexander, 170
McKenney, Thomas Lorraine, 427
McKenzie, Colin, 684
Mackenzie, George M., 387
MacKenzie, Sir George Steuart, 422
McKim, J. Miller, 406
Mackinaw Indians, missions to, 736
McKinley, Alexander, 406
McLean, Archibald, 441
McLennan, John Cunningham, 104
Maclure, Alexander, 428
Maclure, William, 186, 475; letters and papers, **428,** 429

McMaster, James Alphonsus, biog., 438
McMurtrie, Henry, 396
McWilliams, Robert, 9
Madiera family, Philadelphia, 741
Madison, Dolley (Payne), 430, 741
Madison, James (1751-1836), 205, 221, 232, 555; meteorological observations, 430
Magazines, eighteenth cent. American, 183
Magellan, Jean Hyacinthe, 254
Magnetism, 272, 485, 719
Maillet, Benoît de, 431
Maine, folklore, 517
Makower, Henry, 500
Maldonado, Francisco, author, 168
Malecite Indians, natural history terms, 102
Malesherbes, Chrétien Guillaume de Lamoignon de, 234, **432**
Mall, Franklin Paine, 260; biog. data, 651
Mallinckrodt, Edward, 723
Malouin, Paul Jacques, 465a
Mandrillon, Joseph, author, 433
Mann, Horace, 406
Manning, Richard Irvine, 221
Manning, William, 740
Mantell, Gideon Algernon, 422, 475
Maraldi, Jean Dominique, 465a
Marcet, Alexander John Gaspard, 220
Marchant, Henry, journal, 434
Marcoux, Abbé M., author, 435
Maring, Joel, 102
Markham, William, 559, 564
Marsh, Othniel Charles, 14, 406, 597, 598
Marshall, Christopher, 701
Marshall, Humphry, 142, 683
Marshall, John, 13; opinions, 436
Marshall, Moses, 213
Martin, Samuel, 415
Martin, Thomas Commerford, 723
Martin de la Bastide, ——, author, 437
Martineau, Harriet, 741
Mary Canisius, Sister, author, 438
Maryland boundaries, **439, 441,** 566; travel and description (eighteenth cent.), 671, 744
Maskelyne, Nevil, 155, 441
Mason, Charles, 250, 683; Pennsylvania-Maryland boundary, **439, 440,** 441
Mason, John Young, 211
Mason, Otis Tufton, 398
Mason and Dixon Survey, 335, **439, 441, 566,** 683
Maspero, Gaston, 108
Massachusetts, Indian affairs, 442
Massengale, Jean M., author, 443
Massias, Baron Nicholas, 243
Mastodon, 132, 234, 525
Mathematical Association of America, 762
Mathematics, 155, 234, 632; schoolbooks, 659
Mather, Cotton, 640
Mather, Kirtley F., 82a

Matlack, Timothy, 10, 303, 321, 561, 701; accounts, 444
Maule, William, 631
Maumee Indians, missions to, 736
Maury, Matthew Fontaine, 117, 293, 310, 349, 463, 464, 662
Mayan hieroglyphs, 474
Mayer, Brantz, 233
Mayer, Christian, 18
Mayhaw Indians, missions to, 736
Mayhew, Jonathan, 638
Mayo Clinic, 171
Mazalquivir, Africa, 282
Mazzei, Filippo, 254; letters, 445
Mead, Margaret, author, 446
Meade, George, 725
Meadowcroft, William Henry, 723
Mearns, Edgar Alexander, 426
Mease, James, 93, 255, 366, 457, 707, 708
Mecklin, John M., 182
Mecom, Jane (Franklin), 266
Medals, 249
Medical Aid to China, 651
Medical Aid to Spain, 651
Medical education, 280, 332, 471, 648; England, 355, 512, 684; U.S.: 260, Pennsylvania, 625, Philadelphia, 773; Vienna, 387
Medicine, general, 176, 263, 355, 390, 447, 509, 691, 723, 740; Indian, 418, 499, 592, 710; military, 105, 122, 311, 353, 398, 500, 501; Pennsylvania Hospital, 574; practice, 212, 389, 398, 475, 476, 642-647, 650; professional history, 384; research, 171, 260, 501; United States Dispensatory, 776
Meek, Fielding Bradford, 598
Meigs, Charles Delucena, 272
Meitner, Lise, 104
Mellila, Africa, 282
Melmoth, Courtney. See: Samuel Jackson Pratt
Melsheimer, Frederick Ernst, 396, 398
Mendenhall, Thomas Corwin, 398, 723
Menomonee Indians, dictionary, 365
Mentzel, Christian, 448
Mercer, Hugh, 163, 562, 697
Meredith, Reese, 303, 459
Meredith, Samuel, 187, 188
Meredith, Thomas, 187
Meredith, William M., 86
Meriam, Ebenezer, papers, 449
Merriam, Clinton Hart, 426
Merrick, Samuel, 741
Merrill, Ayres Phillips, 389
Merrill, Elmer Drew, 82a, 629
Merriman, Daniel, 233
Merry, Andrew, 640
Metcalf, Maynard Mayo, 372
Meteorological observations, 463, 464; in Arkansas, 729; in Delaware, 450; in New England, 450; in Ohio, 324; in Pennsyl-

vania: 163, 478, 626, Gettysburg, 363, Germantown, 450, Gnadenhütten, 324, Nazareth, 450, Philadelphia, 138, 403, 404, 450, 520; in Upper Canada, 324; in Virginia, 430; on Atlantic Ocean, 450, 600; in South American waters, 450
Meteorology, 141, 740, 766
Methodist Episcopal Church, Indian missions, 451
Mexico, archaeology, 239; botany, 677; Indian languages, 143; natural history, 677; travel and description, 115
Miami-Illinois Indians, dictionary, 393
Michaux, André, 81, 348, **452-454**, 771
Michaux, François André, 248, 453, **455, 456,** 662, 771
Michelson, Truman, 101, 151
Micklé, Samuel, 264
Micmac Indians, language, 496
Middleton, Christopher, 640
Middleton, Peter, 176
Mie, Gustav, 104
Mifflin, John Fishbourne, 457
Mifflin, Thomas, will, 582
Milbank Memorial Fund, 501
Miles, Samuel, 163; papers, 458
Millegan, Robert, 265, 457
Miller, Dayton Clarence, 723
Miller, George G., 324
Miller, Peter, notary public, 459
Miller, Philip, 198
Miller, Samuel, 321
Miller, Thomas Grier, 625
Millhauser, Milton, author, 460
Millikan, Robert Andrews, 82a, 104
Milne-Edwards, Henri, 215, 356, 509
Mineralogy, 283, 475, 678, 695, 726
Mingo Indians. See: Lenni Lenape Indians
Miniature painting, 458
Minnesota, University of, 171
Minto, Walter, papers, 461
Miskey, William F., 748
Missionaries, to Indians, 145, 451, 466; in Spanish America, 420, 515. See also particular Indian tribes
Mississippi River, 588
Missouri, University of, 629
Missouri River, travel and description, 731, 771. See also Meriwether Lewis and William Clark
Mitchell, John, 415
Mitchell, Maria, 119; papers, 463
Mitchell, Silas Weir, 28, 171, 231, 555, 780
Mitchell, William, papers, 464
Mitchill, Samuel Latham, 176, 366, 475, 740, 771
Mixe Indian language, 143
Mörch, O. A. L., 662
Mohawk Indians, grammar and dictionary, 102, 608, 763

Mohegan Indians, language, 658
Mohr, Otto Louis, 473
Monckton, Robert, 170, 262
Monroe, James, 205, 248, 270, 741
Montgomerie, William, of Brigend, Scotland, 465
Montgomery, James C., 124
Montgomery, John Teakle, 124
Montgomery, Thomas H., 465
Montgomery, William, 561
Montgomery family, 465
Montigny, Etienne Mignot de, 465a
Montour, Andrew, 562
Montréal. Séminaire de Montréal, Les Prêtres de Saint-Sulpice, manuscripts, 466
Moore, Ann, 191
Moore, Aubrey Lackington, 356, 467
Moore, E. M., collector, 467
Moore, George Washington, 233
Moore, Ira, papers, 468
Moore, William, 303
Moran, Francisco, author, 469
Moran, Thomas, 598
Moravians, 327
Moray, Alexander, 640
More, Samuel, 638
Moreau de St.-Méry, Mérédic Louis Elie, 685
Morellet, Abbé André, 470
Morgan, Sir Charles, 723
Morgan, George, 586
Morgan, Isabel M., 500
Morgan, John, 163, 303, 338, **471**
Morgan, Joseph, 640
Morgan, Lewis Henry, **472,** 513
Morgan, Thomas Hunt, **473,** 598
Morice, Adrien Gabriel, 100
Morley, Sylvanus Griswold, 380; diary, 474
Morogues, Vicomte de, 465a
Morris, Deborah, estate, 191
Morris, Earl, 380
Morris, Gouverneur, 264, 265
Morris, John Gottlieb, 712
Morris, Margaretta Hall, 396
Morris, Robert, 158, 219, 232, 264, 497, 507, 697; mansion, 578; will, 582
Morris, Robert Hunter, 199, 344, 562, 679
Morris, Roland Sletor, 233
Morris, Thomas, 507
Morse, Jedediah, 173
Morse, Samuel Finley Breese, 14
Morton, Charles, 155
Morton, Henry, 555
Morton, Samuel George, 93, 195, 272, 289, 293, 428, 662; papers, 475
Moscow. Academy of Sciences. See: Academy of Sciences, Moscow
Moseley, Henry Gwyn-Jeffreys, 104
Moseley, Philip Edward, 182
Mottelay, Paul Fleury, 723
Moulinie, J., 216

Mound builders, 405; in Pennsylvania, 174

Mount Vernon, sketches, 539

Mountain Stoney dialect (Sioux Indians), 129

Mower, T. G., 9

Mudd, Stuart, 500

Müller, Johannes von, 293, 382

Muhlenberg, Frederick Augustus, 197, 497; biog., 297

Muhlenberg, Gotthilf Heinrich Ernst, 32, 197, 205, 415, **476-480**, 483, 616

Muhlenberg, Henry Augustus, 483; papers, 481

Muhlenberg, Henry Augustus Philip, papers, 482

Muhlenberg, Henry Melchior, 476, 479, 483

Muhlenberg, John Peter Gabriel, 753; biog., **258**, 481, 483

Muhlenberg, Peter, 483

Muhlenberg family, 483

Muir, James, ledger, 484

Mulhern, Edward, author, 485

Mulliken, Robert Sanderson, 104

Murchison, Sir Roderick Impey, 215, 406, 422, 510; corres., 486

Murillo, Thomas, 469

Murphy, James B., 105

Murphy, Robert Cushman, travel journals, 487

Murray, William Vans, 496

Muséum d'histoire naturelle, Paris, 662

Museums, European, 254

Music, 102, 217, 520, 529, 536, 649, 719; French, 160; Philadelphia, 385. See also: Indians

Muth, Charles V., 388

Mythology, 406. See also: Indians

Napoleon I, 740; wars, 605

National Academy of Sciences, Washington, 272, 629, 651, 762

National Geographic Society, 380

National Institutes of Health, 311

National Research Council, 651, 762

National Science Foundation, 762

Natural history, 113, 132, 153, 199, 253, 254, 272, 293, 301, 311, 356, 394-396, 398, 399, 422, 478, 502, 509, 525, 527-529, 543, 550, 553, 555, 591, 691, 712, 726; Malecite, 102; Mexico, 677. See also particular naturalists, sciences, and places.

Natural philosophy, 520, 632, 751; textbooks, 585, 611. See particular sciences and individual scientists.

Natural selection, 215, 372, 422. See also Evolution

Navaho Indians, ethnomedicine, 102; linguistics, 102

Navarette, M. F., 13

Neagle, John, 488

Nelson, Thomas, 753

Netherlands Antilles, native language, 102

Neuberger, Max, 387

Neumann, Johann von, 104

Neurology, 171

Nevill, Lady Dorothy, 216

Nevins, Pim, journal, 489

New Bern, N.C., defenses (1863), 737

New France, military conquest, 412

New Hampshire. Admiralty Court, 490

New Jersey, charters and laws (seventeenth cent.), 465; currency, 491; laws, 491; Manasquan Inlet, 314; provincial history, 559; provincial troops, 491; Supreme Court, 697

New Mexico, travel and description, 689

New Sweden, history, 492

New York, Commissioners of Indian Affairs, 170; geological survey, 726; Indian missions, 736; Indians, 362, 493, 507, 516; travel and description, 107, 131, 663

New York Botanical Garden, 629

New York City, tuberculosis, 501

Newberry, John Strong, 598

Newberry, Percy Edward, 108

Newcastle, Duke of, 417

Newcastle, Delaware, charter, 227

Newcomb, Simon, 28, 462

Newhouse, Seth, author, 494

Newnan, John, author, 495

Newton, Alfred, 422

Newton, Hubert Anson, 612

Newton, Sir Isaac, 462

Newton, Rejoice, 52

Niagara Falls, N.Y., 131, 777; electricity, 666

Niagara Falls Power Company, 666

Niagara Indians, 170

Nichols, Francis, 11

Nichols, Roy Franklin, 182

Nichols, William Ford, 233

Nicholson, Francis, 640

Nicholson, John, 497

Nicholson, Marjorie, 339

Nicola, Lewis, 10, 303

Nicollet, Joseph Nicholas, 18

Nile River, 108

Nishina, Yoshio, 104

Noailles, Louis, duc de, 234

Nobel prize, 387 (Landsteiner), 473 (T. H. Morgan), 760 (Whipple)

Nobility, history, 291

Noguchi, Hideyo, 105, 500

Nollet, Abbé Jean Antoine, 465a

Non-importation agreements (1765 and 1774), 569

Nooth, John Mervin, 638

Nootka Indians, ethnography, 655; music, 630; texts, 722; vocabulary, 152

Nordal, Johann, 196

Norris, Charles, 772

Norris, Isaac, 559, 563

Norris, Joseph Parker, 52, 584

Norris, William, 741
North America, travel and description, 348, 428
North American Land Company, 497
North Carolina, boundaries, 167
Northrop, John Howard, 144, 629
Norton, Andrews, 119
Norway, World War II, 473
Nottoway Indians, vocabulary, 778
Noyes, Ernest, 178
Nuttall, Thomas, 176, 197, 293, 422, 475, 662, 686; diary, 498

Obstetrics, 332
Oceania, anthropology, 709
Odenheimer, William Henry, 233
Office of Ordinance Research, 762
Ogle, William, 215, 216
O'Gorman, James F., 358
Ohio, boundaries, 131; travel and description, 483
Ohio Valley, Indians, 180
Ojibwa Indians, 615; dictionary, 378; missions, 736; myths, 381
Okonagan Indians, vocabulary, 728
Olbrechts, Frans M., 101; papers, 499
Oldfather, William Abbott, 100
Olitsky, Peter Kosciusko, 105, 260; papers, 500
Oliver, Daniel, 215, 216
Olson, Donald, 102
Oneida Indians, 223
Onondaga Indians, biographies, 140; education, 449; grammar and vocabulary, 783, 784; language, 102
Opie, Eugene Lindsay, papers, 501
Opium War, 125
Oppenheimer, J. Robert, 104
Optics, 155
Oran, Algeria, history, 282; Spanish conquest, 592
Ord, George, 9, 18, 93, 205, 213, 398, **502-503**, 504, 505, 555, 656, 727
Ordway, John, journal, 506
Oregon Indians, missions to, 451, 736
O'Reilly, Henry, collector, 507
Orme, Robert, 562
Ornithology, 138, 253, 426, 430, 502; North America, 132; U.S.: 114, 153, Lancaster, Pa., 478
Osage Indians, 184; missions, 736
Osborn, Henry Fairfield, 260
Osiris (journal), 339
Osler, Sir William, 105, 510
Osten-Sachen, Carl Robert, baron von, 398
Osterhout, Winthrop John Vanleuven, 144; papers, 508
Osterud, Hjalmar Laurits, 372
Ottawa Indians, 615; dictionary, 496; social organization, 102
Ottolenghe, Joseph, 638

Ouachita district, Louisiana Territory, 110
Ourry, Lewis, 163, 170
Owen, Sir Richard, 215, 216, 253, 406, 422, 467; papers, 509
Owen, Robert Dale, 428

Pacific Northwest, Indians, 102
Page, John, 10, 401, 445
Page, Mann, 401
Paget, Sir James, 356, 467, 509; letters, 510
Paine, Thomas, 577, 638
Paleontology, 203, 234, 272, 406, 690, 771
Palisot de Beauvois, Ambroise Marie François Joseph, baron de, 771
Palmer, Innis Newton, 737
Panama canal, 437
Panella, Silvia, author, 511
Papago-Pima Indians, language, 102
Paper making, 665, 668, 671, 672
Papiamento Indians, language, 102
Paraguay, Indian policy, 229; Jesuit missions, 515
Paris, Ferdinand John, 417, 562
Paris, Muséum d'historie naturelle. See: Muséum d'historie naturelle
Paris, travel and description, 203
Parke, Thomas, 346; journal, 512
Parker, Daniel, 394, 616
Parker, Ely Samuel, papers, 513
Parker, George Howard, 508
Parkinson, George H., author, 514
Parras, Pedro Joseph de, 515
Parrish, Jasper, 516
Parrish, John, 586
Parsons, Elsie (Clews), 151; papers, 517
Parsons, Usher, 333
Parsons, William, 344; biog., 747
Parton, James, 233
Partridge, Charles, 310
Paschen, Friedrich, 104
Pasteur, Louis, 467
Pasteur Vallery-Radot, Louis, 260
Pasti, George, author, 518
Patterson, Robert (1743-1824), 9, 11, 44, 366, 584, 724; papers, 519
Patterson, Robert (1802-1872), 253
Patterson, Robert (1819-1909), 520
Patterson, Robert Maskell, 10, 18, 195, 481, 555, 584; papers, 520
Patterson, Thomas Leiper, papers, 521
Patwin Indians, dictionary and grammar, 615
Paul, Peter L., 102
Pauli, Wolfgang, 104
Pauling, Linus, 104
Pawnee Indians, missions, 736
Peale, Albert Charles, 553
Peale, Mrs. Burd, author, 522
Peale, Charles, letter book, 523
Peale, Charles Linnaeus, 675

Peale, Charles Willson, 29, 81, 366, 522, 542, 543, 550, 551, 553, 675; papers, 524-535
Peale, Eleanor May Short, 541
Peale, Eliza Burd Patterson, 553
Peale, Franklin, 525, 542, 543, 549, 553, 675; songs, 536
Peale, Harriet, 553
Peale, James, 554; sketchbook, 537
Peale, Joseph M., 554
Peale, Mary Jane Patterson, 538
Peale, Raphaelle, 555, 675
Peale, Rembrandt, 525, 535, 541, 553, 555, 675; sketchbook, 539; misc. papers, 541
Peale, Rubens, 544, 546, 553, 555, 675; letter books and corres., 542, 543; autobiog., 545
Peale, St. George, 547
Peale, Mrs. T. R., 549
Peale, Titian Ramsay (1780-1798), author, 548
Peale, Titian Ramsay (1799-1885), 272, 395, 502, 505, 525, 553, 555, 675; corres., 549; journal, 552; sketchbook, 550; biog. of C. W. Peale, 551
Peale, William, 554
Peale family, 553-555
Peale's Museum, Baltimore, 543; New York, 542, 543; Philadelphia, 502, 524, 525, 527-529, 542, 543, 553, 555
Pearce, Matthew, 265
Peck, Charles Horton, 230
Peck, William Dandridge, 415
Peckham, Stephen Farnum, author, 556
Peirce, Benjamin, 272, 398, 406, 748
Peking Union Medical College, 651
Pemberton, Henry, 214
Pemberton, Israel, 199, 264, 355, 623; letter book, 557
Pemberton, Israel, Jr., 557
Pemberton, James, 303
Pemberton, Phineas, 520; meteorological observations, 450
Pemberton family, 355
Pendleton, Edmund, 366
Penn, John (1729-1795), 158, 561, 569, 671, 679, 697
Penn, Richard, 558
Penn, Thomas, 307, 562, 684; corres. with James Hamilton, 558
Penn, William, 241, 564; letters and documents, 559
Penn family, estates, 560
Pennant, Thomas, 132
Pennell, Francis Whittier, 137
Pennsbury Manor, 559
Pennsylvania, province: Assembly laws, 564-565; Commissioners for Determining the Pennsylvania-Maryland Boundary, 566; Committee of Safety, 671; Council, 558; Council minutes, 567; Dutch settlements, 561; French and Indian War, military records and accounts, 568; history, 241, 416, 417, 559; Indian affairs, 562, 563; non-importation agreements (1765, 1774), 569; politics, 679; Proprietors, 416, 417, 558; Surveyor-General, 421
———, Commonwealth: Constitutional Convention (1837-1838), 570; State Penitentiary for the Eastern District, 571; taxation, 572, 573, 628
———, Boundaries, 131 439, 441, 566, 626; Democratic Party, 482; geological survey, 406; Germans, 699; Indians, 344, 683, 749; misc. records, 561; slavery, 572; travel and description, 131, 663, 671, 744
Pennsylvania, University of, 81, 171, 260, 272, 408, 413, 501, 519, 520, 561, 575, 636, 732; Academy of Philadelphia, Trustees, 307; College of Philadelphia, student notes, 373; Medical School: 176, 471, lecture tickets, 648, survey, 625
Pennsylvania Academy of the Fine Arts, 408, 525
Pennsylvania Horticultural Society, 29, 81
Pennsylvania Hospital, archives, 574, 578
Pennsylvania Railroad Company, 668
Pennsylvania Vine Company, journal, 402
Penobscot Indians, dictionary, 102, 278; missions, 736
Penrose, Charles Bingham, 482
Penrose, Richard Alexander Fullerton, Jr., 23, 81; papers, 575
Penrose, Thomas, 254
Pentland, Joseph B., 475
Pepper, William (1843-1898), 86, 555
Pepperell, William, 640
Pereira, José Maria Dantas, 18
Perez, Antonio, 576
Perisco, Enrico, 257
Perry, Oliver Hazard, 211
Perry, William Stevens, 233
Pershouse, Henry, letter books, 577
Pershouse, James, 577
Pershouse, John, papers, 577
Peru, Indians, 475
Peter, William, 18
Peters, Richard (1704-1776), 163, 307, 344, 566, 679
Peters, Richard, Jr., (1744-1828), 741
Peterson, Daphne, 645
Petre, Robert James, baron, 198
Pettit, Charles, 355
Pettit, Henry, 39
Petty, William, Earl of Shelburne, Marquess of Lansdowne, 740
Pfeiffer, Louis Georg Karl, 293
Philadelphia, Academy of Natural Sciences. See: Academy of Natural Sciences
Philadelphia, Apprentices Library. See: Apprentices Library Company

Philadelphia, Carpenters Company. See: Carpenters Company, Philadelphia
Philadelphia, Central High School. See Central High School of Philadelphia
Philadelphia, College of Physicians. See: College of Physicians of Philadelphia
Philadelphia, Free Library. See: Free Library of Philadelphia
Philadelphia, Law Academy. See: Law Academy of Philadelphia
Philadelphia, Library Company. See Library Company of Philadelphia
Philadelphia, Photographic Society. See: Photographic Society of Philadelphia
Philadelphia, St. Andrew's Society. See: St. Andrew's Society of Philadelphia
Philadelphia, apprenticeship, 613; City Planning Commission, 578; Committee for the Preservation of Cultural Resources, 413; Common Council, notes, 671; Court of Common Pleas, 244; craftsmen, 606; defense, 274; description, 107; Dr. Franklin's Legacy, 579; education, 199; Friends Academy, 631; music, 385; occupation (1777), 718; Overseers of the Poor, tax book, 581; publishing, 96; riots, 310; shipping, 318; social history, 408; tuberculosis, 501
Philadelphia Assembly, 583
Philadelphia Chamber of Commerce, 32
Philadelphia County, quit rents, 560
Philadelphia Dispensary, 574
Philadelphia Lying-In Charity Hospital, records, 574
Philadelphia Museum Company, 584. See also: Peale's Museum, Philadelphia
Philadelphia Society for Promoting Agriculture, 29, 732
Phile, Frederick, 459
Philips, Oliver, 507
Phillips, Henry, 248
Phillips, John, 215
Phillips, Jonas Altamont, 166
Phlogiston, 604. See also: Chemistry
Phoenician inscriptions in America, 717
Phosphorescence, 141
Photographic Society of Philadelphia, 666
Photography, 549
Physick, Philip Syng, 18
Physics, 113, 377, 611, 719; quantum, 104, 719; textbook, 585; theoretical, 104
Physiognotrace, 543
Piccard, Jean, 719
Pickering, Charles, 93, 406, 475, 727
Pickering, John, 117
Pickering, Timothy, 221, 493; papers, 586
Pickering, William Henry, 723
Pickersgill, Henry William, 348
Pictet de la Rive, François Joseph, 216
Pierce, Catharine J., collector, 587
Pierce, Franklin, 520

Pierce, George, 204
Piersol, George Morris, 105
Pike, Zebulon Montgomery, 457; biog., 589; journal, 588
Pilling, James Constantine, 598
Pima-Papago Indians, language, 102
Pitot, Henri, 465a
Pittsburgh, Pa. See: Fort Pitt, Fort Duquesne
Place names, Indian, 326, 333
Planck, Max, 104, **590**, 662
Plant genetics, 688
Plant pathology, 692
Platt, John David Reynolds, 358
Pleasants, Samuel, 264
Plée, Auguste, sketches, 591
Ploughs, 531
Poinsett, Joel Roberts, 10, 13, 36, 462, 475; collector, 592
Poisons, 234
Poliomyelitis, 105
Polygraph, 525
Polynesian vocabulary, 406
Pomeroy, Fred Elmer, 372
Poole, Thomas, 194
Poor tax, Philadelphia, 581
Porter, Thomas Conrad, 712
Portugal, currency, 116
Post, Christian Frederick, 562; journal, **593**
Postal, Paul M., 102
Potier, Pierre, 594
Potocki, Count Jan, 254; travels, 595
Potter, Alonzo, 18, 119, 233
Potter, George Reuben, author, 596
Potts, Thomas, 306
Poulson, C. M., 662
Powel, Samuel, Jr., 310
Powell, B. Bruce, 358
Powell, John Wesley, 597, 598; survey, 599
Poyntell, William, 600
Prät, Silvestre, 508
Pratt, Joseph Hyde, 723
Pratt, Richard Henry, 624
Pratt, Samuel Jackson, 319
Preble, Edward, 211
Presbyterian Church, missions to American Indians, 759
Preston Retreat, Philadelphia, records, 574
Prestwick, Sir Joseph, 510
Price, Alan, author, 601
Price, Eli Kirk, 636; papers, 602
Price, Richard, papers, 603
Prichard, William, 484
Priestley, Joseph, 10, 18, 29, 42, 155, 176, 254, 604, 662, 740, 741; letters, 605
Priestley, Joseph, Jr., 18, 605
Prime, Phoebe (Phillips), author, 606
Princeton University, 311
Pringle, Sir John, 359
Printing and publishing, London (Strahan), 716; Boston (Ticknor & Fields), 221; New-

port, R.I. (James Franklin, Jr.), 267; Phila-
delphia (Jane Aitken), 96, (Mathew Carey),
172, 173, (Hall, Hall & Sellers), 305-307,
376, (Muir), 484; Williamsburg, Va. (Wil-
liam Hunter), 354, (Joseph Royale), 641;
music publishing, Philadelphia, 385
Prison reform, 603
Pritchett, Henry Smith, 723
Protozoa genetics, 372
Pursh, Frederick, journal, 607
Putnam, Persis, 501
Pyle, Zeba, 671
Pyrlaeus, John Christopher, 608

Quadrant, Hadley's, 711
Quakers. See: Society of Friends
Quantum theory, **104,** 719. (The Society has
published *Sources for History of Quantum
Physics, An Inventory and Report,* by
Thomas S. Kuhn, John L. Heilbron, Paul
Forman, and Lini Allen, which should be
consulted for a complete survey of materials
on quantum physics in the Library.)
Quatrefages de Bréau, Jean Louis Armand de,
215
Quattrocchi, Anna Margaret, author, 609
Quebec, travel and description, 107, 777
Quebec, Université Laval, Séminaire de Qué-
bec, collections, 610
Quekett, William Thomas, 356
Questebrune, John, author, 611
Quetelet, Lambert Adolphe Jacques, corres.,
612
Quimby, Ian M. G., author, 613, 614

Raddi, Giuseppe, 254
Radiation, 719
Radin, Paul, 151; writings, 615
Rafinesque, Constantine Samuel, 93, 154, 415,
478, 496, **617-620,** 727, 755; letters, 616
Raguet, Claude P., 244
Raguet, Condy, 18, 158
Railroads, 310; U.S.: 668, New Jersey, 758
Rainsford, Giles, 199
Ralph, James, 459
Ramage, Adam, 672
Ramsay, David, 176, 525
Ramsay, Sir William, 215, 216
Ramsay, Sumner Morrison, 399
Rand Project, 762
Randolph, Benjamin, 306
Randolph, Thomas Jefferson, 525, 531
Randolph, Thomas Mann, 123
Rask, Christian, 18
Raspe, Rudolf Eric, 254
Rathbun, Frank R., 426
Rathvon, S. S., 712
Rauschardt, Felix Hannibal, author, 621
Rawle, William, 205, 623
Rays Town, Pa., 568

Read, Charles, 623
Read, George, 265
Read, James, 344
Read, John, 187
Read, John Meredith, 482
Réaumur, René Antoine Ferchault de, 465a
Redfield, Robert, 178, 517
Redfield, William Charles, 218
Redman, John, 307
Redwood, Abraham, 416
Reed, Henry, 18
Reed, Joseph, 458, 482
Reed, William Bradford, 272, 708
Rehm, H., 230
Reichard, Gladys Amanda, 100, 101
Reichel, Charles Gotthold, meteorological
observations, 450
Reid, Robert C., 520
Reimarus, John Albrecht Heinrich, 694
Reinbold, T., 196
Reindeer, 734
Reingold, Nathan, 201
Reland, Adriaan, author, 622
Relativity, 719
Religion, 207, 310, 740; Christianity in Brazil,
112. See also Indians
Repplier, Agnes, 82b, 741
Reynell, John, 557, **623**
Rhoads, Charles James, 624
Rhoads, James Evans, 624
Rhoads, Samuel, Jr., 264
Rhode Island, customs, 697
Rice, Edwin Wilbur, Jr., 723
Rich, Obadiah, 428
Richards, Alfred Newton, 629; author, 625
Richards, Benjamin Wood, 18
Richards, Herbert M., 196
Richardson, John, 509
Riché, George W., 723
Ridgely, Charles G., 292
Ridgway, Solomon, 270
Riley, Charles Valentine, 398, 712
Rios Rosales, Juan de, 178
Rittenhouse, David, 10, 232, 366, 458, 462,
626-628, 671, 724
Rivers, Thomas Milton, 387
Roach, Hannah (Benner), 578
Robbins, Frederick Chapman, 105
Robbins, William Jacob, 144, 149, 230; papers,
629
Roberdeau, Daniel, 303
Roberdeau, Isaac, 274
Roberts, Helen Heffron, collector, 630
Roberts, Hugh, 303, 559
Roberts, Joseph, Jr., papers, 631, 632
Roberts, Solomon White, 272
Robie, Thomas, 640
Robinson, Angelica (Peale), 525, 553
Robinson, Benjamin Lincoln, 196
Robinson, Moncure, 86

Rockefeller, John Davison, Jr., 105
Rockefeller Foundation, 629; International Health Division, 501
Rockefeller Institute for Medical Research, 144, 260, 387, 500, 651
Rocky Mountains, geographical and geological survey, 597-599
Rodney, Caesar A., 52
Roenne, Baron, 91
Rogers, Henry Darwin, 272, 406, 486
Rogers, Robert, author, 633
Rolleston, George, 510
Roman Catholic Church, catechism, 112; sacraments, Cakchiquel, 168
Romanes, George John, 215, 301, 302, 467
Romans, Bernard, 415
Rome, antiquities, 310; description, 679
Roosevelt, Theodore, 218
Root, Elihu, 218, 231
Rosenfeld, Leon, 104
Rosenvinge, L. Kolderup, 196
Ross, Betsy. See: Elizabeth Claypoole
Ross, George, will, 582
Ross, P. Campbell, 486
Ross, Sir Ronald, 28
Rosseland, Svein, 104
Rosseter, John, log book, 634
Roth, Johannes, author, 635
Rothrock, Joseph Trimble, letters, 636
Rous, Peyton, 105, 144
Rowland, Henry A., biog. data, 637
Roxburgh, William, 13
Royal Botanic Gardens, Kew, 379
Royal Horticultural Society, London, 9
Royal Society, London, 217, 356; letters on America, 640; minutes of Council, 639
Royal Society of Arts, London, material on America, 638
Royale, Joseph, journal, 641
Royce, Josiah, 28
Rubens, Heinrich, 104
Ruggles, Samuel Bulkley, 119
Rumsey, James, 10
Runge, Carl David, 377
Ruschenberger, William Samuel Waithman, 475
Rush, Benjamin, 10, 158, 188, 190, 355, 366, 401, 461, 603, **642-647**, 649, 662, 740; will, 582
Rush, James, 648
Rush, Richard, 205, 482, 561, 589
Rush, Samuel, 649
Russell, F. F., 500, 501
Russell, Jonathan, 9
Russell Sage Foundation, 762
Russia, travel and description, 595
Ruston, Thomas, 270, 497
Rutherford, Ernest, 104
Rutherford, Lewis Morris, 272
Rutty, John, letters, 650

Sabin, Albert Bruce, 260, 500
Sabin, Florence Rena, 500; papers, 651
Sabine, Sir Edward, 348, 422, 612, 640
Sacco, Luigi, 254
Sachse, Julius F., 38
Sack, William, 496
Saddington, Ronald S., 260
Sadow, A. A., 500
Sagard, Gabriel, author, 652
Sager, A., author, 653
St. Andrew's Society, Philadelphia, minutes, 654
St. Clair, Arthur, 170, 586
St. Clair, Sir John, 170, 262
St. Francis, Order of. See: Franciscan Order
St. George's Hospital, London, lecture tickets, 648
St. John's College, Maryland, 678
Salisbury, Seth, 481
Salzmann, Zdeněk, 102
Sanderson, John, 18
Sanford, E. A., 612
Sansom, Joseph, 36
Santi, Giorgio, 254
Santo Domingo, slavery, 657; travel and description, 403. See also: Cercle des Philadelphes
Sapir, Edward, 100, 151, 709; collector, 655
Sargent, H. E., 151
Sargent, Winthrop, 483
Sarton, George, 339
Saunders, DeAlton, 196
Saunders, Richard. See: Richard Huck-Saunders
Saunders, William, 254
Sauvageau, Camille, 196
Savery, William, 581
Savi, Gaetano, 254
Sawyer, Wilbur A., 501
Say, Benjamin, 701
Say, Lucy Way (Sistaire), 428, 475, 656
Say, Thomas, 10, 154, 428, 475, 550; papers, 656
Sayce, Archibald Henry, 108
Sayle, Charles Edward, 217
Sayre, Stephen, 671
Saz, Antonio del, author, 168
Scaliger, Joseph Justus, 657
Scaliger, Julius Caesar, 657
Scaliger family, papers, 657
Schaeffer, Charles Frederick, 272
Schaum, Hermann, 398
Scheel, Karl, 104
Schenk, Cornelius, 265
Schlaginteweit-Sakülünski, Hermann Rudolph Alfred von, 348
Schlessinger, Walter, 500
Schmick, John Jacob, collector, 658
Schoff, Harry L., 174
Schofield, John McAllister, 119

Schomburgk, Sir Robert Hermann, 293
Schoolbooks, Latin, 97; mathematics, 659
Schoolcraft, Henry Rowe, 13, 233, 462, 475, 513
Schramm, Jacob Richard, 196, 629
Schrödinger, Erwin, 104
Schubert, Friedrich Theodor, 359
Schuh, R. E., 196
Schulz, Theodor, author, 660
Schuyler, Philip, 507, 586
Schuylkill Bank, Philadelphia, 665
Schuylkill River, travel and description, 620
Schwartz, Eugene Amandus, 398
Schweinitz, Lewis David von, 475, 661
Science, history, 201
Sclater, Philip Lutley, 215, 253, 356, 398, 422
Scotland. Society of Antiquaries. See: Society of Antiquaries of Scotland
Scythians, origins, 595
Secretary's handbook, Turkey, 733
Sedgwick, Adam, 422, 509, 662
Sedgwick, S. J., 304
Sedgwick, Theodore, 117
Sedgwick, William Thompson, 231
Seegal, David, 501
Segrè, Emilio, 257
Seidel, Nathaniel, 327
Seler, Edward, 151
Sellers, Ann (1785-?), 675; diary, 633
Sellers, Anna (1824-1908), 675; diary, 664
Sellers, Charles (1806-1898), 674
Sellers, Coleman (1781-1834), 584, 666, 675; letters, 665
Sellers, Coleman (1827-1907), 14, 668, 675; letters 666
Sellers, Coleman, & Sons, 665
Sellers, Cornelia (Wells), 675; letters, 667
Sellers, Elizabeth (Coleman), 675
Sellers, George Escol, 584, 674, 675; memoirs, 668
Sellers, Horace Wells, 554, 666, 668; collector, 669
Sellers, John, records, 670
Sellers, Nathan, 668; records, 671
Sellers, Nathan and Coleman, 672
Sellers, Nathan and David, 671; letter book, 673
Sellers, Sophonisba Angusciola (Peale), 675; accounts, 674
Sellers family, genealogical data, 676; papers, 675; corres., 555
Sellers, Brandt & Co., 665
Seneca Indians, 360; ethnology, 102; history, 513; linguistics, 513; music, 102, 204
Sergeant, John, lawyer, 232, 520
Sergeant, John, missionary, 507
Sessë y Lacasta, Martino de, author, 677
Sevry, J. B., 9
Seward, William Henry, 119, 221
Seybert, Adam, 462

Shakers, New Lebanon, N.Y., 107
Shaler, Nathaniel S., 406
Shamokin, Pa. See: Fort Augusta, Pa.
Shapley, Harlow, 82a, 723
Sharp, Granville, 724
Sharpe, Horatio, 562
Sharswood, George, 86
Sharswood, William, 678
Shattuck, Lemuel, 612
Shaw, Edward B., 260
Shawnee Indians, 562
Sheetz, Henry, 306
Sherard, William, biog., 518
Shils, Edward A., 182
Shipley, William, 638
Shippen, Edward "of Lancaster" (1703-1781), 163, 164, 344, 680, 683; biog., 209; papers, 679
Shippen, Edward, Jr. (1729-1806), 671, 679, 681, 683
Shippen, Joseph, 682
Shippen, Joseph, Jr., (1732-1810), 164, 562, 566, 679; letter book, 683
Shippen, William, Sr., 164, 679
Shippen, William, Jr., 685; journal, 684
Shippensburg, Pa., trade, 164; Library Company, 163
Shirley, William, 562
Shock treatment, 171
Shoemaker, Benjamin, 497
Shope, Richard E., 260
Short, Charles Wilkins, 616, 656, 727; corres., 686
Short, John Cleves, 686
Short, William, 36; corres., 687
Shotwell, James T., 82b
Shryock, John, 672, 673
Shryock, Richard Harrison, 339
Shull, Aaron Franklin, 372
Shull, George Harrison, 149, 218; papers, 688
Sibley, John, 52, 589
Sickles, Daniel Edgar, 649
Siemens, Sir William, 510
Sigerist, Henry E., 500
Silk manufacture, 740
Silliman, Benjamin, Sr., 10, 93, 117, 186, 195, 310, 429, 475, 486, 727
Silliman, Benjamin, Jr., 117, 292, 310, 666, 780
Silviculture, United States, 455, 456
Simcock, John, 559
Simcoe, John Graves, 170
Simpson, George Gaylord, letters, 689; author 690
Simpson, Henry, 482
Simpson, Sir James Young, 510
Sinnott, Edmund Ware, 149, 629
Sioux Indians, missions, 736; Mountain Stoney dialect, 129
Six Nations. See: Iroquois

Skinner, Dorothy P., 174
Skinner, Henry, 745
Skipwith, Fulwar, 205, 270
Slavery, 310, 603; Pennsylvania, 572; Santo Domingo, 657
Sloane, Sir Hans, 198; corres., 691
Smallpox, inoculation, 188
Smallwood, Charles, 640
Smibert, Williams, 338
Smith, Edgar Fahs, 575
Smith, Erwin Frink, papers, 692
Smith, Sir James Edward, 205, 415, 422
Smith, John, 557
Smith, John Jay, 213, 712
Smith, Lloyd Dean, author, 693
Smith, Nicholas N., 102
Smith, Robert, 164
Smith, Theobald, 105, 260
Smith, Thomas Peters, 695; journal, 694
Smith, William, provost, Univ. of Penna., 176, 307, 471, 525, 699
Smith College Genetics Experiment Station, 149, 629
Smithson, James, 254; bequest, 696
Smithsonian Institution, 150, 272, 310, 363, 712; foundation, 696
Smyth, Frederick, papers, 697
Snider, Jacob, 741
Snow, Gideon, 740
Snyder, John Kellerman, author, 698
Snyder, Monroe Benjamin, 723
Social Science Research Council, 762
Sociedad de la Havana, 9
Society for Propagating Christian Knowledge Among the Germans Settled in Penna., minutes, 699
Society of Antiquaries of Scotland, minutes (1780-1782), 700
Society of Friends, 241; Anglo-American relations, 279; "Indian Committee," 702; Philadelphia, 671; Philadelphia Yearly Meeting, discipline, 703; Tortola, B.W.I., 724
Society of Free Quakers, Philadelphia, papers, 701
Society of Jesus, missions in South America, 229, 420, 610
Solander, Daniel, 198, 254
Sommerfeld, Arnold, 104, 662
Sons of Liberty, New York, 569; Philadelphia, 569
Sorby, Henry Clifton, diaries, 704
South America, Indians, 517; travel and description, 348, 515
South Carolina, Reconstruction, 678; travel and description, 135
South Carolina Gazette, name index (1732-1738), 705
Southwest, Indians, 517
Souza Palher, Joao de, author, 706
Sowerby, James, 422

Spain, Paraguay Indian policy, 229; treaty with France (1761), 282
Spangenberg, Augustus Gottlieb, 344
Spanish-America, Enlightenment, 287; law, 592
Sparks, Jared, 13, 119, 233, 462, 740, 741; papers relating to Benjamin Franklin, 707, 708
Sparmann, Anders, 694
Speakman, John, 428
Speck, Frank Gouldsmith, 101; author, 709, 710
Spence, Mary, 645
Spencer, Charles, Earl of Sunderland, 294
Spencer, Herbert, 462, 510, 662
Spencer, Nathan, author, 711
Spielmeyer, Wilhelm, 260
Spiritualism, 310, 356
Spofford, Horatio Gates, 52
Spooner, Henry Joshua, 723
Squier, Ephraim George, 394, 755
Stamp Act (1765), 392, 569, 683
Stanley, Edward George Geoffrey Smith, 14th Earl of Derby, 253
Stanton, Robert B., 599
Stanwix, John, 170, 562
Starr, Betty W., 178
Statistical analysis, 762
Statistics, 762
Stauffer, Jacob, 713; corres., 712
Stay, Benedetto, 155
Steam engines, 234
Stebbing, Thomas Roscoe Rede, 217
Stedman, Charles, 164
Steenstrup, Johann Japetus Smith, 293
Stefansson, Vilhjalmur, 218
Steinen, Karl von den, 151
Steiner, Abraham, 327
Steiner, Lewis Henry, 398
Steinhauer, H., 197
Steinmetz, Charles Proteus, 723
Stephenson, Robert, 510
Stern, Bernhard Joseph, 182
Stetson, Charles Augustus, 555
Steuben, Friedrich Wilhelm Augustus, Baron von, 483, 753
Stevens, Ann (Le Conte), 399
Stevens, Henry, Sr. (1791-1867), 707, 708
Stevens, Henry, Jr. (1819-1886), 462, 707, 708
Stevens, Matilda Jane (Harden), 399
Stevens, William Bacon, 233
Stevenson, Alan, 119
Stevenson, David, 119
Stevenson, John James, 598
Stevenson, Robert, 119
Steward, J. F., 599
Stewart, Thomas Dale, 174
Stewart, Walter, 714
Stewart, Walter B., 260
Stiles, Ezra, 210, 603

Stillé, Alfred, 662
Stimpson, William, 662
Stirling, Walter, 163
Stirling, Earl of. See: William Alexander
Stobo, Robert, 562
Stock-breeding, 740
Stockbridge Indians, missions, 736
Stockler, Francisco Borja Garçao, 18
Stockley, George, 723
Stockton, William T., 715
Stoddert, Benjamin, 211
Stokes, John H., 218
Stokes, Joseph, Jr., 260
Stone Age artifacts, 549
Storms, 310
Story, Enoch, 306
Strahan, William, 269, 305; journals, 716
Stratospheric flights, 719
Stratton, Samuel Wesley, 723
Streeter, Sebastian Ferris, 333
Strettell, Amos, 190
Strettell, Robert, 264
Strettell, Ann, 373
Strickland, Hugh Edwin, 253
Strickland, William, 18, 248
Strong, William Walker, author, 717
Stuart, George, 723
Studer, Bernhard, 216
Stunkard, Horace W., 82a
Sturtevant, Edgar Howard, 100, 101
Sturtevant, William C., 102
Sue, Hiroko, 102
Sugar refining, 559, 766
Sullivan, Thomas, journal, 718
Sully, Thomas, 29, 81, 462, 488, 525, 543
Summer, Jack, 599
Sumner, Charles, 117, 406
Surveying, 421; instruments, 424
Susanna, brigantine, 490
Swadesh, Morris, 101
Swainson, William, 415, 618
Swann, William Francis Gray, 82a; papers, 719
Swanton, John Reed, 100, 101, 151
Swedenborgians, 665
Swift, John, 583
Syng, Philip, 303
Systems Development Corporation, 762

Taft, William H., 171
Talleyrand-Périgord, Charles Maurice, prince de Benevento, 158, 741
Tamil language, grammar, 720
Taney, Roger Brooke, 741
Tappan, Benjamin, 475
Tarascon, L. A., 616
Targioni-Tozzetti, Ottaviano, 254
Tatham, William, 638
Tax, Sol, 178
Taxation, 740

Taylor, Abraham, 558
Taylor, John, author, 721
Teedyuscung, 344
Teeth, artificial, 525
Tegetmeier, William Bernhard, 216
Teit, James Alexander, 151
Temlarh'am, 102
Temperance, 726
tenBroeck, Carl, 500
Tennessee, travel and description, 495
Terry, William A., 196
Tessier, Abbé Alexandre Henri, 254
Tewa Indians, 517
Texas, Aransas Pass, 314
Thebes, Egypt, 108
Thermometrical observations, 148, 299, 772. See also: Meteorological observations
Thiebaut, Arsène, 254
Thomas, Alex, author, 722
Thomas, George, 416
Thomas, Isaiah, 52, 97, 173
Thomas, Jameson L., 449
Thomas, M. Carey, 260; M. Carey Thomas Prize, 651
Thompson, Almon Harris, 598
Thompson, Benjamin, Count Rumford, 640
Thompson, Stith, 517
Thomson, Charles, 307, 462, 562, 563, 685
Thomson, Elihu, 82b, 555; papers, 723
Thomson, J. Edgar, 406
Thomson, Sir Joseph John, 104, 555
Thomson, Silvanus P., 723
Thomson, Sir William, 467
Thomson-Houston Electric Company, 723
Thorne, Sir Thomas Edward, 640
Thornton, William, 10, 366, 496, 555; papers, 724
Thornton, Mrs. William, 724
Thouin, André, 662
Thunberg, Karl Peter, 254, 694
Thwaites, George Henry Kendrick, 215, 216
Ticknor & Fields, 221
Tilden, Samuel Jones, 233
Tilghman, James, 163
Tilghman, Richard, 725
Tilghman, Tench, 119
Tilghman, William, 240, 774; papers, 725
Time Stone Farm, Marlborough, Mass, 296
Tlingit Indians, 226
Tlmecen, North Africa, description, 282
Tocqueville, Alexis de, 14
Todd, David, 723
Tonawanda Seneca Indians, longhouse, music, 102
Torchhammer, Georg, 422
Torrey, John, 93, 186, 197, 346, 475, 616, 620, 686, **726**; autograph collection, 727
Tortola, B.W.I., Society of Friends, 724
Townsend, John, 355
Townsend, John Kirk, author, 728

Tozzer, Alfred Marston, 151
Traill, George W., 196
Transeau, Edgar R., 196
Transit of Venus, 250, 441
Travel and description. See under particular countries, regions, and geographical areas
Treat, John Breck, meteorological observations, 729
Trego, Charles B., 18, 57
Trent, William, 163, 268, 562
Trevelyan, Sir Charles Edward, author, 730
Trevelyan, Sir George Otto, 467
Trigonometry, 621, 632
Troost, Gerard, 475
Tropical Plant Conference (1959), 629
Trudeau, Jean Baptiste, author, 731
Trudeau, Zenon, 731
True, Rodney Howard, 629; papers, 732
Trumbull, John, 724
Trumbull, Jonathan, 561
Truxtun, Thomas, 211
Tsimsyans, 102
Tuberculosis, 171, 501, 651
Tull, Jethro, 234
Tumin, Melvin M., 178
Tupac Amaru II, 592
Turin, Accademia della Scienze. See: Accademia delle Scienze, Turin
Turkey, secretary's handbook, 733
Turner, Dawson, 422
Turner, Edie, 778
Turner, George, 29
Turner, Lucian McShan, author, 734
Turner, Robert, 559
Turner, Sir William, 467
Tuscarora Indians, history, 336; language, 102
Twells. See: Haines & Twells
Tyler, Richard, 358
Tyndall, John, 216, 510, 662
Typhoid vaccination, 171
Typhus fever, 772
Tyson, George, collector, 735
Tyson, Job R., 18

Uber, Fred Murray, 144
Uhlenbeck, George Eugene, 104
Ulke, Henry, 398
Underwood, Oscar W., 218
Union Library Company, 307
Unitarianism, 406, 605, 740, 742
United China Relief, 501
United Church Board for World Ministries, papers on North American Indian missions, 736
U.S. Air Force Systems Command, 762
U.S. Army, 764; Corps of Topographical Engineers, 394, 398; Department of North Carolina (1863), 737; life in Southwest, 115; medical department, 105, 122, 311, 353, 500, 501

U.S. Biological Survey, 426
U.S. Creek agency, 317
U.S. Coast and Geodetic Survey, 119, 272, 520, 748
U.S. Commissioner of Agriculture, 398
U.S. Commissioner of Indian Affairs, 624
U.S. Continental Congress, 671
U.S. Declaration of Independence, 320
U.S. Department of Agriculture, 311; Bureau of Plant Industry, 732
U.S. Exploring Expedition (Wilkes expedition), 475, 502, 550; records, 738
U.S. Geographical and Geological Survey of the Rocky Mountain Region, 597, 598
U.S. Judiciary, Circuit Court, 436
U.S. Military Academy, West Point, 764
U.S. Mint, 272, 549, 668
U.S. Navy, 211; Asiatic Squadron, 118
U.S. Office of Scientific Research and Development, 311
U.S. Post office, 321
United States, American Revolution: 188, 219, 458, 561; accounts, 444, 547; army, 156, 483; quartermaster, 295; Canada, 698; Greene papers, 295; R. H. Lee papers, 401; medals, 249; military journal, 718; J. P. G. Muhlenberg papers, 483; music, 160; orderly books, 156, 714, 754; peace negotiations, 603, 740; Weedon corres., 753;
———, Civil War: 118, 122, 272, 513, 549; medical services, 353, 398; North Carolina, 737
———, Commercial policy, 252; expansion, 310, government buildings (Philadelphia, 1790), 578; immigration, 259, 577; independence, 450; travel and description (eighteenth cent.), 107, 193, 731, 744, 771, 779, (nineteenth cent.), 115, 312, 407, 409, 425, 427, 428, 463, 489, 498, 577, 588, 591, 597, 598, 616, 620, 777; treaties, 165
Universities. See under name of university (e.g., Pennsylvania, University of)
Urey, Harold Clayton, 144
Usteri, Paulus, 349

Vaccination, 501; vaccines, 500
Valenciennes, Achille, 293
Valley Forge, Pa., orderly book, 754
Valltravers, J. Rudolph, 10
Van Der Capellen, Johan Derk, baron, 603
Van Der Osten, Anna L., 105, 260
Van Emburgh, Colonel ———, 772
Van Ingen, S. B., 231
Van Rensselaer, Jeremiah, 154
Van Slyke, Donald Dexter, 144, 260, 501
Van Vleck, John Hasbrouck, 104
Vanuxem, Lardner, 18, 486
Varela, Francisco de, author, 168
Varenius, Bernard, 424
Varlé, Charles, 10

Varley, John, 488
Varlo, Charles, 484
Vasey, G. W., 598
Vassalli-Eandi, Antonio Marie, 254
Vater, Johann Severin, 739
Vattel, Emerich, 234
Vaughan, Benjamin, 186, 640, 62, 707, 708, 741; papers, 740
Vaughan, Charles, 740
Vaughan, Daniel, 117
Vaughan, John, 9, 11, 44, 45, 52, 91, 94, 96, 205, 233, 248, 255, 320, 346, 348, 366, 455, 457, 496, 497, 502, 520, 525, 555, 605, 686, 695, 742, 743, 774; papers, 741
Vaughan, Petty, 310, 707, 708, 740
Vaughan, Samuel, Sr., 740, 741; journal, 744
Vaughan, Samuel, Jr., 210, 740
Vaughan, Sarah, 740
Vaughan, T. Wayland, 82a
Vaughan, William, 9, 117, 310, 708, 740, 741,
Vaughan, William Oliver, 740
Veblen, Oswald, 260
Ventilation, 234
Venturi, Giambattista, 254
Venus. See: Transit of Venus
Vethake, Henry, 13
Vienna, medical schools, 387
Viereck, Henry Lorenz, papers, 745
Viets, Henry Rouse, 339
Viniculture, 402, 616
Virchow, Rudolf Ludwig Karl, 467, 510
Virginia, boundaries, 167; travel and description, 744
Virginia, University of, 520
Viruses, 500, 501
Vitalism, 372
Voegelin, Carl, 709
Voegelin, Erminie (Wheeler), 709
Vogt, Karl Christoph, 216
Voigt, Woldemar, 104
Volney, Constantin François Chassebœuf, comte de, 158, 243, 724
Voltaire, François Marie Arouet de, letters, 746
Vrolik, William, 292
Vuillamy, Benjamin Lewis, 662

Waagen, Gustav Friedrich, 348
Wadsworth, Augustus B., 500
Wagener, Kurt, 500
Wager, Sir Charles, 199
Wagner Free Institute of Science, Philadelphia, 94
Waksman, Selman Abraham, 144, 149
Walam Olum, bibliog., 755
"Walking Purchase," Pa., 749
Walla Walla Indians, vocabulary, 728
Wallace, Alfred Russel, 215, 253, 301, 356, 422, 467, 510, 662
Wallace, Anthony Francis Clarke, author, 747

Wallace, Paul Anthony Wilson, 709
Wallace, William, 264
Waln, Nicholas, 264
Walsh, Benjamin Dann, 215, 398
Walsh, Robert, 205, 640
Wampanoag Indians, language, 222
Warburg, Emil, 104
Ward, Henry Augustus, 292
Ward, Lester Frank, 598
Warden, David Bailie, 10, 771
Warner, John, letters, 748
Warren, Andrew J., 501
Warren, James Collins, 475
Warren, John C., 740
Washington, Bushrod, 366
Washington, George, 158, 219, 321, 366, 401, 458, 483, 525, 561, 685, 724, 741, 753; portrait by Rembrandt Peale, 540, 541, 555
Watermarks, 671
Waterhouse, Benjamin, 741
Waterman, Alan Tower, 629
Waterman, Talbot Howe, 311
Waterton, Charles, 93, 502, 503
Watson, John, 749
Watson, John, Jr., author, 749
Watson, John Broadus, 372
Watson, John Fanning, 213
Watson, Sir Thomas, 510
Watts, Stephen, 303
Waugh, Frederick Wilkerson, collector, 750
Wavran, Abbé C. L. B., 751
Washita. See: Ouachita
Wayne, Anthony, 462, 671, 752
Weatherby, A. G., 598
Weaver, Warren, 144
Webster, Daniel, 13, 18, 233, 482, 513, 602, 741
Webster, L. T., 500
Webster, Noah, 13, 173
Wedderburn, Alexander, 561
Wedgwood, Josiah, 254
Weedon, George, corres., 753; orderly book, 754
Weer, Paul, author, 755
Weigall, Arthur, 108
Weights and measures, 254, 272
Weiser, Conrad, 344, 562
Weisskopf, Victor Frederick, 104
Welch, George, journal, 756
Welch, William Henry, letters to Simon Flexner, 260
Wellcome Historical Medical Library, letters in, 662
Weller, Carl V., 500
Wells, C. W., 501
Werkmeister, William Henry, author, 757
Werner, Oswald, 102
West, Benjamin, 555, 574, 638
West, Byron L., 105
West, George Stephen, 196

West Indies, folklore, 517; history, 294; travel and description, 591, 756
West Jersey and Seashore Railroad, 758
Western Missionary Society of Pennsylvania, records, 759
Westinghouse, George, 555
Wetherill, Charles Mayer, 272
Wetherill, John Price, 18
Wetherill, Samuel, Jr., (d. ca. 1837), 701
Wetherill, Samuel (fl. 1883), 701
Wharton, Lloyd, 482
Wharton, Samuel, 359
Wheatstone, Sir Charles, 510, 612
Wheeler, George Montague, 598
Wheeler, Olin Dunbar, 598
Wheelock, John, 603
Whewell, William, 422, 423, 612
Whipple, George Hoyt, 500; Nobel Prize, 760
Whiston, John, 416
White, Leslie A., 517, 709
White, William, 18, 603
Whitefield, George, 684
Whitehurst, John, 254
Whitfield, J. E., 81
Whitney, Josiah Dwight, 423, 598
Whitney, Willis Rodney, 723
Whittier, John Greenleaf, 14
Whorf, Benjamin Lee, 178
Whymper, Edward, 423
Wichita Indians, paradigms, 102
Wied-Neuwied, Maximilian Alexander Philippe, prinz von, 475
Wien, Wilhelm, 662
Wigglesworth, Edward, 603
Wilbur, Walter K., author, 761
Wild Horse, Chief, 222
Wilder, Marshall Pinckney, 119
Wiley, John, and Sons, Inc., 762
Wilkes, Charles, 398, 475, 640, 726
Wilkes Expedition. See: U.S. Exploring Expedition
Wilkinson, Sir Gardner, 423
Wilkinson, James, 589
Wilkinson, John, 605
Wilks, Samuel Stanley, papers, 762
Willard, Joseph, 603
Willcox, Walter Francis, 100
Willdenow, Karl Ludwig, 348
Williams, Eleazar, author, 763
Williams, Frank, author, 722
Williams, Henry Jonathan, author, 764
Williams, John, 765
Williams, Jonathan, Sr., 766
Williams, Jonathan, Jr., 11, 44, 270, 274, 338, 359, 366, 559, 741; genealogy, 764; papers, 766
Williams, Samuel, 450
Williamson, Miss ——, drawings, 767
Williamson, Hugh, 10
Williamson, John, 265

Williamson, William Crawford, 423
Willing, Charles, 679
Willing, Thomas, 303, 685
Wills, W. R., 423
Wilson, Alexander, 93, 711, 727; letters, 768
Wilson, Edmund Beecher, 629
Wilson, Edwin Bidwell, 149
Wilson, James (1743-1798), 497; accounts, 769
Wilson, James Patriot, author, 770
Wilson, Woodrow, 28, 171, 233
Winchell, Alexander, 462
Winnebago Indians, ethnology, 615; numerals, 378
Winslow, C. F., 748
Winsor, Henry, 406
Winthrop, James, 11
Winthrop, John, Jr., 640
Winthrop, John, IV, 603
Winthrop, Wait, 640
Wirt, William, 221
Wisdom, Charles, 178
Wissler, Clark, 151, 709
Wistar, Caspar, 11, 18, 44, 123, 176, 205, 366, 686, 724, 771, 772-774
Wistar, Catherine (Bache), 774
Wistar, Elizabeth, 774
Wistar Association, 86, 87
Wistar Institute, Philadelphia, 94, 231, 575
Wister, Charles Jones, (1782-1865), biog., 775
Wister, Charles Jones, Jr., author, 775
Wister, Daniel, 163
Wister, John, 11
Witherspoon, John, 232
Witt, Christopher, 640
Witthoft, John, 102, 174
Woglom, William H., 105
Wolcott, Roger, 561
Wollaston, Alexander R., 423
Women's rights, 463
Wood, George Bacon, 18, 25; papers, 776; journal, 777
Wood, John, author, 778
Wood, Searles, 422, 423
Woodbridge, Frederic James Eugene, 151
Woodbury, Levi, 232
Woodmason, Charles, 638
Woodorf, ——, journal, 779
Woodward, Samuel Pickworth, 423
Works Progress Administration, 174
Wormley, Theodore George, corres., 780
Worsaee, Jens Jacob Asmussen, 293
Wound ballistics, 311
Wrangel, Charles, 415
Wright, Asher, 513
Wright, Edward, 199
Wright, James, 11
Wright, Ross P., 174
Wycoff, Ralph Walter Graystone, 500
Wyman, Jeffries, 215, 423
Wyoming, Pa., controversy, 561

Wythe, George, 401, 561

Yager, Robert H., 500
Yale University, 231
Yarnell, William, 253
Yellow fever, 132, 772
Yendo, K., 196
Yoelson, Martin Irving, 358
York, George, W., 388
Youmans, Edward Livingston, 612

Young, Charles, 484
Young, Hugh, author, 781
Young, Thomas, 349

Zeeman, Pieter, 104
Zeisberger, David, 327, 344, 496; grammars, 782-784
Zinsser, Hans, 105, 500
Zirkle, Conway, 709
Zwemer, Raymond Lull, 629